MEDAL OF HONOR™

PRIMA Official Game Guide

Written by: Michael Knight & David Knight

MEDAL OF HONOR

Prima Games

An Imprint of Random House, Inc.
3000 Lava Ridge Court, Suite 100
Roseville, CA 95661
www.primagames.com

Senior Product Marketing Manager: Donato Tica
Product Marketing Manager: Todd Manning
Design & Layout: Marc W. Riegel
Copyedit: Julia Kilmer
Manufacturing: Stephanie Sanchez & Suzanne Goodwin

Prima Games and the authors would like to thank Kevin O'Leary, Geoff Bent, Owen Johnson, Kit Eklöf, Christian Grass, Craig Owens, Lorraine Honrada and Daniel Davis for their support throughout this project.

Important:
Prima Games has made every effort to determine that the information contained in this book is accurate. However, the publisher makes no warranty, either expressed or implied, as to the accuracy, effectiveness, or completeness of the material in this book; nor does the publisher assume liability for damages, either incidental or consequential, that may result from using the information in this book. The publisher cannot provide any additional information or support regarding gameplay, hints and strategies, or problems with hardware or software. Such questions should be directed to the support numbers provided by the game and/or device manufacturers as set forth in their documentation. Some game tricks require precise timing and may require repeated attempts before the desired result is achieved.

ISBN: 9780307469595
Library of Congress Catalog Card Number: 2010936718
Printed in the United States of America

10 11 12 13 LL 10 9 8 7 6 5 4 3 2 1

primagames.com

DAVID KNIGHT

David Knight has been an avid gamer since the days of the Atari 2600 and Commodore 64. His first foray into the gaming industry came in 1995, as a scenario designer for SSI's WWII strategy game Steel Panthers. As online gaming communities sprung up across the Web, David lent his enthusiasm and design skills to many fan sites. In 1998, he co-founded and co-hosted Game Waves, a weekly webcast featuring industry news and game reviews. David's involvement with Prima Games began in the late 90s. Since then, he's contributed to and written dozens of titles for Prima Games.

We want to hear from you! E-mail comments and feedback to dknight@primagames.com.

MICHAEL KNIGHT

Michael Knight has worked in the computer/video game industry since 1994 and has been an author with Prima Games for ten years, writing over 60 guides during this time. Michael has used both his degree in Military History and experience as a high school teacher to formulate and devise effective strategies and tactics for hit titles. Michael has also developed scenarios/missions and written game manuals for SSI, Red Storm Entertainment, and Novalogic.

When he is not busy at work on an upcoming strategy guide, Michael likes to spend time with his wife and six children at their home in Northern California.

We want to hear from you! E-mail comments and feedback to mknight@primagames.com.

CONTENTS

INTRODUCTION

MEDAL OF HONOR

WELCOME TO TIER 1

Operating directly under the National Command Authority, a relatively unknown entity of handpicked warriors are called on when the mission must not fail. They are the Tier 1 Operators.

Over two million Soldiers, Sailors, Airmen, and Marines wear the uniform. Of those, approximately 50,000 fall under the direct control of the Special Operations Command. The Tier 1 Operator functions on a plane of existence above and beyond even the most highly trained Special Operations Forces. Their exact numbers, while classified, hover in the low hundreds. They are living, breathing, precision instruments of war. They are experts in the application of violence. The new *Medal of Honor* is inspired by and has been developed with Tier 1 Operators from this elite community. Players will step into the boots of these warriors and apply their unique skill sets to a new enemy in the most unforgiving and hostile battlefield conditions of present day Afghanistan. There is a new enemy. There is a new war. There is a new warrior. He is Tier 1.

Welcome to the official game guide for *Medal of Honor*. In the latest installment of the popular, long-running franchise you're sent directly into the modern real-world conflict within Afghanistan. Fight today's war as elite Special Forces in a gritty combat campaign using the surgical tactics of Tier 1 Operators combined with the sledgehammer force of Army Rangers. Prepare yourself for unparalleled authenticity as the intense story unfolds with incredible pacing set in the rugged Afghanistan landscape. But the fight doesn't end with the campaign. Multiplayer has been redefined, developed by the world-class team at DICE, makers of *Battlefield: Bad Company 2*. The fast-paced online combat delivers the perfect mix of tactical warfare and all-out action. Whether fighting through the campaign or leveling up online, this guide provides everything you need to achieve Tier 1 status.

THE *MEDAL OF HONOR* LEGACY

The *Medal of Honor* series began with the basic premise of telling a soldier's story. Released on the Playstation back in the fall of 1999, the first title did just that, chronicling the adventures of an OSS field agent fighting behind enemy lines in World War II-era Europe. The success of the first game spawned a long-running and award-winning series of games set in World War II, each telling the story of a soldier risking it all to stem the tide of fascism.

MEDAL OF HONOR

Release Date: October 31, 1999

Platform: Playstation

Inspired by DreamWorks SKG co-founder Steven Spielberg, *Medal of Honor* marked the first World War II action adventure game developed for the Playstation system. The game begins on June 5, 1944, the night before D-Day when the Allied forces launched a massive aerial assault behind German lines. Assuming the role of a young C-47 pilot shot down during the operation, you are recruited into the OSS and begin a new career as a field agent, participating in various covert operations, search and rescue assignments, and commando raids. Each mission is drawn from pivotal historical events that helped shape the Allied crusade in Europe, including sorties involving the development, capture, and destruction of secret war-making technologies. Upon release, *Medal of Honor* was seen as one of the best first-person shooters of its time, garnering praise for its graphics, level design, and original soundtrack, composed by Michael Giacchino.

MEDAL OF HONOR: UNDERGROUND

Release Date: October 23, 2000

Platform: Playstation

Medal of Honor: Underground begins in 1942, not long after Germany crushed the French military and overran the country. You are introduced to Manon who has just witnessed her house destroyed and hometown occupied. With nothing left to lose, she joins one of the many clandestine resistance movements that have taken root throughout her homeland during the early days of the occupation. Over the course of the game, you experience her ascent from a naive volunteer to a seasoned veteran who is ultimately recruited by the Americans for the Office of Strategic Services (OSS), where she eventually plays a key role in the Liberation of Paris.

MEDAL OF HONOR: ALLIED ASSAULT

Release Date: January 20, 2002

Platform: PC

In *Medal of Honor: Allied Assault*, you assume the role of Lt. Mike Powell, member of the famed 1st Ranger Battalion who gets recruited by the OSS and battles through over 20 levels that are based on historical military campaigns of World War II. Set during the most trying years of the war, 1942–1945, *Allied Assault* gives you a sense of the courage it took to survive the landings at Normandy, the assault at Arzew, a rendezvous with the French Resistance outside the village of St. Lo, and the push through the heavily defended border of Germany. As the first title in the series on the PC, *Medal of Honor: Allied Assault* was met with critical acclaim and was soon followed by two expansion packs, *Spearhead* and *Breakthrough*.

SPEARHEAD (EXPANSION PACK)

Release Date: November 11, 2002

Platform: PC

Spearhead was the first of two expansion packs for *Medal of Honor: Allied Assault*. You assume the role of Sgt. Jack Barnes as he endures the final months of World War II, from Operation Overlord to the Battle of the Bulge and culminating with the fall of Berlin. Set during the last year of the war in Europe, June 1944 to May 1945, *Spearhead* gave you a chance to parachute behind enemy lines during Operation Overlord, halt the German counter offensive during the Battle of the Bulge, and engage the Germans as they desperately tried to defend their capital.

BREAKTHROUGH (EXPANSION PACK)

Release Date: September 22, 2003

Platform: PC

Set in the European Theater of Operations from 1943–1944, *Breakthrough* was the final chapter in the popular *Medal of Honor: Allied Assault* series. As U.S. Army Sergeant John Baker, you join the battle at Kasserine Pass in North Africa, race to capture Messina in Sicily, and then finally repel the German army at the historic battle of Monte Battaglia in the heart of Italy. Armed with a new arsenal of weapons, Sgt. Baker fights alone and with squadmates in a rush to stop the Axis powers by striking at the soft underbelly of Europe.

MEDAL OF HONOR

MEDAL OF HONOR: FRONTLINE

Release Date: May 28, 2002

Platform: Playstation 2, Xbox, GameCube

Medal of Honor: Frontline takes you back behind enemy lines with Lt. Jimmy Patterson. In this installment, Patterson and his men use the confusion of the real-world offensive Operation Market Garden to infiltrate the German frontline and steal the HO-IX flying wing, an experimental Nazi weapon so powerful that it could turn the tide of World War II. To help him succeed in his assignment, Lt. Patterson has the assistance of a small squad of soldiers and a slew of new weapons. Together they take on crucial assignments ranging from the assault on Omaha Beach to the epic battle for control of the Nijmegen Bridge.

MEDAL OF HONOR: RISING SUN

Release Date: November 11, 2003

Platform: Playstation 2, Xbox, GameCube

Medal of Honor: Rising Sun gives you the opportunity to turn the tide in the Pacific, and marked the first time the series expanded beyond the European theater. Playing as Marine Corporal Joseph Griffin, *Rising Sun* tells a far-reaching tale of two brothers as Japanese forces sought to expand their dominion over the Pacific. Featuring real-life historical battles like Pearl Harbor and Guadalcanal, *Medal of Honor: Rising Sun* delivered solid action and a compelling story.

MEDAL OF HONOR: INFILTRATOR

Release Date: November 17, 2003

Platform: Game Boy Advance

In *Medal of Honor: Infiltrator,* you assume the role of Corporal Jake Murphy during several daring missions to defeat the Axis in some of World War II's most famous battles. From sabotaging enemy resources, to capturing key personnel, to all-out firefights, there is never any shortage of action. On foot, in a tank, or even in disguise, Murphy engages opponents on the battlefield with a variety of World War II-era weapons including machine guns, grenades, and bazookas. The title also offered connectivity with the GameCube version of *Medal of Honor: Rising Sun*, allowing gamers to access a useful overhead map on their Game Boy Advance.

MEDAL OF HONOR: PACIFIC ASSAULT

Release Date: November 4, 2004

Platform: PC

Medal of Honor: Pacific Assault ushers you into battle against the Imperial Japanese Army, taking you from the shock of Pearl Harbor to triumph on the shores of the Tarawa Atoll. Set in the Pacific Theater of Operations from 1941–1944, you jump into the boots of Marine recruit Tom Conlin as he survives the attack on Pearl Harbor, leads the assault on Guadalcanal, and finally charges up the beaches for the climatic battle at Tarawa. Expert input and advice from the Congressional Medal of Honor Society and war veteran Capt. Dale Dye, U.S. Marine Corps, ensured historical accuracy, making for an authentic gaming experience.

MEDAL OF HONOR: EUROPEAN ASSAULT

Release Date: June 7, 2005

Platform: Playstation 2, Xbox, GameCube

In *Medal of Honor: European Assault*, the story was the star. The year 1942 was a desperate time for Allied forces as the Nazi war machine raged across a devastated European landscape. You assume the role of U.S. Army Lieutenant William Holt, hand-picked by William "Wild Bill" Donovan to be the first field agent of the newly formed Office of Strategic Services—the OSS. You guide Holt through covert operations set in France, North Africa, and the Soviet Union. He even meets up with Manon, the heroine from *Medal of Honor: Underground,* in Belgium.

INTRODUCTION

MEDAL OF HONOR: HEROES

Release Date: October 23, 2006

Platform: PSP

In *Medal of Honor: Heroes*, you fight your way through three campaigns as popular lead characters from past *Medal of Honor* games. This includes a stint as Lieutenant Jimmy Patterson during his time in Holland during Operation Market Garden. Then you assume control of Sergeant John Baker during a sabotage mission on German defenses positioned along the Italian coastline. Next, you try on the officer's cap of Lieutenant William Holt in an OSS mission within the Ardennes Forest during the Battle of the Bulge.

MEDAL OF HONOR: VANGUARD

Release Date: March 26, 2007

Platform: Playstation 2, Wii

Medal of Honor: Vanguard allows you to join the ranks of the elite 82nd Airborne Division as Corporal Frank Keegan. From Operation Husky on the shores of Sicily to the Operation Varsity airdrop inside Nazi Germany, Keegan jumps behind enemy lines to fight the epic World War II battles that turned America's first paratroopers into heroes of World War II.

MEDAL OF HONOR: AIRBORNE

Release Date: September 7, 2007

Platform: Playstation 3, Xbox 360, PC

In *Medal of Honor: Airborne*, you step into the boots of Boyd Travers, Private First Class of the 82nd Airborne Division, and engage in battles throughout Europe, from rocky beginnings in Sicily to war-winning triumphs in Germany. Each mission begins behind enemy lines, with an intense and fully interactive airdrop. The ability to determine your own starting point dramatically changed the way each mission played out, and earned the title high praise from gamers and critics alike.

MEDAL OF HONOR: HEROES 2

Release Date: November 13, 2007

Platform: PSP, Wii

Medal of Honor: Heroes 2 starts on June 6th, 1944, when the war was far from over. You take on the role of OSS Operative John Berg and are tasked with infiltrating Normandy from behind enemy lines to undermine the Nazi regime. As a special agent of the Office of Strategic Services, you use tactics of combat, infiltration, reconnaissance, and sabotage to carry out the covert operations that help defeat the Nazi war machine once and for all.

MEDAL OF HONOR

HOW TO USE THIS GUIDE

That was a nice trip down memory lane, but now it's time to focus on the latest installment of *Medal of Honor*. The information in this guide has everything you need to get the most out of the game's single-player campaign as well as the intense online multiplayer battles awaiting you. Here's a quick look at the guide's contents, along with useful tips on how to use this information to gain the upper hand in every engagement.

BASIC TRAINING

Before you get into the heat of battle, there are several things you need to know to help you be successful. This section covers a variety of information about how the game works and what you need to do to operate more effectively.

INTERFACE

A lot of information appears on the screen as you are playing *Medal of Honor*. This part of the section gives you the scoop on what all of the icons appearing on your Heads Up Display (or HUD) means and how to use it during combat.

COMBAT

It is vital to know how to fight and use the tools at your disposal. This part covers how to increase your accuracy and the damage you inflict on your enemies.

MOVEMENT

Learn about the different stances and types of movement as well as when to use each. This can save your life during a fire fight against hostile forces.

TYPES OF WEAPONS

There are several different types of weapons in *Medal of Honor*. Each has their own strengths and weaknesses. Here you learn the aspects of each weapon type as well as when they are best employed for various situations.

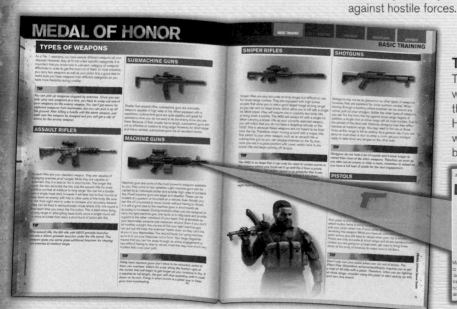

INTRODUCTION
HOW TO USE THIS GUIDE

TACTICS

Combat entails more than just moving and shooting. Tactics combine the two along with methods for decreasing the risks you face during battle while increasing your advantages against the enemy. While Special Operations soldiers are trained to kill, they are also trained to outthink the enemy as well.

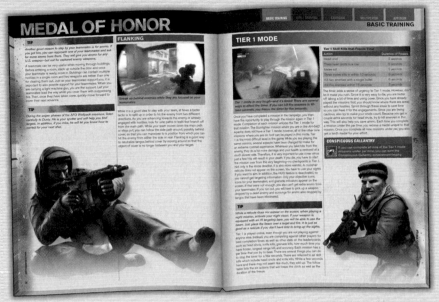

TIER 1 MODE

After you complete a mission in the campaign, you can then play it again in Tier 1 Mode. Find out how this mode is different from the campaign in this section. You will also learn how to overcome the extreme challenges of this mode and emerge both alive and under par.

TIER 1 BRIEFING

During the campaign, you have the opportunity to play as part of four different teams. This section covers each of these teams as well as the enemies you will face. Get to know them before you meet them in combat.

MOTHER
Veteran Tier 1 Operator, AFO Neptune team leader. Skilled warrior who will do anything for his men.

CHARACTERS

Get to the know the members of each of the teams with whom you will be operating while in Afghanistan. The background information on your teammates helps you get to know them. You will also find pictures of your enemies to help you identify them so you know who the hostiles are.

WEAPONS

The weapons used by each of the four teams are included so you are knowledgeable about the tools of your trade. Since you can pick up and use weapons dropped by your enemies, learn to identify them as well.

GLOSSARY AND FOREIGN PHRASES

It is always important to learn the lingo. This section includes a glossary of military terms used by the Special Operations Forces. Frequently used phrases in the languages of the enemies lets you know what the tangos are saying whether they are speaking Pashto, Arabic, or Chechen.

MEDAL OF HONOR

CAMPAIGN

The Campaign chapter provides in-depth walkthroughs of all ten of the single-player missions. Here you will learn how to complete all of the objectives in every mission with step-by-step strategy and tactics. This section also includes some unique features to help you get the most out of each mission.

INTEL REPORT

Right at the start of the mission, find out your main task in the mission briefing. This report also includes the weapons and equipment with which you begin the mission. Finally, the par time for playing the mission in Tier 1 mode is listed, along with the medal you can earn by meeting par.

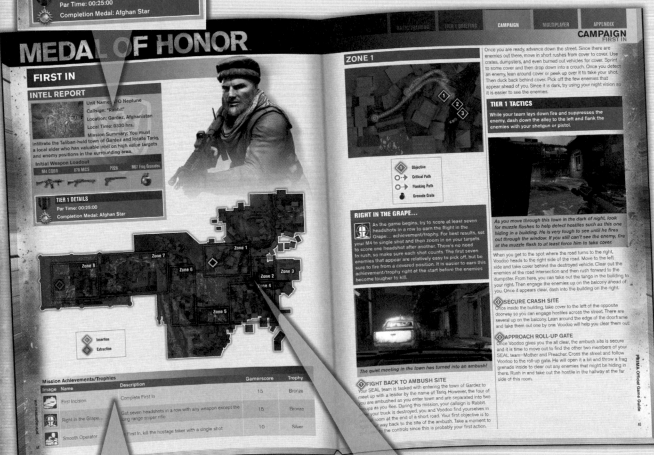

ACHIEVEMENTS AND TROPHIES TABLE

This table lists the achievements or trophies that can be earned during this mission along with the requirements. Knowing the requirements ahead of time helps you be prepared to earn the achievements or trophies during your first play through of the mission.

AREA MAP

The areas in which you will be operating for each mission can be quite large. The area map shows the big picture and includes the insertion and extraction points for the mission, as well as the location of the various zones into which the mission is divided.

INTRODUCTION
HOW TO USE THIS GUIDE

ZONE MAPS

Zone maps provide a zoomed-in view of a portion of the area map that focuses on one or more objectives that you must complete. These maps include the locations of objectives with an icon that corresponds to similar icons imbedded in the text. They also show main movement paths as well as paths for flanking maneuvers. If there are any grenade crates or places where you can earn an achievement, these are also designated on the map with appropriate icons.

TIER 1 TACTICS

While the walkthrough will offer great strategies whether you are playing through the campaign or going through the missions in Tier 1 mode, these boxes within the section offer targeted tips on how play during Tier 1 mode. Since this mode is timed and much more difficult, read these so that you can beat the par time and avoid being killed, so you don't have to keep starting the mission over.

TIER 1 TACTICS

This part of the mission where you go through the dark building is a great place to pick up the pace and save time. Rush through with your shotgun. As long as you keep moving quickly, the enemy will have a hard time tracking and hitting you. You can also freeze the clock here by making melee kills with your knife while maintaining stealth. Another tactic is to use your pistol to make...

FOLLOW VOODOO

"The darkness gives you an advantage, allowing you to enter a room and start firing before the enemy knows where you are. Use the shotgun as your 'room broom.'"

Voodoo leads the way through a hallway. When you come to a doorway to another room, take up a position on the left side of the door. Lean out into the opening and open fire. There are two tangos near the center and one to the left. Blast away at each in turn to clear the room before entering it. Voodoo will usually let you do all the shooting here. Since it is dark, the enemy will have trouble determining where you are at first.

Advance through the room and continue through a doorway on the right side into a kitchen area. There are several enemies in the large storage room. Quickly move through the kitchen and take up a position on the left side of the doorway leading to the storage room. Lean out and take out the enemies you can see. One may be hiding behind some sacks of grain. If he stops shooting for a bit, quickly move in and around to the right to take him out with your knife.

THE SCALPEL & PISTOL PETE SHOWDOWN

The dark building is a great place to start working towards The Scalpel achievement/trophy. You need 20 total knife kills for this award. Since the building is completely dark, rush in fast and knife all the enemies before they know you are there. If you want to start earning the Pistol Pete Showdown achievement/trophy, use your pistol when fighting indoors instead of your shotgun. You will need 30 kills for this award and can easily get at least 10 during this mission. Every little bit helps.

Use your knife to take out tangos

ACHIEVEMENTS AND TROPHIES

So that you can earn lots of achievements and trophies on your first time playing through the campaign, these boxes have been provided to let you know what you need to do within the current zone to earn your awards. Some achievements can only be earned in a specific location or part of the mission. Be sure to read these boxes so you don't miss the opportunity and have to play the mission over again just to earn an achievement or trophy.

TIP

When fighting your way through the interiors of buildings, the shotgun is a good choice for your weapon. Close quarters engagements are quick, so you want to be able to fire fast without having to carefully aim. Shotguns will take out most hostiles with a single shot. Just be sure to reload after each engagement so you are ready for the next fight.

TIPS, NOTES, AND CAUTIONS

These boxes highlight information that can make completing the mission easier or warn you of dangerous threats. Follow these directions to better ensure victory.

THE SCALPEL & PISTOL PETE SHOWDOWN

The dark building is a great place to start working towards The Scalpel achievement/trophy. You need 20 total knife kills for this award. Since the building is completely dark, rush in fast and knife all the enemies before they know you are there. If you want to start earning the Pistol Pete Showdown achievement/trophy, use your pistol when fighting indoors instead of your shotgun. You will need 30 kills for this award and can easily get at least 10 during this mission. Every little bit helps.

Use your knife to take out tangos

MEDAL OF HONOR™

While the campaign is fun, the real action gets underway during online multiplayer matches. In this chapter all aspects of multiplayer are discussed, including classes, weapons, and unlocks. This chapter also contains detailed breakdowns of each map, offering expert tips and tactics for achieving victories in each game mode.

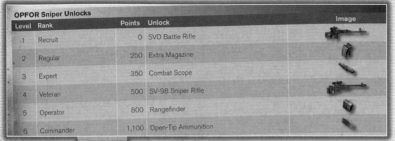

OPFOR Sniper Unlocks

Level	Rank	Points	Unlock	Image
1	Recruit	0	SVD Battle Rifle	
2	Regular	250	Extra Magazine	
3	Expert	350	Combat Scope	
4	Veteran	500	SV-98 Sniper Rifle	
5	Operator	800	Rangefinder	
6	Commander	1,100	Open-Tip Ammunition	

CLASS UNLOCKS

The coalition and OPFOR variants of each class are covered in detail. Study these tables to see what unlocks are in your immediate future.

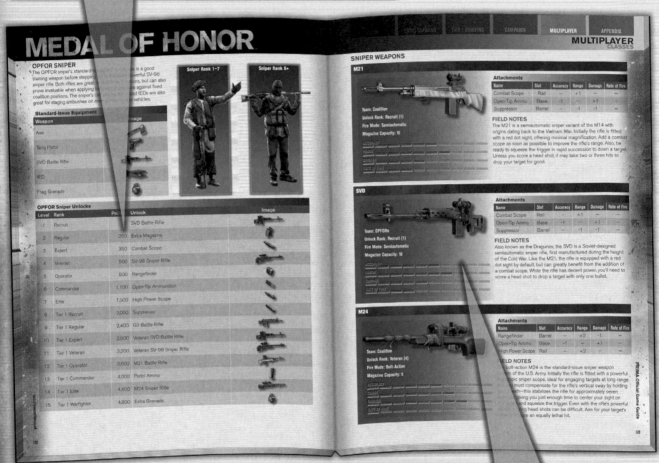

WEAPON STATS

Complete accuracy, range, damage, and rate of fire stats are provided for all weapons and their attachments, giving you a preview of each before you unlock them.

SVD

Team: OPFORs
Unlock Rank: Recruit (1)
Fire Mode: Semiautomatic
Magazine Capacity: 10

Attachments

Name	Slot	Accuracy	Range	Damage	Rate
Combat Scope	Rail	–	+1	–	
Open-Tip Ammo	Base	-1	–	+1	
Suppressor	Barrel	–	-1	-1	

FIELD NOTES
Also known as the Dragunov, the SVD is a Soviet-designed semiautomatic sniper rifle, first manufactured during the he of the Cold War. Like the M21, the rifle is equipped with a r dot sight by default, but can greatly benefit from the additio a combat scope. While the rifle has decent power, you'll nee score a head shot to drop a target with only one bullet.

COMBAT MISSION MAPS

Each Combat Mission map is broken into five areas, each containing a specific objective that the coalition troops must either destroy or control. In addition to showing the objective, vehicle spawn points, and machine guns, coalition and OPFOR bases are also revealed, helping you determine where the enemy is coming from.

TACTICS

Team tactics for every map are discussed in detail, providing valuable insight on how to leverage the environment and its assets to achieve victory in every battle.

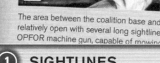

CHOKE POINTS

Each map identifies these narrow, high-traffic areas where you and your teammates can score multiple kills by staging devastating ambushes.

SIGHTLINES

Snipers seeking long-range coverage can utilize these sightlines to pick off enemies at extreme distances. Those caught in the middle of a sightline should get out of the way!

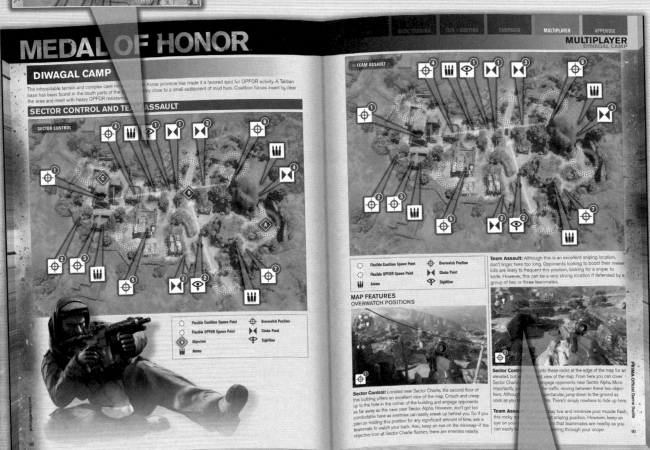

TEAM ASSAULT, OBJECTIVE RAID, & SECTOR CONTROL MAPS

Although these three game modes share the same maps, the layout of objectives and the flow of traffic are different depending on the mode. Therefore, each game mode is covered separately with its own labeled map revealing objectives, spawn points, machine guns, choke points, overwatch positions, and sightlines. Team tactics are also discussed for each mode, identifying flanking paths as well as strong defensive positions.

OVERWATCH POSITIONS

Whether covering your team's advance or defending an objective, these positions are key to suppressing enemy forces, often providing elevated views of the battlefield.

Sector Control: Climb onto these rock elevated, but very exposed, view of the n Sector Charlie as well as engage oppon importantly, you can flank the traffic mov tives. Although the view is spectacular, j

APPENDIX

Flip to the back of the guide for easy-reference tables containing information on the Tier 1 Mode and multiplayer awards. All Xbox 360 achievements and PS3 trophies are also listed in this chapter.

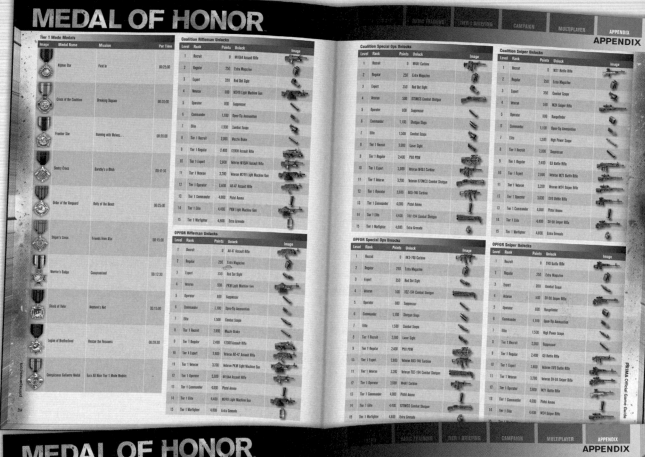

BASIC TRAINING

Medal of Honor is a first-person tactical shooter that puts you in the roles of Tier 1 special operations soldiers. Since the characters you play as are highly trained, it is important to master several aspects of playing the game to get the most out of it and emerge victorious. This chapter will introduce you to several key components of the game, teach you how to maneuver and fight, and finally provide you with the battle-tested tactics to defeat your enemies.

DYNAMIC HUD

Information appears on the screen as it applies, such as when you change stance, fire a weapon, receive a new objective, or press the Dynamic HUD button.

Medal of Honor features a dynamic HUD that lets you focus on the action rather than constant on-screen information. Objective information appears in the top center of the screen. As you change stance, your current stance appears momentarily in the lower left corner of the screen. In the right corner, you can see how many rounds are in your current magazine as well as the total number of rounds you have on your person.

TIP

If you want to check your ammo status and the counter is not on the screen, press the dynamic HUD button.

In addition to the standard info you might find in this type of game, you can also bring up your head's up display by pressing the dynamic HUD button. This will display an icon showing you the direction of your current objective as well as the distance to the objective. Icons will also show you the location of your teammates. If you are not sure where to go or where your teammates have gone, press the dynamic HUD button so you can get back on track.

Tips and icons appear at the bottom center of the screen in order to help you get through the mission. The icons inform you about special types of actions that you must perform at a spot or when you have performed a headshot special kill. The following table shows the various icons that will appear during the game.

HUD Icons

Icon	Name
	Objective
	Objective Complete
	Mount ATV
	Get aboard helicopter
	Breach the door
	Head shot
	Plant an explosive charge
	Buddy boost
	Use machine gun
	Destroy fuse box
	Place beacon
	Use SOFLAM
	Suppress the enemy

STANCE AND MOVEMENT

When sprinting, notice that your weapon is not pointed straight ahead. You can't fire while running.

Stances and Movement

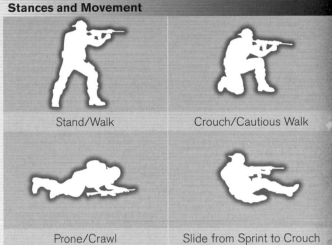

Stand/Walk	Crouch/Cautious Walk
Prone/Crawl	Slide from Sprint to Crouch

You will have to move around in order to complete your objectives. Within the single-player game, you can be in three different stances. These stances affect your speed of movement as well as how large of a target you present to the enemy. While standing, you move at a walking pace. To move quicker, press the sprint button while moving and you will run. While sprinting, you can't fire your weapon, but are more difficult for the enemy to hit. The second stance is a crouch. While crouched down, it is more difficult for the enemy to detect and hit you. However, you move slower than while walking. Finally, you can drop prone onto the ground. If you come under fire while behind low cover, drop prone to make sure you don't get hit—especially if you are trying to recover from some previous hits. Prone also allows you to get under some low obstacles.

One of the cool new mechanics in Medal of Honor is the slide. When you are sprinting, you can slide into a crouch by just pressing the stance button. This will cause your character to quickly drop down into a crouch as he slides to lose momentum. Learn to use this tactic as you are moving from cover to cover. Press the stance button just before you get to the cover and you will slide the rest of the way in. You are then ready to start shooting at the enemy.

TIP

It is always a good idea to sprint across open areas when you are engaged in combat and then drop down into a crouch. You do not need to stand first from a crouch in order to sprint. Pressing the sprint button while moving in a crouch will automatically make you stand up and run. To get into cover quickly at the end of a sprint, keep holding down the sprint button and then press the stance button to cause your character to slide into cover.

COMBAT

Use the weapon sights to increase your accuracy when firing at enemies.

Now that you understand how to get to the enemy, it is vital that you know how to neutralize the hostiles before they kill you. During missions, you will be armed with a variety of weapons. They range from assault rifles to grenades and even a knife. As you find enemies, your job is to kill them. You will not be taking any prisoners. While each weapon has some variation, most of the firearms operate in the same way. When walking around, you will see a crosshair reticule in the center of the screen. This shows you the approximate area your bullets will hit. Firing in this mode is not accurate—especially at medium or long range—because you are essentially firing from the hip without using the weapon's sights to aim. To increase your accuracy, hold down the sights button. This will bring the weapon up to your shoulder and you will be looking through the iron sights or scope, depending on which weapon you are carrying. When looking through the sights, you move slower and lose some of your peripheral vision. An experienced soldier moves around with the weapon lowered and then quickly raises it up to look through the sights before firing.

TIP

If you are getting low on ammo, you can ask a teammate for more. This only works on weapons that you have when you begin the mission. Small bullet icons appear next to a teammate's icon. These represent the number of times he can resupply your ammo. Don't bother teammates if you still have quite a bit of ammo left. They will only give you more when you are low. In addition, they only give you ammo for your currently selected weapon."

TYPES OF WEAPONS

As a Tier 1 operative, you have several different weapons at your disposal. However, they all fit into a few specific categories. It is important that you know how to use each category of weapons effectively in order to get the most out of them. In most missions, you carry two weapons as well as your pistol. It is a good idea to make sure you have weapons from different categories so you have more flexibility during combat.

TIP

You can pick up weapons dropped by enemies. Since you can only carry two weapons at a time, you have to swap out one of your weapons for the enemy weapon. You can't get ammo for captured weapons from teammates, but you can pick it up off the ground. After killing a hostile with the same weapon, just walk over the weapon he dropped and you will get a clip of ammo for the enemy weapon.

ASSAULT RIFLES

Assault rifles are your standard weapon. They are capable of engaging enemies at all ranges. While they are capable of automatic fire, it is best to fire in short bursts. The longer the burst, the less accurate the fire. Use the assault rifle for most outdoor combat at medium to long range. You can kill a hostile with a single head shot, however it will take two to four rounds to take down an enemy with hits to other parts of the body. Be sure to fire from sight view in order to increase your accuracy. Assault rifles can be fired in semiautomatic mode where only one round is fired each time you press the fire button. This is best when firing at long range or attempting head shots, since a single round will be more accurate than even a short burst of automatic fire.

TIP

One assault rifle, the M4 rifle with M203 grenade launcher mounts a 40mm grenade launcher under the rifle barrel. This weapon gives you some great additional firepower for clearing out enemies at medium range.

SUBMACHINE GUNS

Smaller than assault rifles, submachine guns are automatic weapons capable of high rates of fire. When equipped with a suppressor, submachine guns are quite stealthy and great for operations when you do not want to let the enemy know you are there. Because of their smaller barrel length, submachine guns are not as effective at medium to long range. However, for short range and indoor combat, submachine guns are an excellent choice.

MACHINE GUNS

Machine guns are some of the most powerful weapons available to you. They come in two varieties. Light machine guns can be carried by an individual soldier and provide high rates of portable fire. Fixed machine guns are larger and deadlier. These can be located at a position or mounted on a vehicle. Even though you can fire off a hundred or more rounds without having to reload, it is still a good idea to fire machine guns in short bursts as accuracy is increased. During missions when you are assigned to carry the light machine gun, one tactic is to stay back and provide support to the other members of your team. Fire at enemies as your teammates advance and maneuver around. Even if you don't kill hostiles outright, the volume of fire your light machine gun can put out will keep the enemies' heads down so they can't fire at you or your teammates. The second tactic for using machine guns is to put your firepower out in front. Your large magazine means that you can fire away through an entire engagement or two without having to stop to reload. Lead the way mow down any hostiles that cross your path.

TIP

While fixed machine guns don't have to be reloaded, some of them can overheat. Watch for a bar along the bottom right of the screen that will begin to get longer as you continue to fire. If it reaches its full length, the gun will stop operating until it cools down on its own. Firing in short bursts is a great way to keep guns from overheating.

SHOTGUNS

Shotguns may not be as glamorous as other types of weapons; however, they are excellent for close-quarters combat. When moving through a building where enemies can be around any corner, pull out your shotgun. Unlike the other types of weapons, you can fire this from the hip against close-range targets. In addition, a single shot at close range will kill most hostiles. Due to the spread of the shot over distance, shotguns lose their effectiveness at medium range. You may need to fire two or three times at this range to kill an enemy. As a general rule, if you are about to bust down a door to enter a room, get your shotgun ready to take down any tangos on the other side.

TIP

Shotguns do not hold a lot of rounds and it takes longer to reload than most of the other weapons. Therefore, as soon as you take out an enemy or clear a room, remember to reload so you have a full load of shells for the next engagement.

PISTOLS

Your pistol is your backup weapon. Quickly press the weapon select button twice to bring up your pistol. It is often quicker to pull your pistol when one of your other weapons is empty than reloading the weapon. While you have an unlimited supply of pistol ammo, you still have to reload when your clip is empty. Pistols are only accurate at short range and all are semiautomatic. Unless you are going for a head shot, get used to firing three shots at the body of enemies to make sure to kill them.

TIP

Don't only use your pistol when you run out of ammo. The Pistol Pete Showdown achievement/trophy requires you to get a total of 30 kills with a pistol. Therefore, when you are fighting at close range, consider using the pistol to start racking up kills and earn this award.

A Special Prayer for 2011

Heavenly Father, thank you for the blessing of this new year, brimming with hope and possibility.

Grant us the strength, wisdom and enthusiasm to serve those who endure overwhelming hardships, both natural and man-made.

Help promote peace where there is darkness of spirit.

Guide and extend our reach overseas so that all your children may live with dignity.

Amen

GRENADES AND EXPLOSIVES

During most missions, you begin with three frag grenades. These explosives have a five-second fuse that provides a delay before they explode. As soon as you press the grenade button, the fuse starts counting down. To throw the grenade, release the button. Tangos will try to run away when they see a grenade coming towards them. Therefore, it is important to time your throw. For most times you throw a grenade, hold the button for two to three seconds and then release. This is called cooking off a grenade by letting the fuse start counting down in your hand. Then if you time it right, the grenade will explode right when it gets near the enemy and before they can run away. The grenade launcher on the M4 203 fires a grenade without a fuse. Instead, this grenade explodes on impact. The tangos are equipped with rocket propelled grenades or RPGs. This is a tube that fires a high explosive charge. While U.S. forces do not carry RPGs, you can find them in some missions and swap out another weapon to pick up and use RPGs against the enemy.

TIP

Look for grenade crates during missions. They will appear as a light-colored diamond when you are nearby and press the HUD button. You can only use these crates once to fill up your grenades. When you have the M4 203, the grenade crates contain 40mm grenades rather then frag hand grenades.

KNIFE

The quickest and surest way to kill an enemy at very close range is with a melee attack. Just get close and press the melee button to use your knife. It only takes one hit to kill a hostile with the knife. In addition, melee kills are silent. If you are not carrying a suppressed weapon and want to maintain stealth, sneak up behind an enemy and use your knife.

TIP

By using your knife, you can earn The Scalpel achievement/ trophy. You just need a cumulative 20 melee kills with your knife to get this award.

NODS NIGHT VISION

When operating at night or in the dark, use your night vision to see in the dark. This device can give you a great advantage in the dark since the enemy is not equipped with these goggles. Night vision provides an image in various shades of green. In areas where it is very dark, you can move around undetected. As long as you don't fire a weapon, you can move about killing enemies with melee attacks. When you fire a weapon, the enemy can see the muzzle flash and start shooting at your position. While they may not be able to see where you are exactly, they know you are there.

TIP

When using night vision equipment, be sure to deactivate it if you are going into a lit area or if there are illumination flares in the area. These will temporarily blind your view if you don't take off your device in time.

SOFLAM

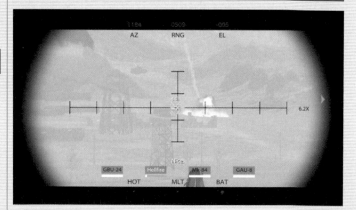

The Special Operations Force Laser Marker allows you to call in air support on the enemy. You can only use this device at certain points during a mission. In some missions, you may have access to only one type of support while in others you can cycle through up to four different air strikes including cannon fire, airborne artillery, bombs, and even guided missiles. With this device, you can destroy lots of heavy targets in a short amount of time.

TIP

When engaging multiple targets, you do not need to continue to target an enemy vehicle or position until the ordinance arrives and destroys it. Instead, just wait until a locked on icon appears on the target. Then you can cycle to a different weapon and begin lasing a new target.

TACTICS

Now that you know about movement and combat, it is time to put them together to form tactics that will help you survive on the battlefield and give you an advantage over the enemy.

COVER

Always use cover whenever you are engaging the enemy.

Today's battlefield is extremely deadly. The enemy you face is heavily armed and out to kill you. Therefore, you need to find some object to position between you and the enemy that will prevent bullets from hitting you. These objects are referred to as cover. Cover can be a wall, a rock, a crate, or even a vehicle. As soon as you come under fire, or even see an enemy in the area, move behind some cover. If it is low, you may need to crouch down behind the cover.

TIP

When you have to move with enemies in the area, always move from cover to cover. Standing still out in the open makes you an easy target and will likely get you killed. In fact, plan which cover you are moving to before you begin to move.

While there is cover between the hostile and you, the enemy can't shoot you. However, you can't shoot him either. While you could move out from cover to take a shot, there is a better and safer way—leaning and peeking. Hold down the peek and lean button and your character's feet stay in one spot. Then when you move to the right or left, your character will lean in that direction. So if you are to the side of a doorway, you can lean into the doorway to see and then shoot enemies. When leaning, you are just moving your upper torso so only your head, shoulders, and arms are exposed. You can still be shot, but it is harder for the enemy to hit you. Moving forward while holding down the peek and lean button will cause you to rise up from a crouch so you can peek over low cover and engage enemies. If you start taking fire, continue to hold down the peek and lean button and stop providing movement inputs. Your character will quickly pull back behind cover.

TIP

While peeking and leaning, hold down the iron sights button. This allows you to peek or lean around cover and still fire with good accuracy. In addition to peeking over objects, you can also peek under cover by moving down rather than up.

TEAMWORK

In each mission, you are a part of a team. Work together with your teammates to accomplish your objectives.

During each mission, you are part of a team. In some you will be with one teammate while in others you will be operating with three other teammates. Teams are important for combat since the members work together to achieve a common objective. It is usually a good idea to stay with your team. Don't take off ahead of them or you may be facing a lot of hostiles on your own. Instead, as you advance, make sure they are coming with you. If they are staying back, they may see a threat ahead and want to engage it from a distance before moving forward. An advantage of staying with your team is their additional firepower. Your teammates will take out tangos along with you—they are not just there for looks. In addition, they can help by calling out threats for you. Listen to what they say, especially if they tell you to target a hostile with an RPG or other heavy weapon.

TIP

Another good reason to stay by your teammates is for ammo. If you get low, you can approach one of your teammates and ask for some ammo from them. They will give you ammo for any U.S. weapon—but not for captured enemy weapons.

A teammate can be very useful when moving through buildings. Before entering a room, stack up outside the door and once your teammate is ready, move in. Buildings can contain multiple hostiles in a single room and two weapons are better than one for clearing them out. Just as your teammates support you, it is important to also provide support for your teammates. When you are carrying a light machine gun, you are the support. Let your teammates lead the way while you cover them with suppressing fire. Then, once they have taken cover, quickly move forward to cover their next advance.

TIP

During the sniper phases of the AFO Wolfpack missions, listen carefully to Dusty. He is your spotter and will help you find targets. In addition, if you miss, he will let you know how to correct for your next shot.

FLANKING

Sneak up behind enemies while they are focused on your teammates.

While it is a good idea to stay with your team, at times a better tactic is to split up in order to hit the enemy from two different directions. As you are advancing towards the enemy or already engaged with hostiles, look for side paths or trails that branch off from the main path. While your team moves down the main path or stays put, you can follow the side path around, possibly behind cover, so that you can maneuver to a position from which you can hit the enemy from either the side or rear. Flanking is a good way to neutralize tangos behind cover by moving around so that the object of cover is no longer between you and your target.

TIER 1 MODE

Tier 1 mode is very tough—and it's timed! There are several ways to affect the timer. If you can kill five enemies in fifteen seconds, you freeze the timer for five seconds.

Once you have completed a mission in the campaign, you then have the opportunity to play through the mission again in Tier 1 mode. Completion of each mission unlocks the Tier 1 mode for that mission. The Gunfighter mission where you are in the AH-64D Apache does not have a Tier 1 mode; however, all of the other nine missions where you are on foot can be played in this mode. Tier 1 is the most difficult level in the game. While you are playing the same mission, several aspects have been changed to make for an extreme combat experience. Whenever you take hits from the enemy, they do a lot more damage and your health is restored at a much slower rate. Therefore, it is very important to use cover since just a few hits will result in your death. If you die, you have to start the mission over from the very beginning—no checkpoints in Tier 1. Not only is the mode deadlier, it is also more realistic. A crosshair reticule does not appear on the screen. You have to use your sights if you want to aim. In addition, the HUD feature is deactivated, so you cannot get targeting information. Only your objective icons, icons for your teammates, and grenade indicators appear on the screen. If that were not enough, you also can't get extra ammo from your teammates. If you run out, you will have to pick up a weapon dropped by a dead enemy and scrounge for ammo also dropped by tangos that have been eliminated.

TIP

While a reticule does not appear on the screen, when playing a night mission, activate your night vision. If your weapon is equipped with an IR targeting laser, you will be able to see the beam. Just place the beam over a target and fire. It is just as good as a reticule if you don't have time to bring up the sights.

Tier 1 is played online, even though you are not playing against anyone else. Instead, you are competing against other players for best completion times as well as other stats on the leaderboards such as head shots, knife kills, grenade kills, how much time you have frozen, longest range kill, and accuracy. Each mission has a par time that you try to beat. There are several things you can do to stop the timer for a few seconds. These are referred to as skill kills which include head shots and knife kills. While a few seconds here and there may not seem like much, they add up. The follow table lists the six actions that will freeze the clock as well as the duration of the freeze.

Tier 1 Skill Kills that Freeze Time

Action	Duration of Freeze
Head shot	2 seconds
Three head shots in a row	5 seconds
Melee kill	2 seconds
Three melee kills in within 10 seconds	6 seconds
Kill two enemies with a single bullet	6 seconds
Kill five enemies within 15 seconds	5 seconds

The timer adds a sense of urgency to Tier 1 mode. However, don't let it make you rush. Since it is very easy to die, you are better off taking a bit of time and using cover. Since you have already played the missions first, you should know where there are areas without any hostiles. Sprint through these areas to save time so you can have it for the engagements. Since you are being cautious, also try to make your shots count. Because you get a couple extra seconds for head shots, try to kill enemies in this way. This will also help you save ammo. Each time you complete a mission under the par time, you receive a medal unique to that mission. Once you complete all nine missions under par, you also get a tenth medal for your effort.

Conspicuous Gallantry

If you can complete all nine of the Tier 1 mode missions under par time, you can earn the Conspicuous Gallantry achievement/trophy.

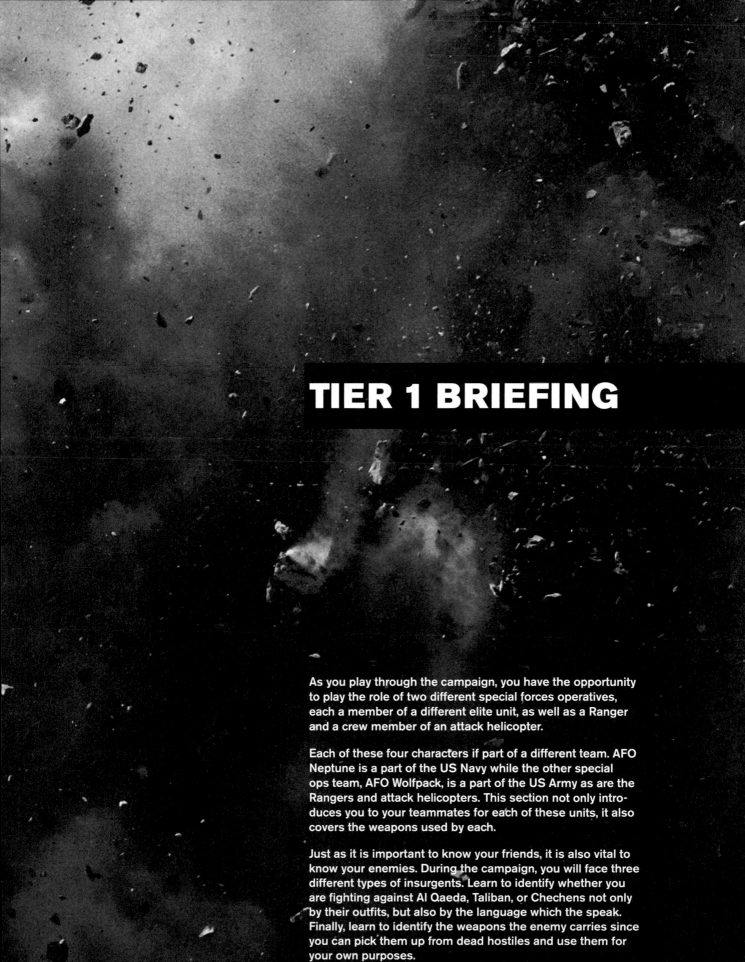

TIER 1 BRIEFING

As you play through the campaign, you have the opportunity to play the role of two different special forces operatives, each a member of a different elite unit, as well as a Ranger and a crew member of an attack helicopter.

Each of these four characters if part of a different team. AFO Neptune is a part of the US Navy while the other special ops team, AFO Wolfpack, is a part of the US Army as are the Rangers and attack helicopters. This section not only introduces you to your teammates for each of these units, it also covers the weapons used by each.

Just as it is important to know your friends, it is also vital to know your enemies. During the campaign, you will face three different types of insurgents. Learn to identify whether you are fighting against Al Qaeda, Taliban, or Chechens not only by their outfits, but also by the language which the speak. Finally, learn to identify the weapons the enemy carries since you can pick them up from dead hostiles and use them for your own purposes.

AFO NEPTUNE (U.S. NAVY)

Neptune is a team of Navy SEALs. This is the U.S. Navy's special operations unit and gets its name because SEALs are trained for combat in the SEa, Air, and on the Land. Due to their training in unconventional warfare, the SEALs were deployed to Afghanistan even though it is not near the ocean. SEALs are deadly no matter in which element they are operating.

MOTHER

Veteran Tier 1 Operator, AFO Neptune team leader. Skilled warrior who will do anything for his men.

PREACHER

Senior AFO Neptune team member. Methodical and quiet in action, but always first to act.

VOODOO

Skilled warrior with combat experience across the globe, he is Neptune's pit bull.

RABBIT

You are Rabbit during the AFO Neptune missions.

TIER 1 BRIEFING
AFO NEPTUNE

AFO NEPTUNE WEAPONS

M4 CQBR

M4

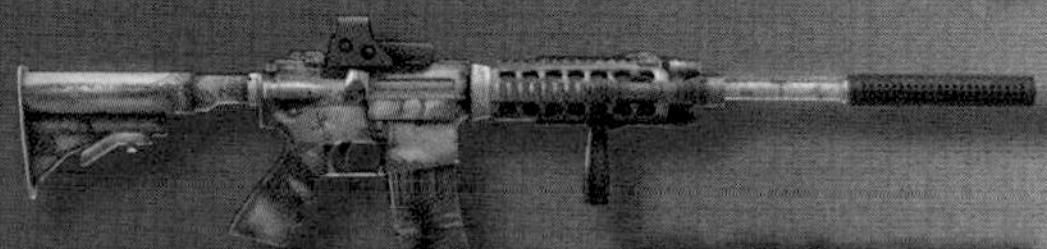

M4 with Suppressor

M14 EBR

870 MCS

M60

PKM

SOFLAM
(Special Operations Forces Laser Marker)

P226

Hilux Truck

SPECIAL FORCES GLOSSARY

30 mike: Slang for rounds fired from the Apache's M230 chain gun or A-10 Warthog's GAU-8 rotary cannon.

40 mike: 40mm grenades, usually deployed from a M203 grenade launcher. The 40mm rounds can also be fired from the AC-130 gunship.

AAA, Triple A: Antiaircraft Artillery. Any improved position that has artillery designed to take down aircraft.

AFO: Advance Force Operations. The "black" special operations team tasked with high-risk missions in hostile territory.

AO: Area of Operation. The geographic location of the combat operations.

BDA: Battle Damage Assessment. Report to aircraft or artillery that tells the success or failure of an airstrike or artillery strike.

CAS: Close Air Support. Any air action from fixed or rotary wing aircraft against hostile forces when friendly forces are in close proximity.

Charlie Mike: Military phonetic alphabet slang for "continue mission."

Contact: A standard marking term used by aviators to acknowledge sighting of a specific reference point. For ground forces, it is when first contact is made with hostile forces. Often yelled, "Contact!"

C-SAR: Combat Search And Rescue.

Delta Hotel: Military phonetic alphabet slang for "direct hit." Acknowledges target destroyed.

Dismounts: Troops that are on foot. They can be enemy or friendly.

DShK: "Dishka." A Soviet-made heavy machine gun that fires large 12.7mm rounds and is used throughout Afghanistan by the Taliban and Al Qaeda.

FARP: Forward Arming and Refueling Point. A safe area where aircraft can refuel that is closer to the area of operation than the base from which they launched.

MEDAL OF HONOR™

AFO WOLFPACK (U.S. ARMY)

Wolfpack is a Special Forces unit of the U.S. Army. These operatives are highly trained in special reconnaissance and unconventional warfare. In Afghanistan, many of the Special Forces grew beards to gain the respect of the locals. According to local customs and culture, beards are a symbol of masculinity.

PANTHER

AFO Wolfpack Team Leader. Lives by the motto "Develop the Situation." Combat experience in Panama, Lebanon, Columbia, Bosnia, Afghanistan, and Iraq. Leads by always listening to the guy on the ground.

DUSTY

Country boy whose hunting skills were honed on his grand-parents' farm. He lives for the hunt.

VEGAS

Panther's right hand man, Ranger, and intelligence guru who speaks seven languages.

DEUCE

When playing the AFO Wolfpack missions, you play as Deuce.

AFO WOLFPACK WEAPONS

MP7A1

M110

M82

G19

ATV

SPECIAL FORCES GLOSSARY

FLIR: Forward Looking Infrared. Infrared technology used in aviation to see in low light in addition to picking up heat signatures.

HVT: High Value Target. An important person of interest who must be targeted or terminated.

IR: Infrared. Often used in low light situations and in conjunction with NODs to mark targets or positions. Can be in the form of strobes or chemical lights.

Lima Charlie: Military phonetic alphabet slang for "loud and clear." Acknowledgement of an order.

LZ: Landing Zone.

"Mujh": Shorthand for mujahideen or "freedom fighter." Refers to any number of factions of armed guerilla fighters in Afghanistan, on either side of the war.

NCO: Noncommissioned Officer. Enlisted soldier above the rank of corporal; usually refers to U.S. Army personnel.

"Nizzos": Component of the male reproductive system.

No Joy: A standard marking term used by aviators to state no visual on the target or reference point.

NOD: Night Optical Device. Sometimes called NVGs, these are used by the military to see in low light situations.

O Dark Thirty: Military slang for the dark hours between midnight and sunrise. Very early.

PC: Precious Cargo. General term used in the SOF community for a tangible objective to be acquired or secured. Can be a person, object, or data.

PID: Positive Identification. Confirmed identification of a target, location, or reference point.

MEDAL OF HONOR

1ST BATTALION 75TH RANGER REGIMENT (U.S. ARMY)

The Rangers are an elite light infantry force of the U.S. Army. They often operate in support of special operations forces.

SGT. PATTERSON

Type A mentality. He is the squad's leader and has seen his fair share of battle in Afghanistan already. Smart and assured, sometimes gruff—when he talks, people listen.

SPC. HERNANDEZ

A Ranger through and through, he is Patterson's most trusted man. Although he is full of Latin bravado, his actions back it up and he is an experienced troop.

TSGT. YBARRA

The squad's U.S. Air Force ETAC (Enlisted Tactical Air Controller) is cool under fire, smart, and doesn't mince his words—the hallmark of a good "com" guy. He's just as handy with a gun as he is with his radio.

SPC. DANTE ADAMS

During the Ranger missions, you play as Dante.

TIER 1 BRIEFING
1ST BATTALION 75TH RANGER REGIMENT

RANGER WEAPONS

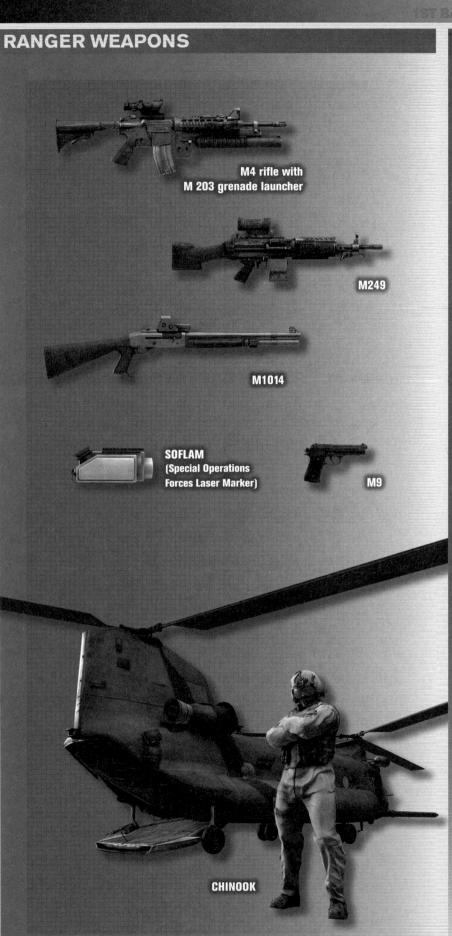

M4 rifle with
M 203 grenade launcher

M249

M1014

SOFLAM
(Special Operations
Forces Laser Marker)

M9

CHINOOK

SPECIAL FORCES GLOSSARY

QRF: Quick Reaction Force. A nimble, at-the-ready force deployed in very short notice, usually under fifteen minutes. The size depends on the threat, but most QRFs are a platoon or a squad.

Roger: "Yes."

RPG: Rocket-Propelled Grenade. Weapon of choice of guerilla forces— it's ubiquitous, portable, and deadly.

SIGINT: Signal Intelligence. All forms of radio, telephone, satellite, or other communication other than personal interaction or human intelligence (HUMINT).

SOFLAM: Special Operations Force Laser Marker. Hand-held laser rangefinder and designator unit used by SOF to mark and destroy enemy targets with laser-guided ordnance.

TADS: Target Acquisition and Designation System. Used on the Apache helicopter, this is the system recognizes targets and designates them for fire missions.

Tally: A standard marking term used by aviators to acknowledge sighting of confirmed enemy target.

Tango Uniform: Military phonetic alphabet slang for total destruction of an intended target.

TOC: Tactical Operations Center. The command center in the area of operation.

TOT: Time on Target. Shorthand for the time before impact of ordnance on a target.

UAV: Unmanned Aerial Vehicle. A pilotless drone that is controlled remotely.

VTC: Video Teleconference. A way for the rear echelon to keep tabs on the guys on the ground. Its benefits are debatable as it has as many detractors as supporters.

WILCO: "Will comply." The shortest, most concise way of saying, "I hear you and will do what you say."

MEDAL OF HONOR™

1ST BATTALION, 2ND AVIATION REGIMENT "GUNFIGHTERS"

This aviation unit of the U.S. Army provides close air support to ground troops and can also be used for independent seek and destroy missions. The unit's AH-64D Apache Longbow attack helicopters can engage all types of targets at a variety of ranges.

CAPTAIN BRAD "HAWK" HAWKINS

During the Gunfighters mission, you play as the front seat gunner in one of this unit's attack helicopters.

GUNFIGHTER AIRCRAFT

AH-64D Apache Longbow

INSURGENTS

As the U.S. and allied militaries invaded Afghanistan in the months following September 11, 2001, they fought primarily against the Taliban, a radical Islamic political group that had ruled the country since 1996. Primarily made up of members of the ethnic Pashtun tribes, the Taliban allowed other Islamic militant and terrorist groups to train and operate within Afghanistan including both Al Qaeda and Chechen rebels. U.S. forces fought against these groups as well as the Afghan Military Forces (AMF).

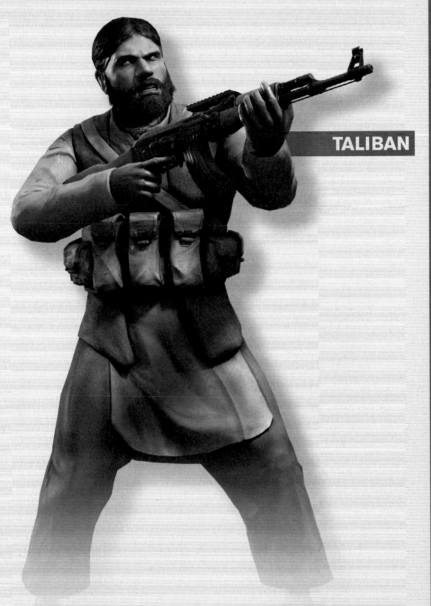

TALIBAN

PASHTO PHRASES

Pashto is the language spoken by the largest and most dominant ethnic group. Pashtuns are mostly Sunni Muslims. Pashto is spoken mostly in rural areas and by the mujahideen and Taliban fighters. All words are spelled phonetically.

Doi halta di!: They are here!

Doi wodarawa!: Hold them off!

Doi wunissa!: Get them!

Dushman!: Enemy!

Dwei wrazi de dey taqaodi ta pati wuh!: He was two days from retirement!

Feire!: Shoot!

Ghol! Doi dalta di!: Shit, they're here!

Hagha wakhla!: Take that!

Halta: Over here.

Hamla!: Ambush! Attack!

Ho, balley, hokey: Yes.

Kafiran!: Infidel!

Lanat!: Damn!

Lasey Bam: Hand grenade.

Mall shey!: Die.

Manana: Thank you.

Melgeray: Friend.

Nah: No.

Saber!: Wait!

Ta da wawrida?: Did you hear that?

Yaw, dwa, drey, za!: One, two, three, go!

Za!: Go!

Ze doi weenum!: I see them!

AL QAEDA

ARABIC

Arabic is the national language of at least twenty countries through Africa and Asia and is the common language of Al Qaeda. This version is sometimes referred to as "gulf Arabic."

Adou!: Enemy!

Al Qaeda: The base.

Ana shayefhon!: I see them!

Hinne hone! Wisloo!: They are here!

Hone!: Over here!

Hujoom!: Ambush! Attack!

Ik'tulhon!: Get them!

Inte smea'to?: Did you hear that?

Intither!: Wait!

Itlek' ennar!: Shoot!

K'umbleh: Hand grenade.

Kawimhon!: Hold them off!

Khara! Wissloo!: Shit, they're here!

Khode!: Take that!

Kuffar!: Infidel!

La'anatoollah!: Damn!

Laa: No.

Moot!: Die!

Na'am: Yes.

Sadeeq: Friend.

Shukran: Thank you.

Ummak kalbeh!: Your mother is a dog!

WaaHid, thnain, thalaatha, yalla!: One, two, three, go!

Yalla!: Go!

CHECHEN

CHECHEN

Chechen is spoken by more than one million Chechen people. Predominantly Sunni Muslims, Chechen fighters have been in Afghanistan for many years fighting with the mujahideen.

Bai yush!: Kill them!

Barkalla: Thank you.

Ca, shih, koh, davale!: One, two, three, go!

Davale!: Go!

Del mostagi!: Infidel!

Dottagh: Friend.

Ee vah tah vezash var!: He should have ducked!

Gerz tokh!: Shoot!

Granaat: Hand grenade.

Ha eca ee!: Take that!

Ha': Yes.

Haa-ha': No.

Halac yush!: Get them!

Hun ee Kheziri?: Did you hear that?

Kagbe yush!: Hold them off!

Le ho!: Die!

Mostagi!: Enemy!

Nya alt khil, Yush kuzah bu!: Shit, they're here!

Sobarde!: Wait.

Sun yush gush bu!: I see them!

Te yagait!: Ambush! Attack!

Tkho ciram dac!: Damn!

Tsigah!: Over here!

Yush kuzah bu!: They are here!

INSURGENT WEAPONS

AK-47

AK-74s

G3A3

PKM

SVD

RPG

DShK

Technical Truck

T55 Tank

CAMPAIGN

INTRODUCTION

Following the terrorist attacks against the United States on September 11, 2001, American intelligence tracked the planning and training for the attack back to a group called Al Qaeda, which was based in Afghanistan. Prior to the invasion of Afghanistan by the U.S. military, highly trained special forces were sent in to pave the way. During the campaign, you will have the opportunity to play as members of various military units. You begin as a Navy SEAL in the Advanced Force Operation task force and then take part in other missions as a special forces operative, an Army Ranger, and even a weapons officer on an attack helicopter. Each of these various units works together as the individual missions make up a larger overall operation.

FIRST IN

INTEL REPORT

Unit Name: AFO Neptune

Callsign: "Rabbit"

Location: Gardez, Afghanistan

Local Time: 0320 hrs.

Mission Summary: You must infiltrate the Taliban-held town of Gardez and locate Tariq, a local elder who has valuable intel on high value targets and enemy positions in the surrounding area.

Initial Weapon Loadout

M4 CQBR	870 MCS	P226	M67 Frag Grenades

TIER 1 DETAILS

Par Time: 00:25:00

Completion Medal: Afghan Star

Zone 1

Zone 7

Zone 8

Zone 6

Zone 2

Zone 3

Zone 4

Zone 5

◇ Insertion

◆ Extraction

Mission Achievements/Trophies

Image	Name	Description	Gamerscore	Trophy
	First Incision	Complete First In	15	Bronze
	Right in the Grape...	Get seven headshots in a row with any weapon except the long range sniper rifle	15	Bronze
	Smooth Operator	In First In, kill the hostage taker with a single shot	10	Silver

ZONE 1

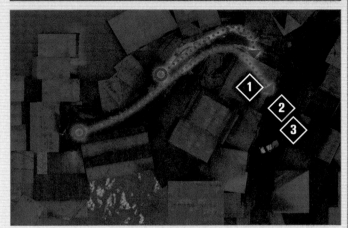

1	Objective
◯⋯▶	Critical Path
◯⋯▶	Flanking Path
🖈	Grenade Crate

RIGHT IN THE GRAPE...

As the game begins, try to score at least seven headshots in a row to earn the Right in the Grape… achievement/trophy. For best results, set your M4 to single shot and then zoom in on your targets to score one headshot after another. There's no need to rush, so make sure each shot counts. The first seven enemies that appear are relatively easy to pick off, but be sure to fire from a covered position. It is easier to earn this achievement/trophy right at the start before the enemies become tougher to kill.

The quiet meeting in the town has turned into an ambush!

① FIGHT BACK TO AMBUSH SITE

Your SEAL team is tasked with entering the town of Gardez to meet up with a leader by the name of Tariq. However, the four of you are ambushed as you enter town and are separated into two groups as you flee. During this mission, your callsign is Rabbit. After your truck is destroyed, you and Voodoo find yourselves in a small room at the end of a short road. Your first objective is to fight your way back to the site of the ambush. Take a moment to get used to the controls since this is probably your first action.

Once you are ready, advance down the street. Since there are enemies out there, move in short rushes from cover to cover. Use crates, dumpsters, and even burned out vehicles for cover. Sprint to some cover and then drop down into a crouch. Once you detect an enemy, lean around cover or peek up over it to take your shot. Then duck back behind cover. Pick off the few enemies that appear ahead of you. Since it is dark, try using your night vision so it is easier to see the enemies.

TIER 1 TACTICS

While your team lays down fire and suppresses the enemy, dash down the alley to the left and flank the enemies with your shotgun or pistol.

As you move through this town in the dark of night, look for muzzle flashes to help detect hostiles such as this one hiding in a building. He is very tough to see until he fires out through the window. If you still can't see the enemy, fire at the muzzle flash to at least force him to take cover.

When you get to the spot where the road turns to the right, Voodoo heads to the right side of the road. Move to the left side and take cover behind the destroyed vehicle. Clear out the enemies at the road intersection and then rush forward to the dumpster. From here, you can take out the tango in the building to your right. Then engage the enemies up on the balcony ahead of you. Once it appears clear, dash into the building on the right.

② SECURE CRASH SITE

Once inside the building, take cover to the left of the opposite doorway so you can engage hostiles across the street. There are several up on the balcony. Lean around the edge of the doorframe and take them out one by one. Voodoo will help you clear them out.

③ APPROACH ROLL-UP GATE

Once Voodoo gives you the all clear, the ambush site is secure and it is time to move out to find the other two members of your SEAL team—Mother and Preacher. Cross the street and follow Voodoo to the roll-up gate. He will open it a bit and throw a frag grenade inside to clear out any enemies that might be hiding in there. Rush in and take out the hostile in the hallway at the far side of this room.

ZONE 2

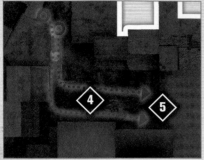

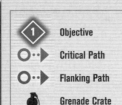

1	Objective
O··▶	Critical Path
O··▶	Flanking Path
🧨	Grenade Crate

◇ SECURE MARKET AREA

Hostiles are at the ground level as well as up on the balconies in the market area.

Follow Voodoo through the dark hallways to the market area. If you have not already activated your night vision, now is the time to use it. You can see Mother and Preacher on the balcony along the right side of the market area. Take cover as soon as you enter this area and begin engaging enemies as you see them. There are a few down at the far end of the area. Pick them off with aimed shots. Once the far side appears clear, go after the enemies up on the second floor of the building just ahead and on your right. Cook a grenade for a couple seconds and then throw it up into the room if you can't get a shot at the enemies. Your teammates will let you know once the area is clear. Until then, move with caution.

◇ BREACH DOOR

You now have to head across the market area to a locked door. Voodoo is waiting there for you. Activate your night vision if you have not done so already and get your 870 MCS shotgun ready. Kick open the door and then be ready to blast the enemy inside.

TIP

When fighting your way through the interiors of buildings, the shotgun is a good choice for your weapon. Close quarters engagements are quick, so you want to be able to fire fast without having to carefully aim. Shotguns will take out most hostiles with a single shot. Just be sure to reload after each engagement so you are ready for the next fight.

ZONE 3

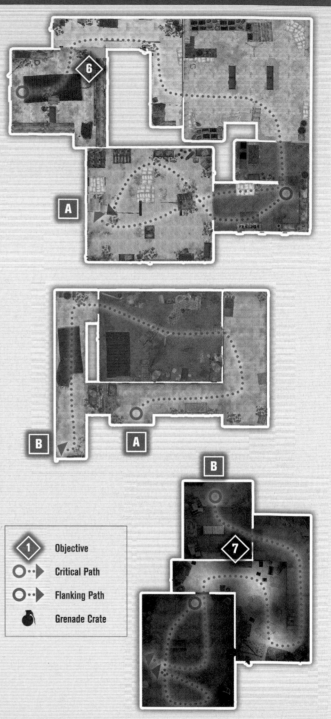

1	Objective
O··▶	Critical Path
O··▶	Flanking Path
🧨	Grenade Crate

◇ DISABLE FUSE

After clearing the room, enter it and head over the to the fuse box. The enemy is not equipped with night vision, so the dark can be your advantage. Activate your night vision if you have not already done so and then hit the fuse box with your knife to kill the lights in the building. Time to move out.

⑦ FOLLOW VOODOO

The darkness gives you an advantage, allowing you to enter a room and start firing before the enemy knows where you are. Use the shotgun as your "room broom."

Voodoo leads the way through a hallway. When you come to a doorway to another room, take up a position on the left side of the door. Lean out into the opening and open fire. There are two tangos near the center and one to the left. Blast away at each in turn to clear the room before entering it. Voodoo will usually let you do all the shooting here. Since it is dark, the enemy will have trouble determining where you are at first.

Advance through the room and continue through a doorway on the right side into a kitchen area. There are several enemies in the large storage room. Quickly move through the kitchen and take up a position on the left side of the doorway leading to the storage room. Lean out and take out the enemies you can see. One may be hiding behind some sacks of grain. If he stops shooting for a bit, quickly move in and around to the right to take him out with your knife.

THE SCALPEL & PISTOL PETE SHOWDOWN

The dark building is a great place to start working towards The Scalpel achievement/trophy. You need 20 total knife kills for this award. Since the building is completely dark, rush in fast and knife all the enemies before they know you are there. If you want to start earning the Pistol Pete Showdown achievement/trophy, use your pistol when fighting indoors instead of your shotgun. You will need 30 kills for this award and can easily get at least 10 during this mission. Every little bit helps.

Use your knife to take out tangos out in the open in the dark. Move fast before they can turn and fire.

Head up the stairs. At the top, turn to the right and rush forward take out the tango in the hallway with your knife. Continue around a corner to the left to a locked door. Time to use your boot. Kick in the door and be ready. There are some more enemies inside. They quickly take cover behind some crates on the opposite side of the

room. If you can't get them with your shotgun, cook a grenade for the count of three and then throw it toward the back wall. This should take out one or two of them. Even if it misses them, it will force them to move out into the open to get away, giving you a chance to gun them down.

Now move through the room and exit through the door on the opposite side. Follow Voodoo down a hall and then out onto a balcony above the market area. Be careful out in the open because an enemy behind a window to the left will open fire. Take him out and then enter the room. Head through the door on the left and then climb up the stairs to the next level. Stay on Voodoo around a couple corners and then clear out a large room where the roof has been destroyed. Watch for tangos behind crates and out on the balcony on the opposite side of the room.

TIER 1 TACTICS

This part of the mission where you go through the dark building is a great place to pick up the pace and save time. Rush through with your shotgun. As long as you keep moving quickly, the enemy will have a hard time tracking and hitting you. You can also freeze the clock here by making melee kills with your knife while maintaining stealth. Another tactic is to use your pistol to make headshots here, which also freezes time, while saving ammo as well.

ZONE 4

①	Objective	
◯··▶	Critical Path	
◯··▶	Flanking Path	
💣	Grenade Crate	

⑧ RALLY WITH MOTHER AND PREACHER

Once the area is clear, exit though a doorway on the side and follow Voodoo outside and across some roofs to where Mother and Preacher are waiting. As you get back down to ground level, your team comes under fire from a machine gun to your left. Switch to your M4 since you are outside again.

9 FLANK MMG GUNNER

Take out the two hostiles on the roof above the MMG who are firing at your teammates.

The medium machine gun is positioned in a building and laying down a dangerous amount of fire. It has to be silenced so your team can continue to advance. Preacher and Mother lay down some covering fire on the machine gun so you and Voodoo can flank it. As soon as your teammates open fire, follow Voodoo forward towards the MMG and then turn to the left. Race across a narrow platform and then up some stairs. Turn to the left and move from cover to cover as you approach the machine gunner. There are some hostiles on the rooftop, so drop them and continue moving towards the sound of the machine gun. As you and Voodoo continue, an RPG gunner will fire at your position and cause the floor to collapse. As you are getting back up, Voodoo will rush forward and take care of the MMG once and for all. Follow Voodoo through a door and down a passageway to exit the building.

10 RALLY WITH MOTHER AND PREACHER

Clear out enemies as you move to the cover of the low wall. Watch for hostiles on the rooftops who will try to fire down on Voodoo and you.

Don't rush right outside. There are several tangos waiting to ambush you. Make sure your magazine is full and then rush out to take cover behind a low wall. Work your way around to the right, clearing out enemies as you go. Head up the stairs and then move to the left. Finally make your way up a wooden ramp to a wall. Voodoo will jump up onto the rooftop and then offer to help you up with a buddy boost. Follow your team into the next area.

ZONE 5

1	Objective
○··▶	Critical Path
○··▶	Flanking Path
🧨	Grenade Crate

11 SECURE COURTYARD

As you continue your advance towards Tariq, you now have to move through a courtyard. However this area has lots of hostiles inside it as well as surrounding it. Follow your team down the stairs. They will continue to the right and take up positions behind cover from where they can fire into the courtyard. Instead of following them, move straight ahead to a spot with an opening in the makeshift wall. From here you can take out the enemies on the balcony area along the right side of the courtyard.

Take out the hostiles on the balcony on the right side while the enemy focuses on your teammates.

Once you have eliminated all of the enemies you can see from this vantage point, move past your teammates and continue to the right side of the courtyard that you just cleared. Move from cover to cover behind a cart so that you can now take out enemies on the left side of the courtyard. Before continuing on, move into the nearby alcove where a grenade crate is located. Pick up some grenades to replace those you have already used.

While you have cleared out the outer courtyard, there are still some enemies inside the inner courtyard, which is surrounded by a wall with a single opening. Advance towards the wall, killing any enemies that stick their heads up over it. Continue to the opening and carefully clear to the left so that the gate on the right covers your back, then clear to the right. As you enter the inner courtyard, the door to the building opposite the opening opens and a tango opens fire. Move to one side and cook a grenade for a couple seconds before throwing it through the doorway to take out this threat. Finally, enter the building and finish off any remaining tangos.

Throw a grenade into the doorway to take out this enemy without exposing yourself to enemy fire. Remember to cook it for two or three seconds before throwing it so the tango doesn't have time to get out of the way.

⑫ RESCUE TARIQ

Once the courtyard is all clear, your team joins up with you. Follow them up the stairs and kick in the door on the top floor. A teammate will move forward to check out Tariq who is tied to a chair. However, this is not him—just a booby-trapped body. Quick thinking by your teammate saves your entire team. Once you recover, follow your team out of the room and through a door to the next area.

ZONE 6

1	Objective
O··▶	Critical Path
O··▶	Flanking Path
🪖	Grenade Crate

⑬ GET TO BALA HISAR FORT

Flank around behind the buildings where the tangos are hiding to take them by surprise while they are focusing on the rest of your team.

Advance down some narrow alleys until you get to a point where it opens up to the left. There are lots of hostiles in this area who will try to ambush your team. Fire at a few, head up the stairs on the left, and then follow the walkway around behind a few buildings. While the hostiles in and around these buildings are firing at your team back where you left them, you can flank the tangos and take them out from the flank. They won't even know what hit them. After moving past the last building, return to the main alley and follow your team up some stairs to the area outside the south door of the fort.

ZONE 7

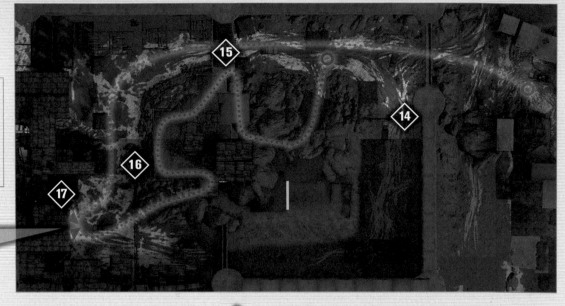

Legend:
- 1 — Objective
- ○··▶ Critical Path
- ○··▶ Flanking Path
- 💣 Grenade Crate

14 WAIT FOR AIR SUPPORT

Your team is not carrying enough firepower to force your way into the fort. However, you have some air support on the way. Stay at a distance from the gate to the fort and the air support will blast the gate to pieces. Advance into the fort and find some cover as you begin to take enemy fire.

15 FLANK AND NEUTRALIZE MMG GUNNER

Enter the cave here so you can move into a flanking position on the MMG.

A machine gun on an upper level fires down on your team and dominates this first area of the fort. You need to take it out. Follow Mother to a cave opening to the left, clearing out enemies as you go. Enter the cave and follow it up and around. Watch out for enemies inside. At the end of the cave, Mother jumps up and helps you with a buddy boost. There is a tango in the doorway up ahead. His back is to you, so sneak up behind him and take him out with your knife. He drops a Dragunov sniper rifle. Switch to your shotgun and then pick up the sniper rifle. Switch back to your M4 and then move in to kill the enemy manning the machine gun.

16 CLEAR A PATH FOR VOODOO AND PREACHER

This vantage point on the upper walkway gives you a great position for sniping on the enemy below.

Switch to the sniper rifle and move along the upper walkway where you are located. Your teammates are moving through the courtyard below and your job is to support them. Take up a position across the from the building and crouch down behind the wall. Peek up over it and kill the hostile in the second floor window of the building. Then continue clearing out all other enemies in this area as well. Then move along the wall to continue to clear the way for your teammates. Mother will lead you to a doorway once the area below is clear. Follow him through the door and down to the ground level.

TIP

If you did not already earn your Right in the Grape… achievement/trophy, this is another great opportunity to try as you snipe at enemies. Just take your time and get your seven headshots in a row.

17 RALLY WITH MOTHER AND PREACHER

Make your way through the chain link gate and into the garage area where the rest of your team is waiting. As you rally with your team, stop to pick up some grenades from the nearby crate. If you need some more ammo for your M4, ask one of your teammates to stock you up.

ZONE 8

Smooth
Operator

 Objective

 Critical Path

 Flanking Path

Grenade Crate

Achievements

⑱ SEARCH FOR TARIQ

Some of the tangos in this large room are hiding behind objects. Shoot as many as you can, then rush in and use the knife on any hideouts.

After your team opens the back door of the garage, head left down the alley. It is clear here, but expect some hostiles as soon as you round the corner to the right. Take cover and engage them. Continue to advance through this outdoor area, clearing as you go. Once all enemies here have been neutralized, follow Mother to the door on the left and enter the building. The first room is empty so move to the second room where you engage enemies on the left while the other half of your team takes care of those on the right. Continue through the room to the alley out back.

⑲ CLEAR LAST BUILDING

Your team regroups and heads to the door at the end of the alley. Kick open the door and then be ready to use your pistol. Be careful not to hit Tariq who is being held hostage. You need to kill the tango holding Tariq first—try for a headshot—and then stop the enemy who is running for the truck. Finally, finish off any remaining hostiles in here to complete the mission.

SMOOTH OPERATOR

It is easy to earn the Smooth Operator achievement/trophy for this mission. As you bust through the door, time slows down a bit, giving you a chance to take careful aim at the hostile holding Tariq hostage. Line up your sight and take the enemy out with a headshot to add this reward to your collection.

MEDAL OF HONOR

BREAKING BAGRAM

INTEL REPORT

Unit Name: AFO Neptune

Callsign: "Rabbit"

Location: Bagram Airfield, Afghanistan

Local Time: 0837 hrs.

Mission Summary: With the enemy located, the key to defeating them begins with securing a former Soviet airbase as your Tactical Operations Center. Alongside AFO Wolfpack and Tariq's local militia, you must penetrate the Taliban's defenses and seize the control tower.

Initial Weapon Loadout

PKM	M14 EBR	P226	M67 Frag Grenades

TIER 1 DETAILS

Par Time: 00:30:00

Completion Medal: Cross of the Coalition

Mission Achievements/Trophies

Image	Name	Description	Gamer-score	Trophy
	Welcome to the TOC	Complete Breaking Bagram	15	Bronze
	The Sledgehammer	In Breaking Bagram, destroy two vehicles with a single 2,000-pound laser guided bomb	10	Bronze

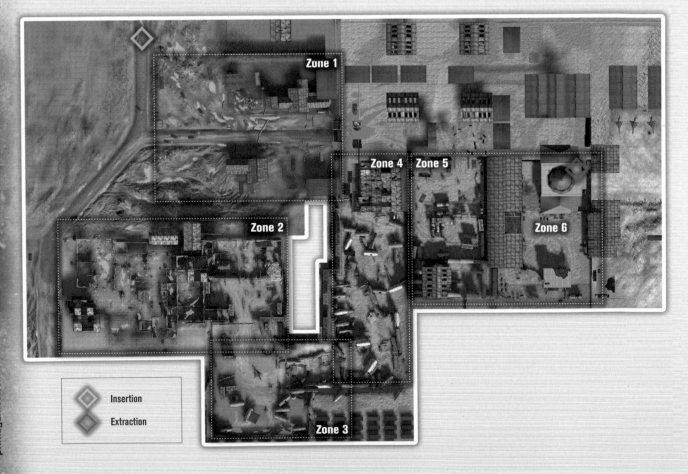

Zone 1

Zone 4   Zone 5

Zone 2

Zone 6

Zone 3

◇ Insertion

◆ Extraction

ZONE 1

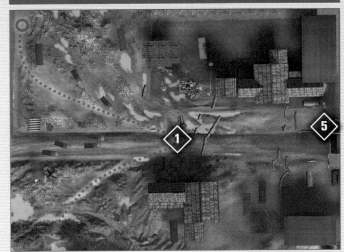

1	Objective
⊙··▶	Critical Path
⊙··▶	Flanking Path
💣	Grenade Crate

Target the threats first. That technical's machine gun can chew you up if you don't kill the gunners first.

When you finally arrive at the front gate of the airfield, the tangos have it barricaded and heavily defended. You automatically climb out of the cab of the truck and man the mounted machine gun. Blast away at the hostiles near the gate. Target the fuel tanks on either side of the gate. When they blow up, they will take lots of enemies with them. The main threats in this area are a technical with a machine gun mounted in its bed as well as the two machine guns in the towers on either side of the gate. Take out the technical and then try to suppress the tower guns.

You are going to have to fight your way to the airfield. Be sure to take out the enemy trucks as quickly as possible.

◆ GET TO THE FRONT GATE

You begin this mission riding shotgun in a pickup truck headed towards the airfield. As you head down the road, some friendly fast movers make an air strike against the airfield's defenders, cutting it a bit too close for your comfort. Shortly thereafter, you reach the enemy truck column that was just bombed and come under fire. Fire right through the shattered windshield to clear out the broken glass and start blasting away with your PKM light machine gun as your teammate keeps driving. While you should shoot at enemies on foot that are firing at you, the main threats are the enemy technicals. These are pickup trucks with enemies loaded up in the back. They will drive alongside your vehicle and shoot at you. Try to take out the hostiles in the back first and then keep firing at the truck to blow it up.

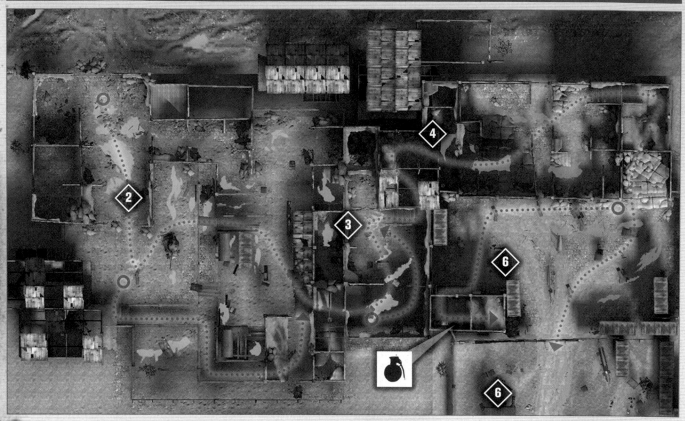

FIND THE MORTAR TEAMS

After a bit, your teammate realizes that it will be too tough to get through the front gate. He backs up the truck and drives you around to the side so that you can try and enter the airfield from another direction. As he crashes through some rubble, gun down any tangos in front of the truck to clear the way. Once the truck comes to a stop, you are ready to proceed the rest of the way on foot.

1	Objective
O··▶	Critical Path
O··▶	Flanking Path
🪖	Grenade Crate

CLEAR THE RUINS

Once you are on foot, take cover behind the rubble ahead of the truck. There are lots of hostiles around the corner to the right. Lean around the corner and fire at any enemies you can see. If you can't engage any, rush forward and take cover behind the stack of three large concrete blocks out in the open. Look for a tango with an RPG on the second floor of the ruin ahead of you. Either mow him down with your PKM or switch to your M14 EBR and snipe at him as well as the other hostiles in the area. More enemies will come at you at ground level. Take them out before they can get in too close.

TIER 1 TACTICS

Tier 1 skips the ride in the truck and begins in Zone 2. As soon as the mission starts, rush to cover and pick off some enemies with headshots to earn some points and time. Then move through the sunken passage quickly to come at the enemy from the flank. You will bypass some enemies, but as they move to respond to your advance, either you or your teammates will have an opening for some shots against them.

Hit the hostiles from the flanks as much as possible while they are concentrating their fire on your team.

After you have cleared out some of the enemies, head to the stairs on your right and take them down to a sunken passageway. Follow it forward and then to the right and you will emerge on the enemy's flank. Continue along the front of the ruined building to an opening that leads to an interior courtyard. Lean around the corner and engage the hostiles inside the courtyard. Clear it out and then advance to the opening on the left side, which leads into another courtyard. There are several tangos inside here. Your teammates will take positions near the opening. Move past them to a small doorway to their right so you can then take out the enemies from a different angle than your team. Advance along the right side of the courtyard to hit the hostiles from their flank. Some of these enemies can be tough to hit as they hide behind cover. Throw a frag grenade over the cover to clear them out.

The SOFLAM lets you call in some very heavy support. A single bomb will leave a crater where this armored vehicle is located.

④ GET EYES ON THE FRONT GATE

Once the courtyard is clear, head up the stairs along with your team. Move through one room and on into a second room. Continue to the edge of the room where the wall has been blasted away and get the SOFLAM (Special Operations Force Laser Marker).

⑤ CALL IN CAS ON THE FRONT GATE

As you are looking through the SOFLAM, target one of the towers on the gate and then fire to designate the target. A bomb dropped by a friendly jet will take out the gate and clear the way. However, don't put down the laser marker just yet. The hostiles bring up an armored vehicle to defend the entrance to the airfield. Wait until another bomb is ready and then target the vehicle and call in another strike. The entrance is now clear.

⑥ FIND AND ELIMINATE THE MORTAR TEAMS

After putting down the SOFLAM, jump down to the ground level and fight your way through some ruins along with your team. There are several hostiles hiding behind walls as well as up on a second floor ahead of you. Take your time to eliminate them all and then make your way up the stairs at the far left corner of the courtyard. Clear out any tangos at the top and then make your way to the far end of this upper level. From this spot you can see the first mortar team. Take them out from this spot and then drop down to the next courtyard.

Clear out the mortar positions from a distance or from an elevated location rather than rushing them and risking a casualty—namely you.

While your team takes cover behind some crates, advance along the right side, rushing from cover to cover to hit the enemies from their flank. Make your way to the stairs leading up to the second floor of a small building. Rush up and clear out any remaining tangos here. Be sure to pick up some frag grenades from the crate on this upper floor. Then move to the edge of this floor where the walls have been blown out and look over the fence to locate the second mortar position. Gun down the enemies there, then drop down to the ground and follow your team through the gate.

TIP

On the top floor, you can pick up an RPG. While you don't really need it, there is a situation later on where it might come in handy. If you decide to do this, leave behind your PKM. You will need your M14 EBR more, and can always pick up another PKM or an AK-47 later after using the RPG.

ZONE 3

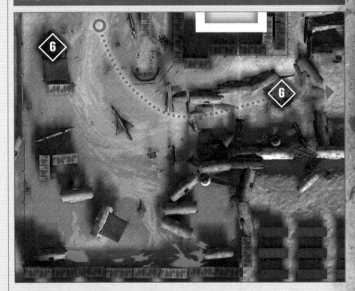

①	Objective
○••▸	Critical Path
○••▸	Flanking Path
💣	Grenade Crate

After passing through the gate, take cover and engage the enemies hiding behind wrecked aircraft and other objects. Advance around to the left, moving from cover to cover. The third mortar position is hidden among the wreckage. Pick off the gunners while staying behind cover. Watch out for other hostiles in the area. Not all are by the mortar. In fact, most are hiding inside the wreckage waiting to ambush you. Clear them out as you push forward towards and then past the mortar position.

ZONE 4

1 ▶	Objective
◯··▶	Critical Path
◯··▶	Flanking Path
🔶	Grenade Crate

7 CLEAR THE AIRPLANE GRAVEYARD

Continue through the maze of wrecked aircraft fuselages. Rush from one position of cover to the next and then scan the area around you. The tangos like to hide inside the fuselages and snipe at you as you move past them. If you start taking fire from your side or from behind, duck into a fuselage yourself and then look for the enemies that are attacking you. Move out into the open occasionally to try and draw some fire and then rush back to cover. Pay attention to the direction the enemy fire is coming from and then let them have it.

Pick off enemies in the airplane graveyard at a distance using your M14 EBR. Try to draw their fire so they reveal themselves.

TIP

Use your frag grenades to clear out those enemies inside the planes who don't want to come out enough so you can shoot them. Be sure to cook the grenade for a couple seconds so the hostiles don't have time to run away from the grenade.

Keep moving through the maze of wrecked planes until you reach the large warehouse. Move along the right side of the graveyard and then turn left at the warehouse so you can hit the enemies in front of this structure from the side. Once you get to the door of the warehouse, walk on inside.

TIER 1 TACTICS

While you usually want to move quickly, take your time indoors in the warehouse, the hangars, and the tower building. There are lots of enemies in close confines. Rushing through these areas will usually end up with your death, making you begin the mission over from the start. Lean around or peek over cover when engaging hostiles so you have some protection. Also try picking up an AK-47. You can reload it quickly and there is plenty of ammo for this assault rifle.

8 SECURE THE WAREHOUSE

As you enter the warehouse, advance to the large open area and take cover. There are several tangos across the area both on the ground as well as on the catwalks above. Clear out a bit and then advance across the floor of the warehouse. As you get towards the middle, a technical will burst in through the opposite door. Shoot the tango on the Dshka machine gun to eliminate this threat. However, if you picked up the RPG earlier, this is the time to use it. Aim for the truck and fire to blow away the gunner. Keep pressing forward to eliminate all of the remaining hostiles in the warehouse.

Kill the gunner on the technical or he can mow you down quickly.

9 GET TO THE TOWER

Head up the stairs on the left side of the warehouse. Then follow the catwalks into a room on the second floor where you can pick up some frag grenades from a crate. Follow your team out another door and down a set of stairs to get to the next area.

ZONE 5

10 GET TO THE HANGARS

As you exit the warehouse, rush to some cover. There are several tangos out here as well as one on a Dshka on a platform next to the hangar. Kill the enemies that man the machine gun as well as those in the yard. As you clear the area, advance from cover to cover so you can get closer to the enemies to kill them. Clear out this yard to complete the objective.

1	Objective
◐··▶	Critical Path
◐··▶	Flanking Path
💣	Grenade Crate

You have to take out that machine gun so you can get to the hangars.

11 CLEAR OUT THE HANGARS

Advance into the hangars and take a left. There are tangos up ahead inside some rooms. Clear off the stairs and head up them to the second floor. Remove the enemies here and then fire down on the enemies in the second part of the hangar. Take out as many as possible before moving down another flight of stairs to finish clearing out the hangars. Once it is secure, join up with your team at the large doors and prepare to exit.

12 ELIMINATE THE SNIPERS

As the door opens, you will take fire from enemies on a tower directly ahead of you. Duck back inside the building and wait for air support to take out the entire tower. Then turn to your left and run for the stairs behind the small two-story building. There are several snipers up on the large control tower to your left. Ignore them for now and get up to the second floor where you can find a Dragunov sniper rifle. Pick it up and get behind some cover. Snipe at the snipers with the Dragunov and clear out as many as possible. Take your time and go for headshots and you can earn the Right in the Grape Achievement/Trophy here if you have not done so already. After you have eliminated the enemies, your team will join you and pop some smoke in front of the tower. This is your chance to sprint across the open area on the ground below and get to the door on the right side. Kick open the door and enter.

ZONE 6

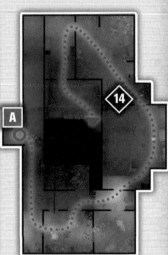

13 CLEAR THE FIRST FLOOR

Upon entering the control tower, you face lots of enemies. Move carefully from room to room. There is a machine gun in the central hallway. Take cover and lob a grenade over the crates to land right behind the machine gun and blow up the gunner. Once the machine gun is silent, rush forward and through the rooms on the right. Once all hostiles have been eliminated here, head up the stairs to the second floor.

1	Objective
◐··▶	Critical Path
◐··▶	Flanking Path
💣	Grenade Crate

⑭ CLEAR THE SECOND FLOOR

Roger. Almost there.

The fighting in the tower building is up close and intense. Try picking up an AK-47 for this fight. You can find plenty of ammo near the bodies of the hostiles you have killed.

Be ready for some more fighting at the top of the stairs. Stay to the right as you engage enemies towards your left. This is a close-quarters battle, so be sure to use cover as you kill several hostiles in the first part of this area. Clear it out and then regroup with your team at a closed door. Kick it open and rush into a room with some more tangos. Hang to the right to try to flank them. Once they are all eliminated, follow your team.

⑮ MOVE INTO THE TOWER

Your teammates will lead you through the rest of the second floor and then up a winding staircase. There are no more enemies in this building, so just race up to the top of the tower.

⑯ GET THE SOFLAM

At the top of the tower, it is time to get busy again. The room is clear, but there are lots of enemies headed your way. Move over by the opening in the tower that overlooks the runways to get the SOFLAM so you can do some laser targeting.

⑰ CALL IN CAS ON THE TALIBAN COUNTERATTACK

The Taliban are sending lots of units your way to try to retake the airfield. You have a variety of support to help you defeat this counterattack. First off, call in strafing runs on stationary targets. A-10 aircraft will fire their 30mm GAU-8 Gatling guns at the targets you designate. While that support is moving into position for another run, switch to Hellfire attacks. These call in guided missiles from AH-64D Apache attack helicopters. Target the moving technicals with Hellfires. Once a lock on box appears on the target, you can begin targeting another enemy vehicle. Destroy the several technicals. You will then gain access to GBU-24 2,000-pound laser guided bombs. As you designate a target, your view then switches to a bomb camera so you can actually steer the bomb onto the target.

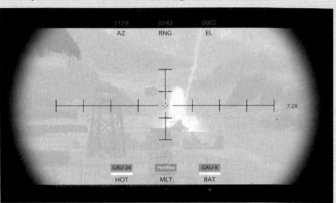

Keep calling in support constantly. While one is recharging, call in another. Not only target vehicles, but also infantry in buildings, towers, and barricades.

The Taliban next sends in several tanks. Alternate between Hellfires and GBU-24 bombs to take them out. By the time you call in one, the next one will be ready to go. The tanks will come from both left and right sides of the village on the other side of the runway. Eventually you gain access to Mk-84 2,000-pound unguided bombs. These will fall where you designate without any guidance, so use them against the infantry in the village who are firing RPG toward you. Keep destroying the enemy until you have successfully fought off the counterattack and completed your mission, earning the Welcome to the TOC achievement/trophy.

THE SLEDGEHAMMER

You can get The Sledgehammer achievement/trophy during the last part of this mission. When you see several technicals or tanks headed towards you in a row, switch to your GBU-24 and designate a target in front of the first vehicle. Then steer the bomb so it lands right between the first and second vehicles to blow them both up. With a 2,000-pound bomb, you don't need a direct hit. Just get close and the enemy is history.

RUNNING WITH WOLVES. . .

INTEL REPORT

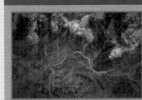

Unit Name: AFO Wolfpack

Callsign: "Deuce"

Location: Gardez, Grid 15501000

Local Time: 0323 hrs.

Mission Summary: Infiltrate the rugged mountains surrounding the Shahikot Valley on stealthed-out ATVs. You will encounter enemy outposts and villages along the way to Observation Post Clementine. It's there where you will rain down tactical air strikes on enemy positions.

Initial Weapon Loadout

M110	MP7A1	M82	G19	M67 Frag Grenades

TIER 1 DETAILS

Par Time: 00:20:00

Completion Medal: Frontier Star

Mission Achievements/Trophies

Image	Name	Description	Gamer-score	Trophy
	Develop the Situation	Complete Running with Wolves...	15	Bronze
	Dropping Deuce	Jump 7.5 meters high on the ATV	10	Bronze

Insertion

Extraction

Zone 1

Zone 2

Zone 3

Zone 4

Zone 5

MEDAL OF HONOR

ZONE 1

As a Special Forces operator, your team will be infiltrating the enemy lines on your ATVs.

1 REACH THE OUTPOST

This mission puts you in control of a different character. You are now part of an Army Special Forces team—AFO Wolfpack. After the team leader gives your orders, climb onto your ATV. Dusty is your teammate during the mission. As he takes off on his ATV, follow him. There are no enemies around at first, so use this time to get acquainted with the controls for the ATV. To help mask your movement, Dusty will take you down into a wadi.

TIP

If you lose track of Dusty, look down at the GPS attached to the handlebar of your ATV. The arrow will point in the direction you need to go. You can also press the dynamic HUD button to bring up an icon showing you the direction to as well as the distance to your next objective.

2 AVOID BEING SEEN BY THE TRUCKS

As you are riding on the ATV, stay down in the wadi and listen to Dusty. He will let you know about obstacles and enemies ahead of you.

Listen carefully to Dusty. Since he is riding point, he will see enemies ahead before you do. After you have been riding for about a minute, he tells you to slow down. Enemy trucks are driving across a bridge over the wadi. Stay back until they pass by. When Dusty gives you the all clear, then move out. Keep following him and as you approach the checkpoint, Dusty tells you to go soft and turn off your headlights. There are some hostiles in a village up ahead. Slow down and go dark. Park your ATV next to Dusty's and dismount.

TIER 1 TACTICS

There is a lot of time spent riding ATVs during this mission. It is important that you stay on the path and not run into a tree or rock, which will force you to stop, back up, and then continue. The faster you can get through the driving sequences, the more time you have for the parts of the mission where you are on foot.

Legend

1 Objective

O··▶ Critical Path

O··▶ Flanking Path

🛢 Grenade Crate

ZONE 2

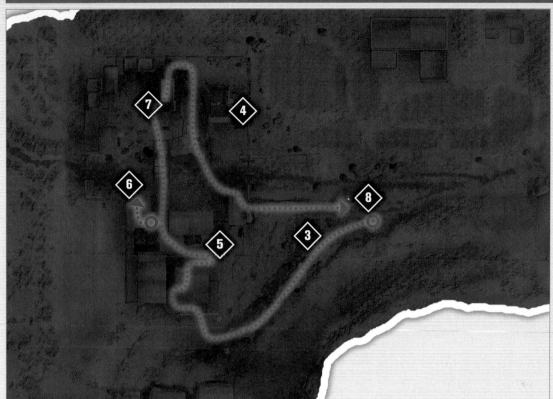

1	Objective
O··▶	Critical Path
O··▶	Flanking Path
●	Grenade Crate

⬥3 SECURE PERIMETER OF OUTPOST

Follow Dusty up onto a ledge overlooking the village. Take some time to look around at the village to get a feel for the layout. It is important that you maintain stealth as much as possible during this mission. Luckily, both your submachine gun and your rifle are equipped with sound suppressors. As you hold in this spot look for the other two members of your team, Vegas and Panther. Cover them as they get into position on the other side of the village.

⬥4 KILL GUARD

Use your silenced rifle to make a long-range shot at the guard in the tower.

Switch to your M110 rifle to look for hostiles around the village. There is a lone guard up on a tower. Take careful aim for a head shot. You want to take out this tango with a single shot before he can raise an alarm or get off a shot of his own. There is no rush, so take your time and focus on accuracy.

⬥5 FOLLOW DUSTY

Once the guard is toast, switch to your MP7A1 submachine gun and follow Dusty along the ridge and down to the village. He knifes a hostile in a short alley and then moves through a small building. Continue outside and down some stairs. There are two enemies to the left of the stairs. Take aim at one of them and fire. Dusty drops the other.

⬥6 ELIMINATE THE FIGHTERS

Follow Dusty to a wooden gate. Here you two separate. While he goes to the right, you must enter the building to the left. Make sure it is clear and then crouch down and move over to the window. Switch to your M110 again and locate the guard up in a tower directly ahead of you. Once again, take careful aim and neutralize the tango with a single head shot. Listen to Dusty as he calls out a second target on the roof to the right. One more shot—one more kill.

Silently take out some more guards. If you have trouble locating the enemies Dusty is calling in to you, press the HUD button to bring up an icon over these targets.

7 RALLY UP WITH TEAM

After taking out the guards, more tangos enter the courtyard in front of you. Don't worry about them. Your team will take them out. Once it is clear, exit the building and move out across the courtyard. Your teammates are waiting in another building. Inside you find lots of enemy intel. It looks like the tangos have a lot more than expected.

8 RETURN TO THE ATVS

It's time to bug out. Follow Dusty back through the village and all the way to the ATVs where you parked them. Climb aboard and get ready to roll. You still have a lot of work to do tonight.

ZONE 3

1 — Objective
O··▶ — Critical Path
O··▶ — Flanking Path
💣 — Grenade Crate

9 FOLLOW DUSTY TO MENJAWAR

Dusty leads the way on his ATV. Follow him as he maneuvers around rocks and other obstacles. He gives you a verbal head's up when there are sharp turns or sudden drops, so listen and be ready for these areas along the path. As you near Menjawar, your other teammates inform you there is an outpost outside of the village that needs to be cleared of enemies.

10 ELIMINATE ENEMIES WITH M82

Bring your ATV to a halt when Dusty stops. As the team sniper, your job is to engage hostiles at extreme ranges. Your M82 sniper rifle has the range and stopping power to kill enemies at long distance with a single shot—whether you get a head shot or not. Since it is night, it can be difficult to find the targets. Switch your scope to white hot mode so that the warm bodies of your targets appear white against the black background. There are a couple hostiles along the right side of the camp—near the fire and the doorway of the building. The third is on a tower to the left. He is tough to see because he is behind some wooden walls. However, you can see his feet using your thermal optics. Aim above his feet and fire. Your .50 caliber round will penetrate the wall and take down this tango. Another tango comes up the stairs to the top of the tower to check on the enemy you just killed. Wait until he stops and then pop him.

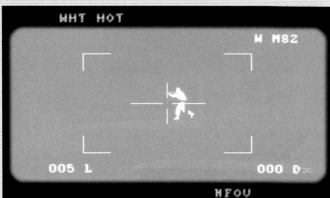

Switch your scope to white hot thermal mode to detect and target enemies more easily.

TIP

When firing sniper rifles as long range, remember that it takes your bullet some time to travel to the target. It is best to shoot at stationary targets so you don't have to lead them. Also, the scope appears to rock up and down—especially when zoomed in on targets. Follow the directions on the screen to hold your breath in order to steady your aim. You can't hold your breath too long or it will start rocking again. Therefore, line up your shot, hold your breath, and then fire when the crosshairs are centered on your target's body.

11 GET TO MENJAWAR

Now that the outpost has been cleared, it is time to ride some more. Follow Dusty all the way to the gates of Menjawar village. Dismount and make sure you have your SMG selected. Dusty leads the way into the village.

ZONE 4

1	Objective
O··▶	Critical Path
O··▶	Flanking Path
🔘	Grenade Crate

⑫ SEARCH FOR TRUCKS IN THE VILLAGE

Follow Dusty through some ruins and down into the village. As you approach some stairs leading down to the ground level, hold while a patrol of enemies walks past the first truck. After they have passed, quietly take out the guard in the doorway on the opposite side of the truck. Dusty will mark the truck with a beacon and then head further into the village. Follow him.

⑬ MARK SECOND TRUCK

You have to plant beacons on two of these trucks. The first one is in the clear. However, you will have to sneak around to the far side of the other so the nearby tangos don't see you.

MEDAL OF HONOR

Stay in the shadows as you approach another open area. There are lots of hostiles walking around out there. Stay near Dusty and you won't be seen. Dusty will let you know when it is all clear. Continue following him into a building. Turn to the left and look through the other doorway to see two tangos located outside. Take aim and kill one of them while Dusty takes out the other. Stay in the doorway while Dusty moves ahead and onto the rooftops. When he calls all clear, move forward, following the pathway around to the second truck. Walk up to it and plant a beacon on it. Two down, one more to go.

Sneak up behind this tango in the building and knife him.

⑭ MARK LAST TRUCK

After you mark the truck, a couple hostiles come walking towards you. Dusty will give you a head's up. Take out one of them while Dusty smokes the other. It is time to get out of this courtyard. Move to the wall with a lit lantern hanging nearby. Dusty will give you a buddy boost up. Follow him until he tells you to halt. There are more tangos in the area around the last truck. Wait for the patrols to pass. When Dusty gives you the all clear, move quickly and quietly across to the building on the opposite side. Enter and knife the hostile standing near the other doorway. Stay low and move up to the truck to plant the beacon.

⑮ RETURN TO ATVS

You now have to backtrack all the way to Dusty. As you enter the building again, another tango is inside. Sneak up behind him and take him down with your knife. Before exiting the building, wait for a hostile outside to walk away and then make your way back to Dusty who will give you another buddy boost. Follow Dusty back towards the second truck and then through a building. The hostiles are out in the courtyard and on the upper levels of the building on the opposite side of the courtyard. Stay in the doorway, using it for cover, and shoot at the hostiles in those locations. Move forward onto the patio area and clear out more enemies while taking cover behind the low wall. Once it looks clear, head down the stairs to the left and move through the courtyard. There may be one or two tangos hiding in corners, so be ready to take them out.

Roger. D, step it up.

You have to fight your way out of the village. There are a couple areas where groups of hostiles block your way and you will have to clear them out.

Head around to the left and then up the stairs. Follow the balcony walkway around. Knife the hostile with his back to you along the way and continue to the end where you overlook another courtyard. There are more hostiles down below. Pick them off before dropping down and crossing to the gate. Dusty opens it for you. Follow him past the first truck and back through the way you first entered the village. Get a boost from Dusty to get to the top of a wall, and then help him up as well. Continue back to the ATVs and mount up.

TIER 1 TACTICS

Most of the mission requires stealth. However, as you are headed back to the ATVs, you are going to kill some tangos along the way. Forget sneaking around and move quickly. Also try to knife enemies as much as possible or get head shots to earn yourself some extra time. The first courtyard has enough hostiles in it for you to stop the timer for a bit if you can kill them all quickly enough.

ZONE 5

Dropping Deuce

①	Objective
○··▶	Critical Path
■	Achievements

⑯ RALLY UP WITH TEAM

Ride your ATV along a narrow path to get to the rally point where Panther and Vegas are waiting for you.

All you have to do now to complete the mission is to follow Dusty as he leads the way on his ATV. Keep going until you reach the rest of your team who are waiting for you. Completing this mission earns you the Develop the Situation achievement/trophy.

DROPPING DEUCE

As you get close to the rest of your team, you will see Dusty go over a steep drop and tell you to hang on. Keep driving your ATV as fast as you can over this drop. Right after it you will hit a bit of a ramp before a second drop. If you are going as fast as you can, your ATV will jump high enough to earn the Dropping Deuce achievement/trophy.

primagames.com

64

DOROTHY'S A BITCH

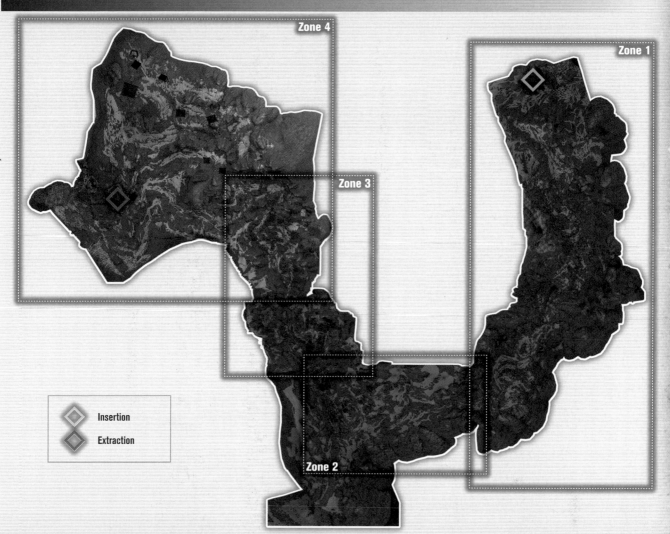

Zone 4
Zone 1
Zone 3
Zone 2

◇ Insertion
◈ Extraction

INTEL REPORT

Unit Name: AFO Neptune

Callsign: "Rabbit"

Location: Shahikot Valley, Grid 19009210

Local Time: 0438 hrs.

Mission Summary: Push into the snow-capped peaks of the Shahikot Valley on foot, take out Taliban and Al Qaeda fighters in close-quarters battles, and eliminate AAA positions with the support of the AC-130 gunship Reaper 31, all on the way to Dorothy, your final OP.

Initial Weapon Loadout

M4 Suppressed	M14 EBR suppressed	P226	M67 Frag Grenades

TIER 1 DETAILS

Par Time: 00:17:30

Completion Medal: Sentry Cross

Mission Achievements/Trophies

Image	Name	Description	Gamer-score	Trophy
✈	Unexpected Guests	Complete Dorothy's a Bitch	15	Bronze
	Fear the Reaper	In Dorothy's a Bitch, destroy the entire AQ camp with the AC-130	10	Silver

ZONE 1

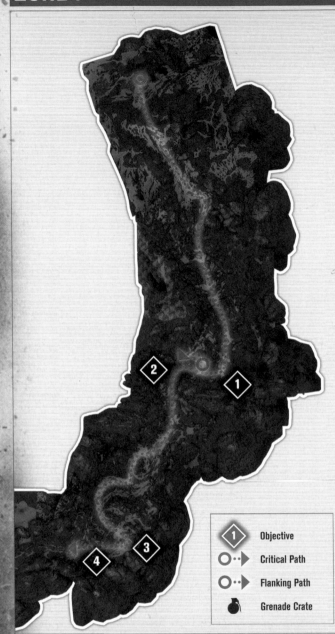

![1]	Objective
○··▶	Critical Path
○··▶	Flanking Path
🛢	Grenade Crate

Your SEAL team must work their way up the mountain to their assigned observation point.

① MOVE TO OP DOROTHY

You are a SEAL once again. The area through which you must advance is mountainous. Keep a careful eye out for enemies hiding in the rocks and be sure to use those same rocks for cover when you get into a fire fight. After a teammate knocks out a shepherd, follow your team up the mountainside along a ridgeline. After a bit of a walk, you come across a group of hostiles. Stay low and wait to see if they will lead you back to their base. Since they are staying put, you have to take them out. Wait for your teammate to give the order to fire on your first shot. Take careful aim and drop one of them. Your team takes care of the rest.

TIER 1 TACTICS

There is quite a bit of combat during this mission. However, you also move through a large area. To save time, sprint as much as possible. After playing through this a time or two, you will know where the enemies are located and that you can move quickly along paths. Don't wait for your teammates to lead the way.

② ELIMINATE TALIBAN SCOUTS

Up ahead, you see a light. It looks like another patrol with a flashlight. Stay low and follow your team. Don't engage the enemies yet since they are moving and may lead you to something bigger. Keep following them and you will find a campfire with five hostiles around it. These scouts must be neutralized before they can warn others of your presence. The rest of the team will wait for you to take the first shot. Rather than staying put and shooting from where you first saw the camp, move around to the right to hit the enemies from the flank and ensure your team takes them all out quickly.

TIP

With several enemies close to one another, this camp is just begging for a frag grenade. Cook one off for two to three seconds and then throw it right at the campfire. You should be able to take out at least three of the tangos with a single grenade. Be ready to shoot any survivors.

Since you are sneaking up on these Taliban scouts, take careful aim and go for a head shot with your first shot. Then just drop the rest however you can.

③ ELIMINATE AAA POSITION

Continue following your team. Up ahead you can see an enemy antiaircraft artillery gun firing at American aircraft. You need to silence that gun. As you advance, stay high and to the right. There are several hostiles guarding the way and they know you are in the area. Start firing at them. While you can use your M4, it is easier to engage them at long range with your M14 EBR. Take cover behind a rock and then lean out from behind it to take your shots. If you start taking fire, duck back behind cover. Clear out all of the enemies you can see, then switch back to the M4 and advance. Again, stay high and to the right as you approach the gun emplacement from the rear. As soon as you detect more enemies, take cover and return fire. Finally, move in and clear out any remaining hostiles hiding out. Once the area is clear, place a demolitions charge on the AAA, move back, and blow it up.

Blow up the AAA at this position so you can call in some air support later during the mission.

④ RALLY UP WITH TEAM

As you were taking care of the AAA, your team moved forward a bit to get out of the blast area. Move to where they are waiting for you. A teammate will give you a buddy boost up a rock wall so that you can all continue.

ZONE 2

⑤ MOVE TO OP DOROTHY

Keep moving along with your team across the ridgeline. Keep going until you see some trucks ahead in the distance.

①	Objective
○·▸	Critical Path
○·▸	Flanking Path
🍃	Grenade Crate

⑥ TARGET TRUCKS WITH SOFLAM

Switch on your night vision and you can see infrared blinking strobes on these trucks. AFO Wolfpack (you in the previous mission) has marked these trucks as targets. They are carrying surface-to-air missiles, which will be deadly to American aircraft. They need to be destroyed. Move forward to the edge next to Mother and use the SOFLAM. Target the truck in the middle and the AC-130, callsign Reaper 31, will let loose with a barrage of 105mm artillery fire.

Use the SOFLAM to mark the second truck in the convoy and the gunship will take care of the rest.

⑦ RALLY UP WITH TEAM

Follow Mother along the trail towards a village. As you enter, take cover behind a wall of a ruined building on the right side.

⑧ CLEAR THE VILLAGE

Several hostiles are in this village. A patrol is headed your way. Stay low and take aim, waiting for them to get closer. When it looks like they might see you, open fire and take out as many as you can. Stay along the right side as you advance, hitting the enemy in the flank. Then cut across to a central building with a roof and enter it. Move through it to the opposite doorway and hold there while you engage more enemies in the village. Keep advancing along with your team until you have eliminated all tangos here.

TIER 1 TACTICS

Quickly kill all of the enemies headed your way and you can halt time for a bit, allowing you to rush through the village and earn extra time with head shots or even melee attacks.

Ambush this group of Taliban as they are walking towards you. Your teammates will hit them from the sides as you hit them head on.

ZONE 3

9 CONTINUE TO OP DOROTHY

Keep following your team through the burned out part of the village. Along the way, a Taliban fighter ambushes you. Your teammates will take care of him, however. As you come to a still burning structure that blocks your way, kick down the door and move right on through. On the other side, you will see an entrance to a cave. Activate your night vision and move on in. There is a single hostile inside, so take him out and then continue to the exit. As you leave the cave, you will come across a Taliban camp. Stay to the right and move up onto a ledge overlooking the camp. Take some cover, switch to your M14 EBR, and start sniping at the tangos below. The rest of your team moves in to clear out the camp while you provide fire support.

1	Objective
O··▶	Critical Path
O··▶	Flanking Path
🔶	Grenade Crate

This Taliban camp is a target-rich environment. Start picking off enemies here.

10 MOVE TO OP DOROTHY

Your teammates will let you know when the camp is clear. Hop down from your ledge and move through the camp to where your team is waiting. Then follow them along the path. There is an AAA up ahead, but Reaper 31 will take care of it for you.

ZONE 4

11 TARGET ENEMY POSITIONS WITH SOFLAM

You have to be quick to destroy all of the targets in the Taliban base before your gunship support leaves the area.

Down below you is a Taliban base. Follow your teammate up to a ledge and use the SOFLAM. There are nine targets, which include AAA guns, ammo dumps, and supplies. You can call in 25mm, 40mm, and 105mm attacks. You don't have a lot of time before Reaper 31 has to return to base due to sunrise. Therefore, you have to call in your targets quickly. Lase one target, then quickly switch to a different weapon support and lase another target. You don't have to wait for one strike to hit before calling in another. Try to use the 105mm against the AAA if possible.

FEAR THE REAPER

This is a tough award to earn. You have to lase targets as quickly as possible. As soon as one target is locked on, switch to another weapon and lase again. Press the HUD button in order to see where some of the targets is located. However, in order to earn this award, you have to destroy all parts of the camp as well as all of the Al Qaeda so wipe them all out.

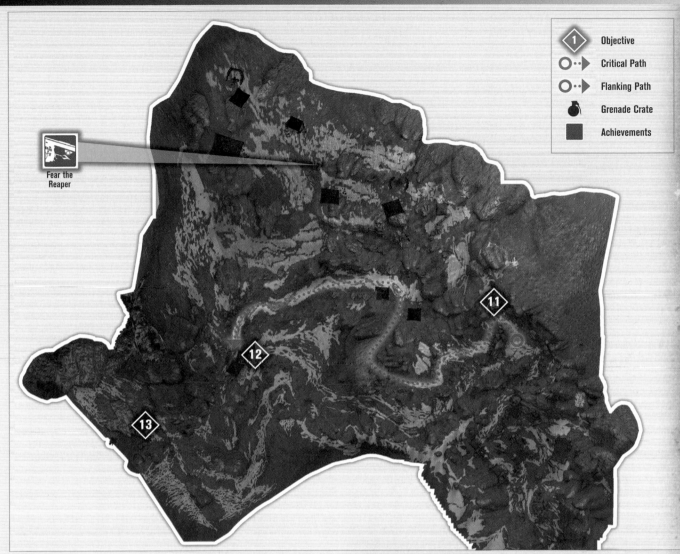

Legend:
- **1** Objective
- ○··▶ Critical Path
- ○··▶ Flanking Path
- Grenade Crate
- ■ Achievements

Fear the Reaper

12 CONTINUE TO OP DOROTHY

Now that the camp is in flames, follow your team along the path to a wooden door at the entrance to another cave. Switch on your night vision and enter. There are no hostiles inside, so continue through the cave and exit into the still burning camp. As you follow your teammate along the path, you see that Reaper 31 has come under fire. Keep running all the way towards the weapons stockpile.

13 DESTROY REAPER'S ATTACKER

As you approach the stockpile, shoot several of the hostiles moving about on the ridge ahead of you. They will try to shoot you if you don't take them out first. Now pick up the RPG on the table. The AAA is hidden behind some large rocks. However, there is an ammo dump nearby. Take aim and fire the RPG at the center of the crates. The resulting explosion will not only destroy the ammo but the AAA as well. Reaper 31 is able to escape safely and your mission is complete. For your excellent work, you will receive the Unexpected Guests achievement/trophy.

Fire the RPG at these crates of ammunition and you will blow up the AAA in the process.

BELLY OF THE BEAST

INTEL REPORT

Unit Name: 1st Bn 75th Ranger Regt.

Callsign: SPC. Dante Adams

Location: Shahikot Valley,
Grid 17809020

Local Time: 1310 hrs.

Mission Summary: Inserted into the Shahikot in heavy lift helicopters, you and your platoon must fight your way to the high ground and eliminate the enemy's firing positions. It's what you do—you're Rangers!

Initial Weapon Loadout

M249	M1014	M9	M67 Frag Grenades

TIER 1 DETAILS

Par Time: 00:25:00

Completion Medal: Order of the Vanguard

Zone 4

Zone 1

Zone 3

Manic
Suppression

Zone 2

◇ Insertion

◈ Extraction

Mission Achievements/Trophies

Image	Name	Description	Gamerscore	Trophy
	Full Battle Rattle	Complete Belly of the Beast	15	Bronze
	Manic Suppression	In Belly of the Beast, defeat the DShK in under two minutes	20	Silver

ZONE 1

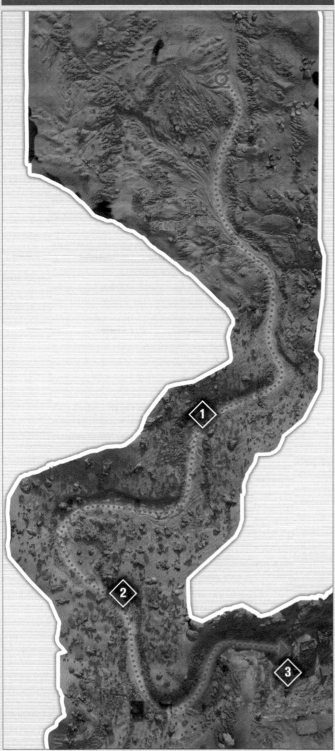

As the transport helicopters are taking off after delivering the Rangers to the LZ, the enemy begins their attack. You must regain the advantage. "Rangers lead the way!"

① MOVE THROUGH WADI WITH TEAM

Your platoon is under fire right from the start. You are armed with the M249 Squad Automatic Weapon or SAW. As such, you are the heavy firepower of the platoon. Unlike the previous missions, you will not be moving out in front or flanking. Instead, you need to concentrate on finding some good cover for yourself and then laying down fire on the enemy while your platoon maneuvers in to finish them off. However, at the beginning, just follow your platoon down into the wadi and then through it. Don't waste time returning fire. Just keep running.

② CLEAR WADI OF TALIBAN FIGHTERS

When your platoon stops and takes cover, it is time to fight back. Crouch down behind rocks and then either lean around the side or peek up over the top. Your SAW is outfitted with a scope that increases your accuracy at long range. Use the scope to pick off hostiles with short bursts. As your platoon advances, wait until they reach cover, then dash forward to some cover of your own. Keep moving along, taking out tangos as you go until you have cleared out the wadi.

TIP

With the M249, you can pick off enemies with accurate fire by using your scope. In addition, this weapon is also great for suppressing tangos. Without using the sight, fire in the main direction of hostiles to force them to take cover. This allows your platoon to advance. Once they are in position behind cover, then resume more accurate fire. No matter whether suppressing or direct targeting, keep your bursts short to conserve ammo as well as accuracy. This weapon takes a while to reload, so make sure you load a new belt of ammo before you get into a firefight. You don't want to be reloading in the heat of combat.

◇ 1	Objective
○··▶	Critical Path
○··▶	Flanking Path
🧨	Grenade Crate

Pick off hostiles with accurate fire. Don't try to mow down everyone or you will run out of ammo quickly.

PRIMA Official Game Guide

TIER 1 TACTICS

Don't rush through the wadi or you are likely to get killed. Stay behind cover and take aim at enemies. Go for head shots to earn some extra time.

③ RALLY WITH TEAM AT VILLAGE

Continue to follow your platoon along the wadi. When you get to a small bridge over the wadi, climb up out of the wadi and head along a road to the left past an old destroyed Soviet tank from a previous invasion of Afghanistan. Push on to the village where the rest of your team will regroup with you to prepare for the next objective.

ZONE 2

①	Objective
⦿⋯▶	Critical Path
⦿⋯▶	Flanking Path
💣	Grenade Crate

④ CLEAR ENEMY VILLAGE

Put your shotgun to good use in the village. Hostiles will jump out at you, so shoot quick.

Move with your team to the edge of the village and take out some hostiles that run out to engage you. Now move into the village. Switch to your M1014 shotgun. It is much more effective for close-quarters fighting. There are tangos hiding in buildings, so move in and take them out. Your knife can also come in handy for this type of combat.

THE SCALPEL & PISTOL PETE SHOWDOWN

 If you have not earned the Pistol Pete Showdown achievement/trophy, use your pistol when fighting through the village instead of your shotgun. In addition, you can also get several melee kills by rushing forward and using your knife to help you earn The Scalpel achievement/trophy. Take advantage of the many tangos at close range to get in some kills, which will get you closer to both of these awards.

⑤ RALLY UP WITH TEAM

After clearing out the first part of the village, follow your team to a hut. As one of your platoon breaks down the door, rush in and blast away at the enemies inside with your shotgun. Hold here for a bit so that your team can rally up before continuing.

⑥ MOVE THROUGH UPPER VILLAGE

Your SAW is great for clearing out the pathways ahead of your team as tangos move to ambush you.

Follow your platoon through the narrow walkways. Switch back to your M249 while you are outside so you can engage enemies as they lean out from behind cover to attack. Try to check each building as you go, using your shotgun when entering. Some tangos like to wait for you to walk by and then shoot you in the back.

⑦ CLEAR HUT

Follow your team to a hut. After they break down the door, move inside. There are no hostiles inside; however, you will find a crate of grenades. Pick up some if you have already used frags so far in this mission. Once you are ready, continue outside with your team and take cover behind a low rock wall.

ZONE 3

MANIC SUPPRESSION

Manic Suppresson is an easy achievement/trophy to earn during this mission. As long as you keep the gun position suppressed, your Rangers can move forward to place the smoke. Not only do you need to suppress the gun, but also pick off tangos that fire on your team from the nearby buildings. The more you take down, the faster your Rangers can get in close, pop the smoke, and then get out of there. If you can help them complete this objective in under two minutes, the award is yours.

⑨ RALLY UP WITH TEAM

After the gun position is a crater, move forward to join up with your platoon. Take some time to reload your SAW, since you will need it again in just a little bit. If you are getting low on ammo, be sure to ask one of your teammates for some more. You will definitely need it, too. Follow your teammates through the last part of the village and back out into open terrain.

⑧ SUPPRESS DSHK FOR TEAM

The enemy has a DShK ahead. You don't have the firepower to take it out. However, one of your platoon is calling in an airstrike. Your team just needs to pop some red smoke grenades on the position to mark it for the F-15s. Your job is to provide covering fire and keep the position suppressed so some of the Rangers can get close enough to put the smoke on it. Make sure your M249 is fully loaded and then take aim at the DShK position. Fire short bursts right at it. As enemies move out in front of it, take them out as well. Be careful not to hit your Rangers as they advance in front of you towards the gun. You may want to move up a bit and take cover behind some rocks—just be careful to suppress the gun first and then sprint to cover. After you see the red smoke, keep suppressing so that the Rangers can withdraw before the airstrike hits.

①	Objective
O ··▸	Critical Path
O ··▸	Flanking Path
🔨	Grenade Crate

Use short bursts to suppress the gun position.
Clear the way for your Rangers.

MEDAL OF HONOR

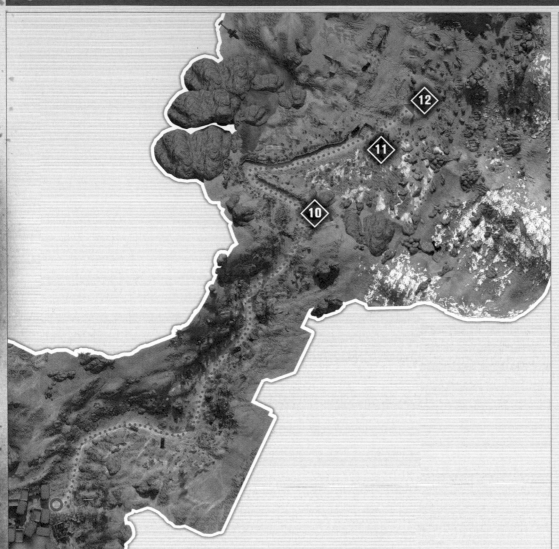

1 — Objective

○··▶ — Critical Path

○··▶ — Flanking Path

🖤 — Grenade Crate

⟨10⟩ MOVE TO LZ BETTY

Follow your platoon down another wadi. As before, find cover and provide suppressing fire as they advance. Tangos seem to pop up all over—down in the wadi as well as up along the edges. Watch out for hostiles with RPGs up on the hills. They will fire down on your platoon, so follow the smoke trails back to the enemies and take them out. Advance through this winding pass until you reach the end and can look down on LZ Betty.

The wadi can be dangerous with hostiles in front of you as well as on the sides. Keep your eyes open and look around in all directions.

11 SECURE LZ BETTY

Continue down a path to a building. The walk is clear, but you need to ensure that there are no hostiles in the building. As your platoon kicks it open, the building explodes. The enemy set a trap. You are injured, but your fellow Rangers drag you into the building for cover. There are more enemies on the way.

12 DEFEND YOUR POSITION

Take cover behind the walls and start firing at enemies coming at you from the hills. Many of them are at a distance, so use the scope to pick them off. As your platoon moves to a hut which provides more cover, follow them. Now you can fire out of windows with walls that will help protect you. Your teammates will call out targets to you. Pay attention when they let you know about RPGs. Take those out quickly or they will kill you. The attackers begin coming down the hill along the right side. Engage them and then watch for more coming from the left side. They will fire RPGs and take out part of hut, reducing your cover. Keep killing hostiles to keep them away from your position.

TIER 1 TACTICS

This is a very difficult firefight since there is so much lead in the air that it is easy to get killed. Use cover and be sure to watch for enemies in close. It is important to take out the RPGs, so listen for your teammates to call in enemy positions.

There are tangos everywhere—and they just keep coming. Don't fixate on one spot. Keep looking around and firing away.

The enemies will send a pickup truck filled with explosives down into your position. When you see it rolling, get out of the way before it destroys the rest fo the hut. As you move out of the destroyed hut, watch out for tangos coming from the far right. As the fight continues the enemies will become bolder and try rushing the hut. Don't let them get in close if you can help it. Eventually they will be able to flank you and sneak up from behind your position. When this occurs, try to move back into the building so you have some cover from at least a couple sides.

TIP

If you start taking hits and seeing red, duck down behind cover until you regain your health. Then be ready to attack the enemies in that direction. This is the toughest part of the mission. You just have to stay low and keep shooting. Eventually, when things look pretty grim, the cavalry will arrive in the form of a couple AH-64D Apache attack helicopters. As they help defeat the enemies in the hills, stay vigilant as some tangos may still be up close. Finish them off to earn the Full Battle Rattle achievement/trophy.

The Apaches arrive just in time and make short work of the hostiles.

GUNFIGHTERS

INTEL REPORT

Unit Name: 1st Battalion 2nd Aviation Regt.

Callsign: Cpt. Brad "Hawk" Hawkins

Location: Shahikot Valley, Grid 15109160

Local Time: 1514 hrs.

Mission Summary: You're the front seater of an AH-64D Apache on mission with your companion aircraft, Gunfighter 11. Together you will go "Switches hot" on Taliban mortar teams, Al Qaeda RPG gunners, and AAA positions with the Apache's deadly arsenal of high-tech weaponry.

Initial Weapon Loadout

AH-64D Apache with 30mm chain gun	70mm Hydra rockets	Hellfire ATGM

Mission Achievements/Trophies

Image	Name	Description	Gamer-score	Trophy
	Bad Guy Jamboree	Complete Gunfighters	15	Bronze
	It Takes a Village…Out	In Gunfighters, destroy 30 buildings in the village	10	Bronze

You are switching from being one of the Rangers on the ground to being the gunner of one of the Apaches that came to the rescue at Objective Betty.

① TEST FIRE WEAPONS

As the gunner for your Apache, your job is to identify and then destroy hostile targets. Your pilot will do all the flying for you, so concentrate on using the weapons systems to cause as much damage as possible. You have several different weapons available to you. As you are flying towards your first target, test fire the 30mm cannon. It is slaved to your visor, so it will fire at whatever you look at and center under the targeting reticule. As you fly over some technicals below, try to destroy them with the 30mm. Next, test out the Hydra rockets. These unguided rockets only fire straight ahead.

TIER 1 TACTICS

This mission is not available for play in Tier 1 mode.

The 30mm cannon is more than capable of tearing up technicals and even structures. You can target enemies to either side of the Apache as well as directly ahead. If you can see it, you can kill it.

② DESTROY MORTAR TEAMS

The Special Forces team has located some enemy mortar teams up in the hills. There are three different mortar positions that you must destroy. For these targets, you will be using the Target Acquisition and Designation System or TADS. This lets you detect and target enemies at a distance in all types of visual conditions. As you are viewing the enemy below, Gunfighter 11 will designate a target for you. Once you get a solid targeting box, move the reticule into the box and hold down the secondary fire button until the bar at the top fills and the target is locked. Then release the button to fire a Hellfire missile. This guided missile is fire-and-forget, so as soon as it leaves the rails, you can begin going after other targets. Use the 30mm gun to finish off any tangos near the position.

Move the TADS to the far right and down a bit to locate the second mortar team. Once again, Gunfighter 11 will designate the target. Lock on and fire another Hellfire. Two mortars down, one to go. Finally, move the TADS to the bottom and to the left to find the last mortar. Lock on and fire to complete this objective.

Use the TADS and Hellfire missiles to take out the mortar teams from a safe distance.

③ CLEAR VILLAGE OF COMBATANTS

You receive intel on some trucks filled with weapons headed for a village. As you approach the village, keep an eye—and your targeting reticule—focused on the bridge. As soon as you see the white trucks crossing the bridge. Let loose with a barrage of 30mm cannon fire and take out those trucks. Your pilot will then circle around the village. The hostiles inside will open fire. The village is fair game as a target. Use the 30mm cannon to attack tangos. Especially watch out for those with RPGs. Take them out first before they can fire on your Apache. Fire Hydra rockets at all of the buildings to level the village and prevent it from being used as a Taliban base in the future.

Stop those trucks from entering the village!

There is a fortified building in the center of the village. Its gray color stands out among all of the brown buildings. Fire lots of rockets at this structure. As you do, the tangos inside will launch RPGs at you. Keep firing until this structure is destroyed. Then mop up any remaining enemies to finish clearing out the village. During the attack, Gunfighter 11 took some damage from an RPG. Their weapons have been knocked out; however, they can still fly and designate targets for you.

This building is a tough nut to crack. Hostiles are holed up inside with lots of RPGs. Take it out to clear the village.

IT TAKES A VILLAGE...OUT

It Takes a Village . . . Out can be an easy achievement/trophy to earn if you really focus on it as soon as you approach the village. Use your Hydra rockets to blow up at least 30 of the buildings in the village. Since you can only fire these rockets straight ahead, you have to make the most of each pass your pilot makes over the village. Blowing up the buildings will also kill nearby hostiles, so as you are focusing on the buildings, you will be clearing out the village at the same time.

④ DESTROY MORTAR TEAMS ON THE WHALE

As your pilot flies toward the next target, Gunfighter 11 has detected some more enemy mortar teams. When you pop up over one hill, you will find a hostile camp. Blast away at the technicals as you fly past. Gunfighter 11 will then designate an enemy mortar position. Move your reticule into the targeting box and let loose with a Hellfire missile. Fire another missile at a second target Gunfighter 11 finds for you.

You have to be quick on the trigger in order to take out many targets of opportunity as you fly past them.

⑤ DESTROY EMBEDDED MORTAR POSITION

Gunfighter 11 has found an enemy camp with dug-in mortars. It is defended by lots of tangos, some of whom have RPGs and are not afraid to use them. Shoot to the side with your 30mm cannon as you fly by. When the Apache is facing targets, launch rockets. Destroy the mortars covered with camouflage netting. Then, as you fly up over the top of the mountain, look for a Hellfire target box. Gunfighter 11 is designating an RPG position behind some rocks. Fire a missile to destroy it before it can fire. Mow down other tangos as they scatter about. Fire a second Hellfire as soon as you get a lock on another targeting box. Mop up any remaining tangos with the 30mm cannon.

Target the netting with rockets to destroy the embedded mortars.

⑥ DESTROY EMBEDDED MORTAR POSITION

As the two Apaches are flying back towards base, Gunfighter 11 takes a hit. There is a hidden camp on another mountain top. Gunfighter 11 will designate one of the mortar positions for you to hit. If you can launch a Hellfire quickly, do so. Otherwise, focus on taking out the antiaircraft artillery as quickly as possible before it can cause a lot of damage to the Apaches. Destroy the technicals as well as other hostiles. Gunfighter 11 will designate another dug-in mortar, so send a Hellfire at it. Clean out the rest of the hostiles before you return to base. You will be awarded the Bad Guy Jamboree achievement/trophy for your efforts.

Take out that AAA on the mountaintop before it can shoot you down. Then go after the mortars.

FRIENDS FROM AFAR

INTEL REPORT

Unit Name: AFO Wolfpack

Callsign: "Deuce"

Location: Shahikot Valley, Grid 28509540

Local Time: 1725 hrs.

Mission Summary: The previous night's air strikes were a success. Now you and Dusty move higher up the mountains to hunt dug-in Al Qaeda fighters. Conceal your movement and watch your noise discipline or the hunter will become the hunted.

Initial Weapon Loadout

M82	MP7A1	M110 Sniper Rifle	G19	M67 Frag Grenades

TIER 1 DETAILS

Par Time: 00:15:00

Completion Medal: Sniper's Cross

◇ Insertion

◈ Extraction

Zone 1

Zone 2

Zone 3

Mission Achievements/Trophies

Image	Name	Description	Gamerscore	Trophy
	Friends from Afar	Complete Friends from Afar	15	Bronze
	Like a Surgeon	While long range sniping in Friends from Afar, hit one of every body part	10	Silver
	Have a Good One	Finish all of Deuce's missions	15	Bronze

MEDAL OF HONOR

ZONE 1

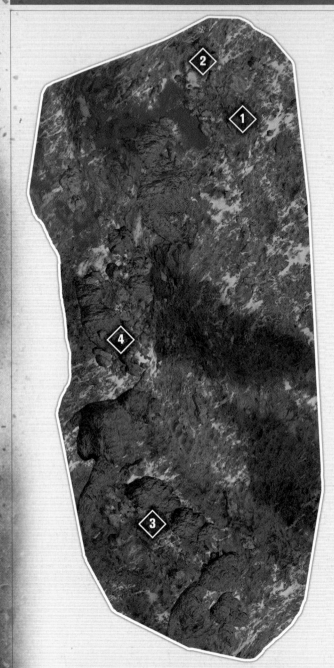

The hostiles you will be engaging with your sniper rifle are nearly one kilometer away. Therefore, it is important you take careful aim before firing.

1 HUNT AND KILL CAMPED ENEMIES (FIRST CAMP)

You and Dusty are lying prone on a ridge, ready to snipe at enemies on an opposite ridge. Panther and Vegas, your other two teammates, are positioned on another ridge and have detected some enemy camps. They don't have a good angle for the shot, so it is up to you. You are already looking through the scope of your M82 .50 cal. sniper rifle. Listen to Dusty as he helps you find targets. If you find Panther and Vegas, go up from them to find three hostiles putting out their laundry to dry near some runoff from the melting snow. Zoom in on them, take aim, hold your breath, and fire. Take out all three as quickly as possible.

TIP

Press the HUD button in order to bring up a cursor that will help you find your targets in the distance. They can be hard to find with just your eyesight. Also use the thermal imaging on your scope since the warm bodies of the tangos will stand out against the cooler surroundings.

LIKE A SURGEON

The Like a Surgeon achievement/trophy is easiest to get right at the start of the mission. To earn it, you must hit different body parts with your M82 sniper rifle. When firing at the first three hostiles, aim for a leg of the first one. As they scatter, shoot a second one in the arm and then go for a head shot on the third. Now all you have to get is a shot into the center of another enemy's body and you can add another award to your collection.

TIER 1 TACTICS

This is a tough mission for Tier 1. You have no HUD cursors to help you locate targets. Therefore, it is important that you use your thermal vision. This will make the hostiles stand out from their cooler surroundings so you can find them quickly and then kill them.

1	Objective
O··▶	Critical Path
O··▶	Flanking Path
🧨	Grenade Crate

② HUNT AND KILL CAMPED ENEMIES (SNIPER)

After clearing out the first camp, Dusty detects a glint of light from a scope. There is a sniper out there and he is looking for you and your teammates. From the first camp, pan to the right and then up. Use the thermal sight to quickly find him. The sniper is prone, so you have a smaller target to hit. Take him out as soon as you can line up the shot.

③ HUNT AND KILL CAMPED ENEMIES (SECOND CAMP)

There is another sniper in the second camp. Be sure to locate him hiding off to one side and kill him.

There is another camp. Pan to the left to locate it. Target the three tangos near the campfire and neutralize one of them. Let the others be for a second. There is another sniper here. Look to the right. He is positioned under a tree between the tents and a large rock. Kill him before he can take a shot at you. Now finish off the last two hostiles at this camp.

④ HUNT AND KILL CAMPED ENEMIES (MORTAR POSITION)

Now you have a mortar firing at you. Kill the crew to end this threat.

Your position is about to come under mortar fire. Pan to the right to find a couple hostiles manning a mortar. Quickly take them out because they are already firing. Stay on the mortar after the first two are dead since a third will run up to try to lob some rounds at you. Once the mortar crew is history, look to the right and down a bit. There is a sniper taking shots at you. Use thermal sights to quickly locate and then eliminate him.

ZONE 2

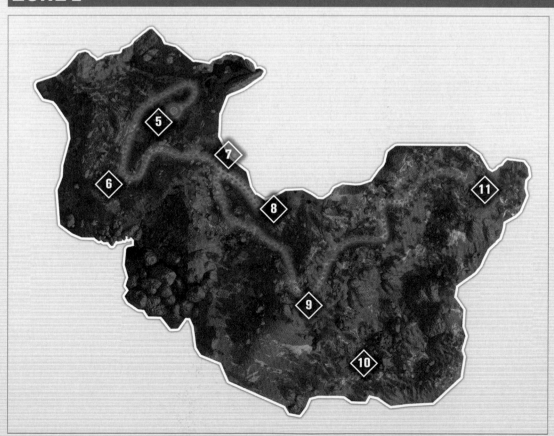

1 — Objective

O··▶ — Critical Path

O··▶ — Flanking Path

— Grenade Crate

⑤ DEFEND HIDE FROM APPROACHING FIGHTERS

Dusty detects another sniper on the far ridge when one of the claymores he positioned below you detonates. You have hostiles headed in your direction. After lowering the M82, switch to your MP7A1 SMG and stay low. The enemy does not know where you are exactly. Let them get a bit closer and then open fire. Take out as many as you can. When the last claymore detonates, it is time to bug out. Follow Dusty up a trail to another position. Take cover behind some rocks and then engage the enemy below.

Take out the tangos headed up the hill toward your position. Be sure to stay low and behind cover.

⑥ RALLY WITH DUSTY

Once the tangos have been neutralized, Dusty heads down the hill. Follow and meet up with him near the body of a tango. From the looks of it, these guys are well equipped and ready for action.

⑦ AMBUSH APPROACHING FIGHTERS

It appears one of the enemies was only wounded and got away. Maybe he can lead you to others. Dusty follows the blood trail to see where he went. Stay on Dusty. Once you find the wounded hostile, Dusty decides to set up an ambush for them.

⑧ FOUND A BETTER HIDE. PREPARE FOR AMBUSH

Not satisfied with the current position, Dusty heads up a trail. Follow him to a better ambush spot. You are uphill from the wounded enemy. Stay low. You can either continue using your SMG or switch to your M110. Wait for all of the tangos below to come into view. Dusty will count down when to fire. Target the tango with the RPG first and then finish off the rest.

As the hostiles come to get their wounded comrade, spring the ambush and mow them down.

⑨ FOLLOW DUSTY

The area around you is now clear. It is time to resume your sniping. Follow Dusty around until you come to another good overwatch position from which you can engage hostiles at very long range. Drop prone and crawl forward to the edge to view the enemy camp below and deploy your M82.

⑩ CLEAR ENEMY CAMP

There are four tangos in the camp below. You are fairly close to them, so you want to be able to kill them all quickly. Even though you can see them fairly well in regular light, switch to thermal mode. This allows you to quickly pick out each target and engage them without wasting time trying to locate each. As soon as the first hostile goes down, the others will start moving around. After the second or third is dead, expect fire on your position. Once the camp is clear, pack up your M82 and get ready to move.

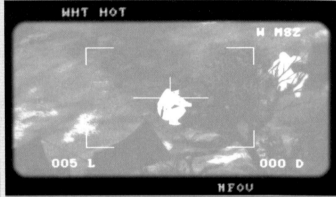

Four enemies are taking it easy in their camp. When you are done, there will be none left.

⑪ GET TO OVERWATCH POSITION

Follow Dusty as he leads the way up the ridgeline to another overwatch position. You have to do some crawling to get under rock ledges and get to this spot where you will do some more sniping in support of the SEAL team.

ZONE 3

1	Objective
◯·▸	Critical Path
◯·▸	Flanking Path
🛢	Grenade Crate

12 AID NEPTUNE'S MOVEMENT

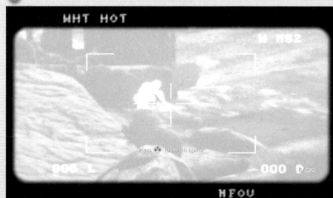

The tangos attacking the SEALs are hiding behind cover. However, they don't know that you are behind them and have a clean shot at them.

The RPG gunners are easy to see as they are silhouetted against the ridgeline. Kill both of them before they can hurt Neptune.

The SEAL team, Neptune, is in trouble on another ridge. They are taking cover behind a wall with lots of tangos converging on their position. Use thermal sights to quickly locate the enemies. The SEALs have flashing infrared beacons on them so you can easily identify them as friendlies. Start picking off hostiles firing at Neptune. Some are taking cover near the buildings while others are coming at the SEALs from the right side. The biggest threat to the SEALs are a couple of tangos with RPGs up on the ridgeline behind them. As soon as you see them, drop those two. That will allow Neptune to move on up the ridge to try to make their escape. Keep engaging enemies as the SEALs withdraw and you will earn not only the Friends from Afar achievement/trophy for completing the mission, but also the Have a Good Day achievement/trophy for completing all of Deuce's missions.

MEDAL OF HONOR™

COMPROMISED

INTEL REPORT

Unit Name: AFO Neptune

Callsign: "Rabbit"

Location: Shahikot Valley, Grid 20508890

Local Time: 1800 hrs.

Mission Summary: In the southern end of the Shahikot, Al Qaeda and Taliban fighters take the bait and walk into your iron as you draw them closer with tactical fallback maneuvers.

Initial Weapon Loadout

M4	M14 EBR	M60	P226	M67 Frag Grenades

 TIER 1 DETAILS

Par Time: 00:12:30

Completion Medal: Warrior's Badge

Mission Achievements/Trophies

Image	Name	Description	Gamer-score	Trophy
	Cliffhanger...	Complete Compromised	15	Bronze
	Feeding the Pig	In Compromised, get 15 kills with the M60	15	Bronze

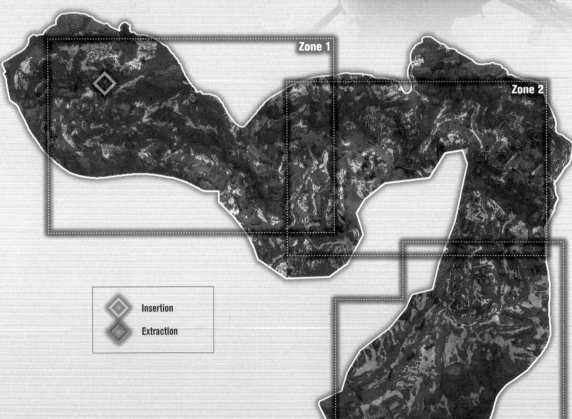

Zone 1

Zone 2

Zone 3

◆ Insertion

◆ Extraction

ZONE 1

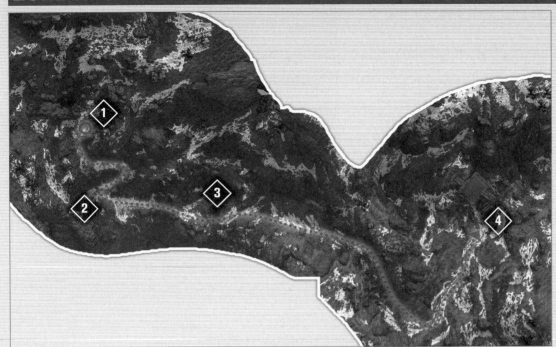

①	Objective
○∙∙▶	Critical Path
○∙∙▶	Flanking Path
💣	Grenade Crate

The enemy is following your team. Try to hit as many as you can while they are silhouetted against the sky at the top of the ridgeline and without any cover.

① DEFEND POSITION

This mission takes place immediately after the previous mission; however, you are now one of the SEALs in Neptune and moving away from a mass of Taliban fighters. Take cover behind a log and start firing at hostiles as they come over the ridgeline. Expect to take a lot of fire. Be sure to duck down behind cover when reloading or when you start getting hit. When your teammates call out positions of RPG gunners, target them immediately, since one hit by that weapon can kill you.

TIER 1 TACTICS

Usually during a Tier 1 mission, you want to rush. However, since it doesn't take many hits to kill you, it is important to use cover and then either lean around it or peek over it. Consider using the M14 EBR and getting extra time by making head shots on the enemy.

② FALL BACK ON SMOKE GRENADE

After killing many tangos, your team is ready to pull back. One of them will deploy a smoke grenade. Keep firing at the enemies while your team gets ready. As soon as they tell you to move, leave your position and sprint towards your teammates. Don't waste time turning and firing at the enemy behind you. Just keep moving until you get to some ruins and then take cover.

③ DEFEND POSITION

As your team is withdrawing, you also want to eliminate as many enemies as possible. Therefore, you are holding at the ruin for a bit to kill some tangos as well as make arrangements for an extraction. The first hostiles will come from the direction you just moved. Stay low in the ruin and take them out. However, as more Taliban arrive, they will try to flank you on the right side. Watch for RPG gunners on the ridge to your right and kill them. Pull back from the ruin and take cover behind some rocks along the path. They will give you better protection against fire from the right flank. Stay put until your teammates are ready to bug out from this spot.

The tangos are trying to flank your position. Take them out and then pull back a bit to better cover.

4 FALL BACK TO HELO

The helicopter is coming to pick you up at the primary LZ. It is just a short distance away. Your teammates pop some more smoke grenades and then take off. Follow them down the trail and then around a corner towards another ruined building. The helicopter is trying to land. However, there are hostiles at the LZ and the slope is causing a bad updraft that prevents your ride from setting down. Clear out the tangos—especially the one with an RPG—and then move into the structure for cover.

Get to the bird! Prowler 1, hold at the LZ. We are on the way!

The LZ is hot and the helicopter is not able to land. Take out the enemies so they don't shoot down your way out of here.

ZONE 2

5 FIND SECONDARY LZ

Follow your team out the back door of the structure and rush across an open area to another set of ruins. Once again, take cover. Be ready to engage enemies who are following you.

1	Objective
◯··▶	Critical Path
◯··▶	Flanking Path
💣	Grenade Crate

6 CALL IN CAS ON ENEMY HUT

Once in the ruins, move over by your teammates and you will automatically pick up the SOFLAM. Aim at the hut you just moved through near the primary LZ and designate it as a target. Some jets will fly over and drop a bomb on it, killing all the hostiles inside and near it.

Call in some close air support by lasing the hut so that the flyboys can deliver a bomb on the enemy's cover.

7 DEFEND POSITION

The air strike took out several hostiles, however more are on the way. Stay put in the ruins, find good cover, and be ready to defend your position. Stay behind the wall and then peek up through a window to take shots. Try using your M14 EBR to pick off targets at a distance—especially those with RPGs. Just follow the smoke trails back to the hostiles firing the RPGs.

8 MOVE TO SECONDARY LZ

Your teammates have called in another air strike. However, for this weapon, you are too close. Move to the back wall of the ruin and your teammates will give you a buddy boost up. However, the second bomb hits just as you are getting to the top. The concussion from the blast blows Voodoo off his feet, dislocating his shoulder. While he can still move, there is no way he can handle the M60. You are now the machine gunner for your team. Head out to another ruined hut and take cover. There are enemies in the village ahead of you. Lean out from the doorway and start shooting at them. Keep up the fire. When your teammates move forward, follow them towards the village and then past some buildings to a spot overlooking the rest of the village. Reload your weapon while you are moving. Take cover behind some rocks and start firing on enemies.

TIP

When firing the M60, stay crouched and stationary to improve accuracy. Also fire it in short bursts rather than just holding down the trigger.

As your team moves forward, stay back and provide covering fire. Then once they are behind cover, rush forward and duck behind a wall in the middle of the pathway before resuming fire on the enemy. From this spot, you can mow down hostiles as they try to move to cover to advance towards you. Stay here for a while and just kill tangos.

Stay behind this ruin and lean to the left to attack enemies on this side of the village. At this position, you will be safe from fire from the right and have a perfect shot at enemies as they move from the structures to the large rocks.

FEEDING THE PIG

 As long as you find a good position for firing the M60, this is an easy achievement/trophy to earn. You only have to kill 15 hostiles with the M60 to earn this award. With all of the tangos moving around, you will have no trouble getting this award as long you keep using the M60 and have good cover.

ZONE 3

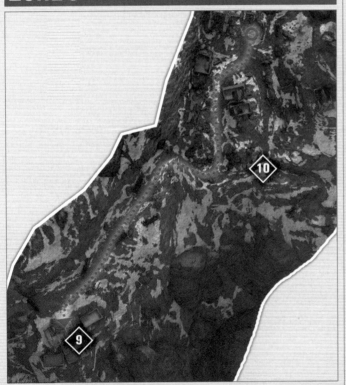

9 GET ON TO THE HELO
When you get the word that your ride has arrived, leave your cover and start moving through the village, then out the other side. You will have to take out some tangos as you go. Follow your teammates until you see the helicopter and then sprint for it. Don't stop until you are up onto the ramp.

1	Objective
O··▶	Critical Path
O··▶	Flanking Path
💣	Grenade Crate

The helo is hovering over the roof of a building. Run right up onto the ramp as quickly as possible.

10 COVER TEAM'S MOVE TO LZ
Once on the ramp, get onto the door machine gun and start firing at the enemy. Voodoo and Preacher don't get on before the helo has to lift off. Kill the enemy near your teammates on the ground so they can start moving to another LZ. The pilot will slip the helo to the side so you can continue supporting Voodoo and Preacher by killing the hostiles moving through the village. As usual, watch for the telltale smoke trails of RPGs and kill the tangos firing them. Your helo will eventually take a hit and need to move away, leaving your two teammates alone in hostile territory. Keep shooting as long as you can and you will earn the Cliffhanger... achievement/trophy.

Mow down the hostiles as you provide covering fire for two of your teammates. Aiming can be difficult when firing from a moving helicopter, however keep up the fire. If you don't kill all of the enemies, at least you got some of them.

MEDAL OF HONOR

NEPTUNE'S NET

INTEL REPORT

Unit Name: AFO Neptune

Callsign: "Rabbit"

Location: Shahikot Valley, Grid 20508890

Local Time: 0200 hrs.

Mission Summary: Two of Neptune's team members are left on the mountain. You ignore the order to return to base and reinsert at night on top of Takur Ghar to get your men back.

Initial Weapon Loadout

M4	P226	M67 Frag Grenades

TIER 1 DETAILS

Par Time: 00:15:00

Completion Medal: Shield of Valor

Mission Achievements/Trophies

Image	Name	Description	Gamer-score	Trophy
	S.E.R.E.	Complete Neptune's Net	15	Bronze
	The Quiet Professional	In Neptune's Net, eliminate 13 enemies without alerting anyone	15	Silver
	Never Quit	Finish all of Rabbit's missions	15	Bronze

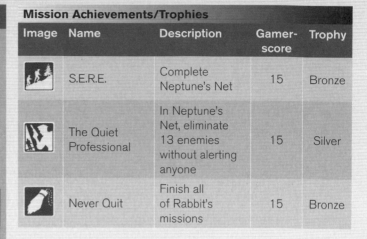

◇ Insertion

◇ Extraction

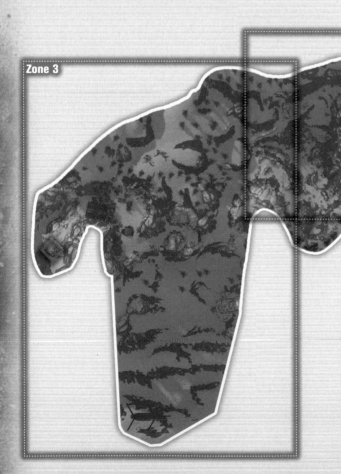

Zone 2

Zone 3

Zone 1

ZONE 1

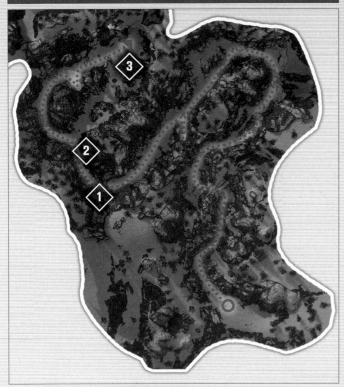

Sneak up on this enemy and give him the blade.

◇1	Objective
○··▶	Critical Path
○··▶	Flanking Path
🖤	Grenade Crate

Pick up the tango's AK-47 rifle. However, you only want to use this as a last resort. You are on your own with lots of enemies in the area. Stealth is your best weapon. Switch to your P226 pistol, which is equipped with a silencer. This will be your weapon of choice—along with your knife—as you advance on your way to Mother. Up ahead, you can see a tango up along a side trail to the right. Stay quiet and get behind him. Kill him with either your knife or a head shot with your pistol. Pick up some ammo for the AK-47, then drop down to the main trail.

This tango has his back to you. Sneak up and take him out quietly.

THE QUIET PROFESSIONAL

In order to earn The Quiet Professional achievement/ trophy, you have to kill 13 enemies in a row without alerting anyone. In this first part of the mission, you can easily kill four and get a good start on this award. Whenever you come across hostiles later, try to either knife them or take a head shot with your pistol. As soon as you alert anyone in this level, you are detected and can't earn the achievement.

You are on your own in the dark and have to start off with just a knife. Stay quiet if you want to stay alive.

◇1 RALLY UP WITH MOTHER

You and Mother have reinserted to try and find Preacher and Voodoo. However, your helo comes under attack right after Mother jumps out. By the time you are able to jump, the helo has moved to evade and your rifle went flying out the back. As you pick yourself up off the ground, you have your knife and an injury that won't let you run for now. Crouch down and begin to move forward. You are in communications contact with Mother, and he will help guide you. As you see some light up ahead, move quietly to sneak up behind a hostile with his back to you. Wait until another one walks past, then move in and kill the one by the lantern with your knife.

Continue a bit further and you come to a couple hostiles with their backs to you. Sneak up behind them. Take careful aim at one for a head shot. Then, as soon as you fire, target the other one and take him down. It is important that you kill all of these enemies without them raising an alarm. Once again, pick up some more ammo from their dropped guns. Head along a narrow ledge to the left to another snowy pathway.

Mother radios you that a patrol is headed your way. Quickly move forward and look for a path that leads up and to the left. It dead ends at the top, but puts you in a spot where you can hide. Drop prone and wait for the patrol to walk past. They have a flashlight, but won't look in your direction. After they pass by, head back down to the main trail and go left.

Mother calls in and says the enemy has found your rifle. If you activate your night vision, you will see your IR laser on your rifle shining up into the sky like a beacon. Head towards it, and as you get close, you will slide down a slope. Stay silent at the bottom. While the tangos are looking at your rifle, Mother moves in and takes them out. Now move forward and pick up your rifle. It is equipped with a silencer, so you can use it and still stay quiet.

2 FOLLOW MOTHER

Time to move out. Follow Mother up a slope to an open area. The enemy has set up a camp here. It is not going to be easy to get through here.

3 ELIMINATE FIGHTERS AT ENEMY CAMP

Silently kill the enemies up on the ridge since they look down on the camp and will alert the others if they see any of the tangos by the campfire go down.

The only way to get past this camp is to eliminate all of the hostiles inside. Continue to follow Mother. He leads you around the left side of the camp. Take cover behind some rocks that overlook the campfire below. Mother sneaks up behind a tango near you and silently knifes him. Take aim at one of the tangos on the ridge at the other side of the camp. There are a couple tangos on it that move across a small bridge. Wait until he stops, then drop him with a head shot. Do the same for the other tango on the ridge. If you have been careful, the enemy still won't know you are there and should have dispersed a bit. Try to take out more hostiles down below by picking off those who are not in view of the others. Eventually, the enemy will detect you. Stay behind cover and continue killing them until the camp is clear.

TIP

Press the HUD button while at the camp and icons will appear where each of the tangos is located. This helps you determine which are on the perimeter looking into the camp so you can neutralize them first.

ZONE 2

1	Objective
◯··▶	Critical Path
◯··▶	Flanking Path
🧨	Grenade Crate

4 SEARCH FOR VOODOO AND PREACHER

Stay out of sight as enemy patrols walk past you.

Follow Mother out of camp. He will give you a buddy boost up onto a ledge. Continue along the path and slide down a slope. You now have to go prone and crawl under a ledge. After this, use caution. You have to move under a couple bridges. Crouch down under the first one and wait for a patrol to walk across both bridges. Do not engage them. Just let them pass. This is not the time to fight. After they have passed by, stay on Mother as he advances. When he goes up to the right, stay to the left. Hold as you approach another bridge. A patrol is walking across it. Wait for them to continue. A couple hostiles stay on the bridge. You will have to take them out. Target one and shoot him with a head shot while Mother deals with the other. Now move under the bridge and turn right to walk up to the trail and meet up with Mother.

As you move into some woods, stay quiet. There is another patrol ahead. These two hostiles are not moving. Target one and kill him while Mother ices number two. Move forward some more until you come across yet another patrol. This time there are three tangos. Try to get the first one with a head shot and then go after a second. Mother takes care of the third. You and Mother are now splitting up. While he heads up high, follow the HUD icon and drop prone so you can crawl through a small tunnel. As you emerge, you are in some serious trouble. There are lots of tangos up on a ledge and they have their flashlight and weapons pointed right at you.

⑤ CLEAR ENEMY CAMP

Get up onto the ledge where you will find crates of weapons. Pick up one and start engaging the enemy headed your way.

Mother has a plan. If you have your night vision activated, turn it off. Mother throws a flare right by the hostiles and distracts them. Rush forward and take cover behind a rock. Start picking off enemies up on the ledge. When it looks clear, run around the rock to the left and then up the ledge to your right. At the top are several crates of weapons. Pick up either the PKM machine gun or the Dragunov sniper rifle. Then take cover behind a crate or rocks at the edge of the ledge. Hostiles are coming down the hills towards you. Take them out. Mother will let you know when another flare is coming, so be ready to take off your night vision goggles quickly if you use them when it gets dark.

Mother will join up with you. Hold at your position on the ledge and watch for hostiles trying to flank you on the left side. Use grenades if you need to hit enemies hiding behind rocks or other cover. If you run out, there is a grenade crate in the cave behind the weapons crates. Keep firing at the enemies until you have eliminated all of them.

MEDAL OF HONOR

ZONE 3

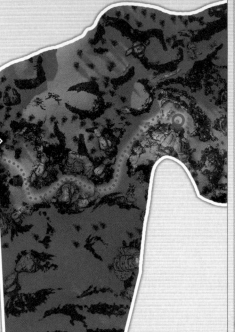

Use your pistol to take out the hostiles rushing into the building.

The enemy knows you are in the building and starts firing through the wooden walls. Try to take cover. An RPG round blasts a hole in the building, knocking you to the ground. Mother grabs you by the collar to pull you out. However, you have to engage tangos as they rush in to kill you. Use your pistol to take them out. Don't worry about head shots. Just fire several times right into their chest to put them down. Keep this up until Mother gets you out of the building.

⬧ EVADE ENEMY PURSUERS

Once you are outside, get up onto your feet and move as quickly as possible away from the building. Mother will provide some covering fire. Keep going until you get to the edge of the cliff. Hostiles are on your tail. The choice is between broken bones or bullets. You and Mother decide on the first and jump. While you survive the fall, you are in no shape to resist the enemies that move in and surround you. As a reward for surviving, you get the S.E.R.E. and Never Quit achievements/trophies.

1	Objective
⬤··▶	Critical Path
⬤··▶	Flanking Path
💣	Grenade Crate

⬧ MOVE TO PEAK

This building is near the peak of the mountain. Move inside to see if you can find your missing teammates.

Head left up a snowy slope as Mother leads the way. At the top, turn right and Mother will give you a buddy boost up to the top of a ledge. Continue along the path to a building. It seems quiet, but be ready as Mother opens the door and enters. Follow him inside. Voodoo and Preacher aren't here. However, there are some dead tangos. Don't get too comfortable. It is about to get real busy.

RESCUE THE RESCUERS

INTEL REPORT

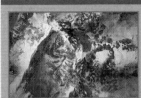

Unit Name: 1st Bn 75th Ranger Regt.

Callsign: SPC. Dante Adams

Location: Takur Ghar, 20508890

Local Time: 0732 hrs.

Mission Summary: The TOC has lost contact with Neptune, and Wolfpack is three mountains away. With time running out, there is only one option—send in the Quick Reaction Force (QRF). You once again step into the boots of Ranger SPC. Dante Adams and are inserted on top of Takur Ghar to find Neptune.

Initial Weapon Loadout

M4 w/M203	M1014	M9	M67 Frag Grenades

TIER 1 DETAILS

Par Time: 00:28:30

Completion Medal: Legion of Brotherhood

Mission Achievements/Trophies

Image	Name	Description	Gamer-score	Trophy
	Eight Heroes Aboard	Complete Rescue the Rescuers	15	Bronze
	Timber!	In Rescue the Rescuers, chop down five trees with the minigun	10	Silver
	Rangers Lead the Way	Finish all of Dante's missions	15	Bronze
	The Battle is Won	Finish the game on Easy, Normal, or Hard	50	Bronze
	...But the War Rages On	Finish the game on Hard	75	Silver

ZONE 1

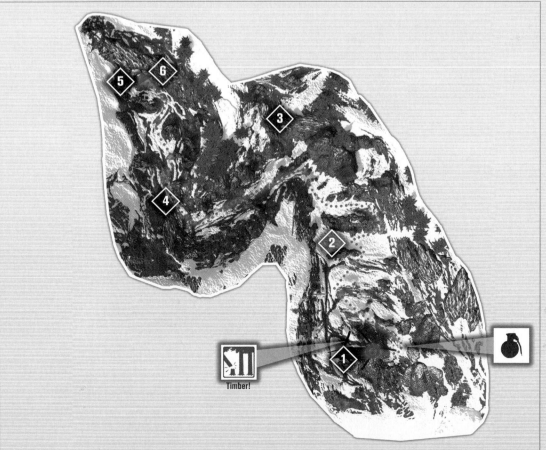

1	Objective
O···▸	Critical Path
O···▸	Flanking Path
🛢	Grenade Crate

Timber!

The RPG gunners are marked with diamond icons. Shoot them quickly. If they hit the fuel tanks on the helo, you are toast.

① DEFEND THE CRASH SITE

The helicopter carrying the Ranger QRF was attacked and shot down. A handful of the Rangers is all that survived. As the wounded are being extracted from the downed helo, you are ordered to man the side door minigun. This weapon puts out a shower of lead and will mow down the enemy. It will keep firing as long as you hold down the trigger, but it can overheat. You don't need to shoot in short bursts, since it can take a bit to get the barrels rolling and the weapon shooting. However, give it some time to cool off if you don't see any enemies. The main threats are the RPG tangos. They appear with a diamond icon over them in your HUD and teammates usually give you a verbal warning as well. Be sure to kill these hostiles quickly. Keep up the fire. Eventually an RPG round will hit the helo and knock you to the ground. Time to get out.

TIMBER!

 While you are defending the crash site, target some of the trees along with the tangos. If you cut down five trees with the minigun, you will earn the Timber! achievement/trophy.

② RALLY UP WITH TEAM

After getting up, quickly move out of the helicopter. Take cover behind some rocks and start firing at enemies. Your rifle is equipped with a grenade launcher. To switch to the grenade launcher, press the grenade launcher button to cycle back and forth between your rifle and the attached grenade launcher. Try this weapon out and fire some grenades at enemies behind cover. If you need more grenades, there is a crate near the helo. Use your HUD to see where you need to move to rally with your team. Since you will be under fire, sprint from cover to cover to get to the team.

TIP

This area is deadly with enemy fire. There are lots of hostiles just waiting for you to stick your head up above cover so they can take it off. Always stay low and lean around cover rather than peek up over it when possible. The enemy has a few RPGs that will kill you with one hit. When you do have to move out in the open, sprint and then quickly drop down into a crouch as you reach cover.

TIER 1 TACTICS

You actually have quite a bit of time to complete this mission to make par. Therefore, it is vital that you take your time and really use cover throughout. The mountains are filled with enemies that use grenades and RPGs as well as several spots with machine gun positions. Advance cautiously throughout this mission. You don't want to get near the end and get killed, forcing you to start over from the beginning.

③ RAIN CAS ON FIXED POSITION

The machine gun in this position is preventing your team from advancing. Call in some air support to take it out.

Once you have met up with your team, it is time to deal with the main threat in this area. The enemy has a fixed position up on the hillside with a machine gun. It is protected by some ad hoc armor plating. You will need some heavy firepower to take it out. Luckily there is an AC-130 gunship, callsign Clash 01, in the air overhead. Meet up with Tech. Sgt. Ybarra and get a SOFLAM from him. Use it to designate the fixed position. The gunship will then take it out with one of its cannons. As soon as you take out the target, take cover behind the rocks. More tangos will be trying to kill you.

④ MOVE UP WITH TEAM

Watch for the smoke trails from RPG gunners. Follow the smoke trail back to the gunners and kill them.

After you have cleared out the immediate area, follow your teammates forward. As you come under fire, take cover behind some rocks. There is another RPG gunner, so take him out. As you continue around a corner to the right, watch for tangos on the snowy slope above the draw through which you are moving. Neutralize them with long-range fire and advance along with your team.

⑤ RAIN CAS ON FIXED POSITION

Scratch one more machine gun position.

There is a second machine gun position up on the hillside ahead of you. Check your HUD to see where you need to be with the SOFLAM and move there. Take aim at the position and lase it for Clash 01. After the machine gun is silenced, clear out any remaining tangos in the area and then follow your team up to the position you just destroyed.

⑥ CLEAR BUNKER WITH TEAM

The bunker was protecting this entrance to a cave.

As you get to the position, there are some sheets of metal covering a hole in the side of the hill. It is an entrance to a cave system. As your team walks up to the cave and tries to open the door, Hernandez is shot and wounded by hostiles inside. Another teammate blasts open the entrance with a frag grenade. Time to head into the dark.

ZONE 2

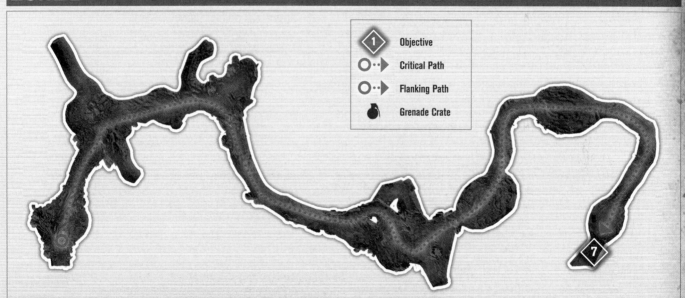

①	Objective
⊙··▶	Critical Path
⊙··▶	Flanking Path
💣	Grenade Crate

⑦ SEARCH CAVES FOR SEAL TEAM

The cave is filled with tangos. Move through cautiously and kill all of them along the way.

Enter the cave and switch on your night vision. You will encounter hostiles in the areas where the cave widens out. There are plenty of crates and rocks behind which you can take cover. As you move through these areas, be sure to check to the sides and any corners where enemies could be hiding. You don't want to be shot in the back as you continue through the cave, so clear as you go. In one area, your teammate will call out "Flares!" Quickly switch off your night vision or you will be temporarily blinded. The tangos have thrown flares in the large area so they can better see you. The flares also allow you to see them. Take cover and neutralize them. Head up a small ladder to continue through the cave. Keep fighting tangos as you advance. As you get to the end of the cave, there are some friendlies up ahead. You have found Voodoo and Preacher, two of the SEALs.

ZONE 3

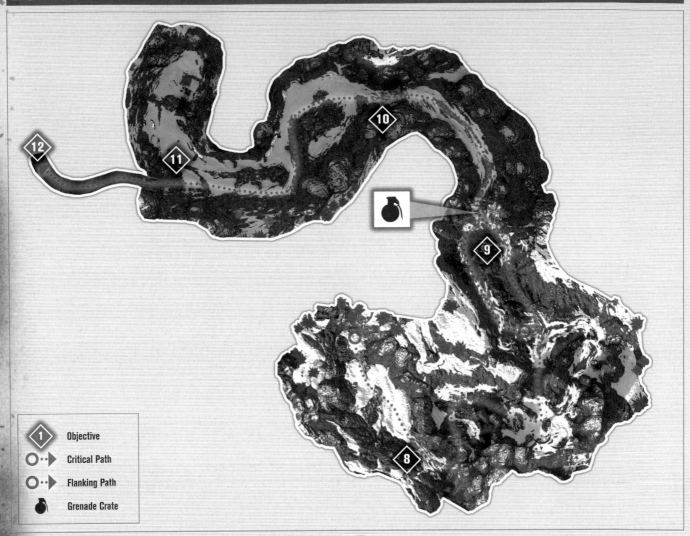

1	Objective
O··▶	Critical Path
O··▶	Flanking Path
🛢	Grenade Crate

8 CSAR WITH SEALS

Upon exiting the cave, follow the SEALs as all of you perform a Combat Search and Rescue (CSAR). Right before you drop down from a ledge, you will find a Dragunov SVD sniper rifle on the ground. While it is not necessary for the mission, if you like sniping, switch your M1014 for the sniper rifle and take it with you. Catch up to the SEALs at the bottom of the snowy slope and get ready to fight.

The Al Qaeda camp has lots of rocks and stone walls behind which you can take cover. Use it so you don't die.

9 ELIMINATE AQ CAMP AND FIGHTERS

As you turn to the corner to the left, you find an Al Qaeda camp. There are lots of hostiles here. Take cover and begin engaging the enemy. The first part of the camp has some close engagements. Head around to the left and then go to the right, as you move towards the large open area. Once you have cleared the first part of the camp, find a good spot from where you can engage enemies out in the larger, more open area. If you picked up the sniper rifle, this is a good place to put it to use. On the other hand, as groups of tangos move behind cover, blow them up with a grenade from your launcher. You can pick up some more grenades later.

The grenade launcher works well in the open area at the camp. Aim at the ground as tangos run towards cover and you can take out two or three with a single round.

TIP

The hostiles in the camp will throw grenades at you. Be ready to move out of the way if a grenade comes towards your position.

After you clear the open area, head left through a gap in the rocks and move towards an area with camouflage netting. Instead of fighting your way through that area and getting shot at from enemies above, head up a narrow slope to the left so you can flank the enemy. Kill all the enemies in this upper area and fire down on those below. Keep pushing to the end of the camp where you will find a crate with some grenades for your M203 launcher.

10 CONTINUE CSAR

Now that the camp is cleared out, take some time to restock your grenades. If you need ammo, ask a teammate for some. When you are ready, get a buddy boost from a teammate and then follow the SEALs along a path. After dropping down from a ledge, you will start taking fire from the enemy.

11 ELIMINATE AQ FIGHTERS

The enemy has some hardpoints up ahead with a machine gun and some RPGs. They can really hurt you if you don't take cover.

Quickly take cover behind some rocks. Pick off enemies above you and to the left. Clear the area immediately in front of you and then advance. There is a machine gun position in the distance as well as RPGs. Don't stay in one place too long and sprint when

moving. Follow the path around to the left so you can approach the enemy while staying behind cover. Kill tangos along the way while advancing on the hardpoints. As you get close to the first position, hide behind a stone wall. Drop prone and then lean to the left to take shots at the hostiles inside. Pick off as many tangos as you can see by the machine gun. This will allow your teammates to move forward to help out. Eventually, you will receive some air support that takes out the hardpoints and clears the way for you to advance.

12 FIND THE SEALS

Say low behind this stone wall and launch grenades at the enemy in the hardpoint.

Follow your teammates forward towards a cave behind the closest hardpoint. Move through the cave to the end where you find a closed door. Kick in the door to find the two captured SEALs and complete the mission and the campaign. You will be rewarded with the Eight Heroes Aboard, Rangers Lead the Way, and the Battle is Won achievements/trophies.

Kick in this door to find Rabbit and Mother.

MULTIPLAYER

Medal of Honor multiplayer puts two teams of twelve players against one another on custom-made maps in the unforgiving Afghan mountains, valleys, and city ruins with modern-day weaponry. As the coalition forces and the local OPFORs clash, your skill and determination will help win the day. This chapter covers all aspects of multiplayer, including the different classes, weapons, game modes, and maps.

MEDAL OF HONOR

BEGINNER'S GUIDE: GETTING STARTED

You're only a few seconds away from starting your multiplayer career. If you'd prefer to jump into the action immediately, follow these quick and easy steps to get started. However, you may want to browse through this chapter at least once before taking the fight online. The online action is fast-paced and can be a bit intimidating to a first-time player. But if you're experienced with online first-person shooters, you should have no problem picking up the gameplay.

1: CHOOSE MULTIPLAYER

When you first launch the game, you're prompted to choose between the single-player campaign and multiplayer. Each game mode is separate and loads independently of one another. At this point, select Multiplayer to load the online component of *Medal of Honor*. Also, if playing on a console, make sure you're signed in with your Playstation Network or Xbox Live Gold profile.

2: ACTIVATE EA ONLINE PASS

Before you can join a multiplayer match for the first time, you must first log in with your EA.com account profile. If you already have an EA.com account, simply enter your e-mail address and password to proceed. If you aren't registered with EA.com yet, you can do it all from this screen. Simply enter your e-mail address and create a password. Agree with the terms and conditions to continue.

3: SELECT QUICK MATCH

You're now at the multiplayer main menu. From here you can choose from a variety of options. Take a moment to browse through the different submenus under Career. Since you haven't played yet, you haven't accumulated any stats or unlocks, but you can remedy that by joining your first match. The quickest way to jump into the action is by choosing the Quick Match option.

4: CHOOSE GAME MODE

From the Quick Match menu there are a few more options, allowing you to specify one of the four game modes, as well as Hardcore mode—don't choose that one quite yet. If you have a specific game mode you'd like to play, select Combat Mission, Sector Control, Objective Raid, or Team Assault. If you have no preference, select the Any Game option. This will automatically connect you to the best available server running any of the four game modes.

5: SELECT CLASS AND PLAY!

You've most likely joined a match in progress and are automatically assigned to the team with the least players. Before you spawn on the map, choose which class you'd like to play. The rifleman class is the most versatile and probably the best choice for now, but feel free to try out the special ops or sniper class as well. You can also customize your weapons from this screen, but if this is your first match, you have no customization options yet. Don't worry, you'll unlock some new gear soon enough. Finally, you're ready to join a match. Press the button/key shown at the bottom of the screen to deploy at your team's base. You're now ready to begin your online career.

INTERFACE

Objective Icon: Objective icons appear on both the HUD and the minimap. On the HUD, these icons are accompanied by a number, showing the objective's distance in meters.

Weapon Reticule: Place this reticule over your target and fire to score a hit. Reticules expand and contract based on your movement and stance. A small reticule reflects improved accuracy, so always try to fire from a stable and crouched position. Using a weapon's iron sights or scope yields even better accuracy.

Ammo Crate Icon: The bullet icons on the minimap represent the location of an ammo crate. These icons don't appear on the HUD, so use the minimap to pinpoint their location. You can stock up on ammo, grenades, rockets, and explosives at each ammo crate. Simply stand next to one of these wooden crates spilling over with bullets to replenish your ammo.

Points Awarded: Every point you earn appears here, near the top of the screen along with a text notification describing the action that earned you these points.

Ribbon Award: If you perform an action meeting a specific criteria, a ribbon is awarded, showing up here momentarily. Medals are awarded only at the end of a round.

Most Wanted Ribbon

Game Mode Info: Each game mode features specific information in this corner of the screen. This may include items such as a timer, team health, team scores, and other items specific to each game mode.

Kill Notification: Every time you kill an opponent, a string of text appears on the bottom of the screen identifying the name of your victim as well as the weapon used to score the kill. Similar kill notifications appear below the minimap when teammates kill or are killed by opponents.

Ammo in Magazine: This number represents how many rounds are remaining in your weapon's current magazine.

Reserve Ammo: This is how much extra ammo you're carrying, not including the bullets in your currently loaded magazine.

Minimap: The minimap is your own personal satellite view of the battlefield. Use it to find ammo, objectives, teammates, and even enemies. For more details, refer to the minimap section.

Available Support Actions: The available offensive and defensive support actions appear here, differing based on your achieved scorechain level. You can only choose one support action per level, so choose carefully. Support actions remain available until selected, even if you die.

Grenade Count: How many grenades you're currently carrying.

Scorechain: The number on the left is your current scorechain. If you die, this number resets to zero. The number on the right is the score you must attain to reach the next scorechain level.

CONTEXTUAL ACTIONS

Press the button/key shown on screen to take control of machine guns and vehicles.

During gameplay, you have the opportunity to interact with a few objects. At these times, instructions appear on the screen. For example, when you are near a weapon on the ground or next to a vehicle, a note appears in the middle of the screen stating which button you need to press to pick up the weapon or to get into the vehicle. Interacting with objectives (in Combat Mission and Objective Raid) makes you initiate a timed explosive charge used to destroy the crate. You can even take control of fixed weapons, including heavy machine guns and rocket launchers.

HEALTH

If this is what your screen looks like, find cover fast!

In *Medal of Honor* there is no health bar showing you how close you are to dying. Instead, as you take damage, the HUD's perimeter turns red with splotches of blood and your vision blurs. Whenever this happens, seek cover immediately before you die. While in cover, you slowly heal over time and the HUD returns to its default pristine condition. But reaching cover before dying is easier said than done. The weapons in multiplayer inflict heavy damage, rarely giving you the chance to take evasive actions. If you do survive the first barrage, find cover immediately instead of trying to seek out your attacker.

MINIMAP

Activating the UAV defensive support action reveals the locations of enemies on your minimap for 30 seconds.

The minimap is your best friend. Not only does it give you a top-down view of your surroundings, but it also relays vital real-time information including the positions of your teammates and enemies. The white triangle icons on the minimap represent your teammates. Knowing where your friends are at all times is a vital tool in any combat situation. Try to stay in an area where there are several white triangles around you. If you see no white triangles on the minimap, find a good hiding spot as this indicates you're potentially deep in enemy territory. It's safe to assume areas that aren't occupied by friendly forces contain enemies. The minimap is a great way to gauge the distance between you and your teammates. While it's a good idea to stay within sight of your buddies, clustering too tightly together can make you vulnerable to explosive attacks such as mortar strikes. Keep an eye on the minimap to make sure you're not presenting the enemy with a tempting target for offensive support actions.

Orange triangles on the minimap represent enemies. These icons appear briefly whenever your opponents fire unsuppressed weapons. Watch for these orange triangle icons popping up on the minimap and use this information to hunt down nearby opponents. Activating a UAV defensive support action also reveals the locations of all enemies for approximately 30 seconds. This information is shared with all members of your team via their minimaps, so if your team has a UAV in the air, there's nowhere for the enemies to hide. Take advantage of this intelligence while the UAV is still active.

TIP

If you have a suppressor attached to your weapon, your position is not shown on your opponents' minimaps while firing. However, a suppressor will not prevent you from being spotted by a UAV.

MOVEMENT

Moving around the battlefield is fairly straightforward. On consoles, the left stick controls forward and backward movement as well as strafing to the left and right. Strafing is a lateral move where the direction you are facing does not change. It is useful for moving out from cover to fire and then back behind cover for protection. The right stick controls where you look—turning left and right as well as looking up and down. The peek and lean feature in single-player mode is not available in multiplayer. You will need to physically move in and out of cover.

CROUCHING AND SPRINTING

Your weapon is lowered while sprinting, preventing you from firing. However, you can reload your weapon while sprinting.

There is more to movement than just walking. Try crouching for greater stealth and stability. While crouched, you move slower. However, since you are lower, you make a smaller target for the enemy to hit and you can more easily duck behind cover. When advancing against an enemy position, it is usually best to move crouched, as it is harder for the enemy to detect you. Crouching also causes the reticule to tighten up, indicating an increase in weapon accuracy. Make a habit of dropping to a knee (and aiming) before firing a shot.

At times, it is better to move fast. Hold down the left stick while moving to sprint. You can't use weapons or equipment while sprinting, but you are much more difficult for the enemy to hit. Sprint when you have to cross a dangerously open piece of ground as you move from one position of cover to another.

CAUTION

Unlike single player mode, you can not go prone in multiplayer. The lowest you can get is a crouched stance.

COMBAT

While moving about the battlefield is a major part of gameplay, the sole purpose of movement is to place you in a position where you can use your weapons to engage and eliminate the enemy. As a Tier 1 operator-in-training, you have access to different types of weapons. However, the controls for using these weapons are fairly common. For specifics on weapons, see the Classes section, which covers this topic in greater detail.

FIREARMS

The reticule on the HUD exhibits a subtle bloom animation when your bullets strike your target.

As mentioned earlier, the reticule in the center of the screen is your aiming point for using weapons. Most of the weapons you use are direct fire, meaning that the projectile you fire travels in a straight line from your weapon to the target. Using these weapons is simple. Place the reticule directly over the target and then press the fire button. For semi-automatic or single-shot weapons such as pistols, shotguns, and sniper rifles, each time you press the fire button, you fire a single round. However, for automatic weapons such as submachine guns, assault rifles, and light machine guns, they will continue to shoot as you hold down the fire button until they are empty.

TIP

When firing automatic weapons, the longer the burst, the less accurate your fire. Therefore, to maintain greater accuracy and still put out a lot of lead, fire in short bursts. You are more likely to kill your target, especially at medium to long range, with a few accurate rounds rather than an entire clip spread all over.

IRON SIGHTS AND SCOPES

The bloom animation also appears when hitting targets through your weapon's iron sight or scope view.

When you fire a weapon using the reticule to aim, you are essentially firing from the hip, with the butt of your weapon in the crook of your arm. This is not very accurate and should only be used at close range. To increase your accuracy, press the zoom button. This will bring up the iron sight view, where you are actually looking through the weapon's sight to aim. The butt of the weapon is brought up to your shoulder, giving you greater stability and accuracy. Simply put the sight's front post over your target and squeeze the trigger to score a hit. If your weapon is equipped with a scope, the zoom button provides a view through the scope rather than the iron sight.

TIP

It's a good idea to get in the habit of pressing the zoom button to bring up your iron sight just before firing. This not only is more accurate, but it also provides a zoomed-in view of the target. To further increase accuracy, crouch down and remain stationary while firing. In the console versions, an aim assist function snaps your aim to a nearby target, making it much easier to score hits, even if your initial aim is slightly off.

GRENADES

If you suspect an opponent is hiding in a building or other confined space, toss a grenade inside before entering.

Grenades require a bit more skill to use effectively since they are either thrown or launched. Unlike a bullet or rocket, which travels in a straight line, grenades travel in a parabolic arc due to their lower speed and the effect of gravity. In the case of a grenade launcher, the farther away you are from the target, the higher you need to aim. That is why the reticule for a grenade launcher has several horizontal line aiming points. For a short-range shot, use the top line. The farther away your target, use the lower lines. By using a lower aiming point, you are essentially aiming the weapon up higher to lob the grenade towards the target.

Hand grenades work a bit differently. They are thrown rather than launched. When throwing a grenade, the reticule on the screen turns into a tiny white dot. Use this dot to adjust your aim before letting go of the grenade. The longer you hold down the grenade button, the farther your throw. A quick press of the grenade button will toss the grenade right in front of you while a long hold on the grenade button before release will send it flying some distance. However, the longer you hold down the grenade button, the shorter the fuse on the grenade. This is called cooking a grenade, ensuring it explodes shortly after landing, giving opponents little time to run away. If you hold down the fire button too long, the grenade is automatically thrown after a few seconds, preventing it from exploding in your face.

NOTE

When using grenades, it is important to understand how they work. Rifle grenades fired from a launcher explode on impact. Hand grenades, in contrast, have a five-second fuse. As a result, you can bounce hand grenades around corners or roll them down a slope.

ROCKET LAUNCHERS

Never attack an M3 light tank from the front. Instead, try to ambush it from the side or rear where its crew can't see you.

Rocket launchers are carried exclusively by the special ops class. The OPFOR RPG-7 and the coalition AT4 function identically, firing a high explosive rocket capable of taking out infantry, fixed weapons, and vehicles. While carrying a rocket launcher, there is no reticule icon on the HUD. To fire these weapons accurately, you must aim through the weapon's iron sight. When properly aimed, the rockets have surprising range and accuracy, flying in a relatively straight line from the weapon to the point of impact. You don't need to compensate for drop, so aim directly at your target to increase the chances of scoring a hit. Rocket launchers are particularly effective against the coalition M3 Cavalry Fighting Vehicle in the Combat Mission game mode. When squaring off against these light tanks, try to hit their weak side or rear armor to maximize damage.

EXPLOSIVES

Explosives are devastating against all targets. Just make sure you're far away before detonating them.

The snipers are the explosive experts in *Medal of Honor*, each carrying a few remotely detonated explosive devices. The coalition C4 and OPFOR IED function identically and are readily available to recruit-level snipers. Simply equip your explosive device and press the fire button to throw on down. These devices can also be stuck to surfaces such as walls and even ceilings. Pressing the fire button a second time detonates the explosives, so make sure you're a safe distance away to avoid blowing yourself up. Explosives are great for staging ambushes at narrow choke points, such as bridges and alleyways. Or you can use them to defend critical positions, like flags in Sector Control, or objectives in Objective Raid. They're also perfect for sneaky sabotage actions against fixed heavy machine guns. If you're feeling brave, sneak up on an M3 light tank and stick a few of these devices to its side and rear armor to take it out, along with its two-player crew.

SCORING AND STATS

There's more ways to earn points than scoring kills. Each action performed (and points awarded) appears in white text at the top of the HUD.

Almost every action you perform in multiplayer earns you points. The points you earn are tallied from round to round, accumulating over time, ultimately determining your rank in each class. Players gain experience for their chosen class by performing actions that result in points on the field of battle. Points are gained by performing a wide range of actions and by completing certain game mode-specific goals. Leveling up unlocks new weapons and attachments for players. Each class levels separately from the others, so if you wish to gain access to new weapons or abilities for a class, you must play as that class to earn experience. The level of your class is independent of your faction. So if you are a level 7 rifleman when playing as an OPFOR, you will be a level 7 rifleman when playing as a coalition soldier.

The classes, including their ranks and unlocks, are covered in detail in the next section. In the meantime, scan the following table to get an understanding of exactly what actions award points.

Multiplayer Scoring

Name	Description	Points
Kill	Kill an enemy	10
Head Shot	Head shot bonus	5
Vehicle Kill	Destroy vehicle	10
Avenger Kill	Kill an enemy that recently killed a teammate	5
Driver Kill Assist	Points awarded when your machine gunner kills someone	5
Passenger Kill Assist	Points awarded when your driver kills someone	5
Savior Kill	Kill an enemy that almost killed a friendly	5
Kill Assist	Damage an enemy that is killed by a friendly (60% damage)	5
Vehicle Kill Assist	Sit in a vehicle that someone is killing an enemy from	3
Destroy Vehicle Assist	Help destroy a vehicle	5
Vehicle Damage	Damage a vehicle	5
Double Kill	Kill two enemies within .4 seconds	10
Triple Kill	Kill three enemies within .6 seconds	15
Multiple Kill	Kill four enemies or more within .8 seconds	25
Tier 1 Kill	Bonus for killing a Tier 1 soldier if you aren't one yourself	5
Suicide	Kill yourself	-10
Teamkill	Kill a teammate (Hardcore mode only)	-15
Team Damage	Injure a teammate (Hardcore mode only)	-10
Objective Destroyed	Destroy the objective in Objective Raid or Combat Mission	30
Objective Disarm	Disarm the objective in Objective Raid or Combat Mission	15
Objective Defense Kill	Kill an enemy around the objective in Objective Raid or Combat Mission	3
Objective Arm	Arm the objective in Objective Raid or Combat Mission	15
Crate Defend Kill	Kill an enemy around the crate in Objective Raid or Combat Mission	3
Crate Attack Kill	Kill an enemy around the crate in Objective Raid or Combat Mission	3
Flag Defense	Kill an enemy within the flag radius in Sector Control	3
Secure Objective	Secure an area in Combat Mission	30
Flag Capture	Capture a flag in Sector Control	20
Defensive Support Action 1	Points for activating UAV/Intel (Level 1)	30
Defensive Support Action 2	Points for activating Match Ammo (Level 2)	40
Defensive Support Action 3	Points for activating Flak Vest (Level 3)	40
Defensive Support Action 4	Points for activating FMJ Ammo (Level 4)	50
Defensive Support Action 5	Points for activating Jammer (Level 5)	50
Defensive Support Action 6	Points for activating AP Rounds (Level 6)	60
Defensive Support Action 7	Points for activating Kevlar Vest (Level 7)	100

NOTE

When you score enough points to level up, a badge appears on the right side of the HUD, along with the name of your new rank. Next time you're in the spawn screen, cycle through the weapon customization options to see what you've unlocked. Achieving certain ranks can also earn you achievements and trophies.

SKILL LEVEL

You can see your current skill level, and those of your peers, on the global leaderboards.

In *Medal of Honor,* multiplayer skill is highly rewarded and measured with a special skill value ranging from zero to 3,000 (or even higher). Anything that gives you score, such as defeating enemies or clearing objectives, will potentially help raise your skill. But it is calculated in relation to other players, so defeating good players makes you gain more skill. Losing fights you should really win might decrease your skill instead. A high skill value represents the ultimate bragging rights.

SCOREBOARD AND LEADERBOARDS

The scoreboard can be viewed at any time during a match, showing you where you rank among your teammates.

Want to see how you stack up against your the competition? During a match you can access the Scoreboard at any time. This shows your ranking within your team based on your points earned. It also shows your skill level and kill/death ratio. The Global Leaderboard offers a much broader view of the competition, ranking every player on each respective platform. Choose the Leaderboards option in the main menu (under Career) to sort through this dynamic collection of data. By default, the player with the highest skill level appears atop the Global Leaderboard. But these rankings are fluid and can also be sorted to show the player with the highest score, kills, or play time—recorded in days, hours, and minutes. If you want to see where you rank among your friends, choose the Friend's Leaderboard. This is a much smaller version of the Global Leaderboard, limited to the players on your friend list.

STATS AND AWARDS

The My Stats screen shows you just about everything you need to know about your multiplayer career.

For greater detail on personal performance during your multiplayer career, choose the Stats and Awards option under Career from the main menu. The My Stats screen shows you more specifics about your profile, including your score, kills, deaths, time played, skill level, next unlock, and class progression. The Awards screen shows you which ribbons and medals you've already earned. But you can also view the requirements necessary to earn the awards you don't have yet.

SCORECHAIN AND SUPPORT ACTIONS

All points earned apply to your scorechain. Each scorechain level allows you to choose an offensive or defensive support action. If you die, the scorechain resets to zero.

Use the binoculars to call in offensive support actions. Make note of the distance to the designated target area to ensure you're outside the incoming ordnance's blast radius.

The scorechain system rewards skilled players with an increasing powerful array of offensive and defensive support actions. You earn points by shooting other players or by performing certain in-game actions, as described in the previous section. Once you begin accruing points, the scorechain begins. The scorechain builds as long as you remain alive, but is reset to zero when you die. At certain intervals, players are awarded support actions, which can be activated to provide an offensive or defensive boost to the team.

There are two types of support actions, offensive and defensive. Offensive support actions are different forms of artillery, like mortars or close air support, provided by fighter aircraft. Defensive support actions help you and your entire team by supplying intel, armor, and enhanced ammunition. You trigger offensive support actions with your binoculars—just aim where you want the incoming munitions to hit and press the fire button. Defensive support actions are called in using your radio or cell phone—equip it and press fire. The defensive support actions influence all members of your team, but they don't stack. Offensive support actions give you extra points if you manage to kill enemies with it, but defensive actions guarantee you a specific amount of extra points with each deployment.

Scorechain Support Actions

Level	Scorechain	Offensive		Defensive	Defensive Bonus Points
1	50	Mortar Strike		Intel/UAV	30
2	100	Rocket Attack		Match Ammo	40
3	175	Guided Missile		Flak Vest	40
4	250	Artillery		FMJ Ammo	50
5	350	Strafing Run		Jammer	50
6	450	Air Strike		AP Rounds	60
7	600	Cruise Missile		Kevlar Vest	100

NOTE

Bonuses granted by defensive support actions are cleared when a player dies. After attaining level 7, no more support actions are available, but every point you earn afterward is multiplied by 2x. The point multiplier remains in effect until you die.

Support actions are extra military assets that can be used against the opposition, such as artillery or better ammunition. If you die while you have a support action that has not yet been activated, you may use it when you respawn. If you want to gain a different support action, you must rebuild your scorechain to the necessary level. A meter in the lower right-hand corner of the screen displays the current level of your scorechain and the requirement for the next level. Using a granted support action will not cancel your scorechain, and you will keep getting better ones as long as you manage to stay alive. Make a habit of using your support actions as soon as they're awarded. The points earned through activating these support actions can help build up the points required to achieve the next scorechain level.

OFFENSIVE SUPPORT ACTIONS

LEVEL 1: MORTAR STRIKE (50 POINTS)

Projectiles: 5

Blast Radius: 7 meters

Damage in Center: 150HP

As the first offensive support action, the mortar strike is the weakest. But it can still be effective with accurate targeting. For best results, aim at the ground beneath your target when peering through the laser-designating binoculars. This will ensure the mortar rounds land exactly where you want them to, hopefully taking out any enemies within its modest blast radius.

LEVEL 2: ROCKET ATTACK (100 POINTS)

Projectiles: 6

Blast Radius: 12 meters

Damage in Center: 150HP

The rocket attack is a slight upgrade from the mortar strike, offering more projectiles and a significantly larger blast radius. As with the mortar strike, target high concentrations of enemies and target the ground beneath them to ensure an accurate strike. In addition to infantry, rocket attacks are very effective against the M3 Cavalry Fighting Vehicle and fixed weapon positions.

LEVEL 3: MISSILE ATTACK (175 POINTS)

Projectiles: 1

Blast Radius: 8 meters

Damage in Center: 1,000HP

While the missile attack is initiated by aiming through the binoculars, once the attack is launched, you gain control of the actual missile. Use the missile camera view to fly it into your enemies, appearing as orange triangles on the HUD. You only have a few seconds before impact, so make the most of this time, centering the missile's crosshairs on the largest concentration of enemy troops. While the missile has a relatively small blast radius, it kills everyone within eight meters. Even hiding in a concrete-reinforced bunker won't protect you from this attack.

LEVEL 4: ARTILLERY STRIKE (250 POINTS)

Projectiles: 6

Blast Radius: 12 meters

Damage in Center: 250HP

The artillery strike is basically a much more powerful version of the rocket attack. Using the binoculars, target the ground beneath a group of enemy units and watch the incoming shells saturate the kill zone. The artillery strike doesn't have the penetrative power of the missile attack, so players hiding in fortified structures may survive the barrage of exploding shells.

LEVEL 5: STRAFING RUN (350 POINTS)

Projectiles: 30

Blast Radius: 12 meters

Damage in Center: 200HP per bullet

Upon activating this support action with the binoculars, a jet swoops down and strafes the target area. This is a more linear attack than the other support actions and is best focused down narrow streets, bridges, or alleyways. Also, make sure you're well outside the target area. Strafing runs are effective against exposed targets, but have no effect against enemies hiding inside buildings.

LEVEL 6: AIR STRIKE (450 POINTS)

Projectiles: 6

Blast Radius: 15 meters per bomb

Damage in Center: 250HP per bomb

The air strike is one of the most effective offensive support actions, so be careful not to waste it. For best results, wait until a friendly UAV is in the air so you can target the largest concentration of enemies. Move to an elevated position and use the binoculars to zoom in on the target zone. Aim at the ground beneath your enemy's feet, call in the air strike, and then sit back and watch the fireworks—preferably from a very distant position.

LEVEL 7: CRUISE MISSILE (600 POINTS)

Projectiles: 1

Blast Radius: 40 meters

Damage in Center: 1,500HP at center

Reaching level 7 is difficult, but so worth the effort. The cruise missile functions just like the missile attack, but with a much larger blast radius and kill potential. Approximate the target area with the binoculars and then take control of the cruise missile, flying it into the largest concentration of orange triangle icons, representing your opponents. The cruise missile is extremely powerful, so make sure you're well outside its 40 meter blast radius, otherwise you'll be joining your victims back at the spawn screen.

TIP

Immediately after targeting an area for a missile or cruise missile strike through the binoculars, get ready to take control. The HUD view immediately changes to a black-and-white camera view positioned in the missile's nose cone. At this point you can fly the missile. Identify enemy targets on the ground (appearing as orange triangle icons) and fly the missile directly at a large group. The missile's crosshair sight at the center of the HUD makes it easy to line up the missile with the intended point of impact.

DEFENSIVE SUPPORT ACTIONS

LEVEL 1: INTEL/UAV (50 POINTS)
Description: Spots all enemies on the map for 30 seconds

Activation Points: 30

At level 1, the UAV is much more valuable than the mortar strike, and will often yield you more points, putting you only two kills away from attaining level 2. This is one of the most powerful support actions, revealing all enemies to you and your teammates via the minimap. But the UAV is only active for 30 seconds, so make the most of this time, using this intel to ambush and hunt down your unsuspecting opponents.

LEVEL 2: MATCH AMMO (100 POINTS)
Description: 1.2x damage bonus for all living teammates

Activation Points: 40

This ammo upgrade slightly increases the damage caused by your team's weapons. For best results, activate this support action when the bulk of your teammates are alive and on the map. Players who are dead or in the spawn screen do not benefit from this action. Increasing the damage output of your team's weapons is always welcome, but the 40 bonus points for activating this support action are even nicer.

LEVEL 3: FLAK VEST (175 POINTS)
Description: +50HP for all living teammates

Activation Points: 40

Dying too frequently? Consider activating this support action to gain some bonus health. Flak vests are shared with the rest of your teammates too, assuming they're alive when the support action is activated. The bonus health afforded by these vests can make the difference between life and death in close-quarters duels, giving your whole team a significant advantage in each fire fight they experience.

LEVEL 4: FMJ AMMO (250 POINTS)
Description: 1.5x damage bonus for all living teammates

Activation Points: 50

Just like match ammo, Full Metal Jacket (FMJ) ammo increases the damage output of your team's weapons. However, these bonuses aren't stackable. If match ammo is still active, FMJ ammo replaces it. But don't worry, the 1.5x damage multiplier is significant enough to notice a difference in the performance of your team's weapons. As usual, wait until the majority of your team is alive before activating this action.

LEVEL 5: JAMMER (350 POINTS)
Description: Jams enemy UAVs for 30 seconds

Activation Points: 50

The jammer doesn't just jam UAVs, but it also scrambles your opponents' minimaps, removing all objective and ammo icons. This also means that your team's positions don't appear on their minimaps when firing. Although it only lasts for 30 seconds, this is a very powerful support action and is best deployed when an enemy UAV is in the air. Take advantage of this blackout to make a move on an objective or other enemy-controlled location.

LEVEL 6: ARMOR-PIERCING ROUNDS (450 POINTS)
Description: 2x damage bonus for all living teammates

Activation Points: 60

This is an extremely powerful support action, especially when deployed on a skilled team. Armor-piercing rounds effectively double the damage dealt by your team's weapons, turning even the weakest weapons into fearsome killers. So even if you have FMJ ammo active, the armor-piercing rounds are well worth the upgrade.

LEVEL 5: KEVLAR VEST (600 POINTS)
Description: +100HP for all living teammates

Activation Points: 100

Despite the generous health bonus and activation points, the Kevlar vest remains a hard sell since the devastating cruise missile is also available at this level. However, if you're looking for points over visceral thrills, the Kevlar vest is the wisest choice. Not only do you get 100 points up front, your whole team gains the benefit of bonus health. While it's possible to score more than 100 points with a cruise missile, it isn't as easy as choosing the Kevlar vest.

NOTE

When you die, you can see the defensive support bonuses applied to your killer, appearing as blue icons on this card. The card also identifies the name of your killer, their rank, and the weapon (plus attachments) they used to send you back to the spawn screen.

GAME MODES

Medal of Honor offers several multiplayer gameplay modes that support up to twenty-four players for twelve-on-twelve combat. Each mode is accessible via pre-set playlists residing on a dedicated server. Playlists are set by the server's host and can be composed of several gameplay modes, which are cycled randomly in online matches.

If there are not enough players present on a server, the match begins with a Preround. This gives players a chance to get a brief preview of the map. No points are tracked in the Preround, though players can move and shoot. The Preround continues until the minimum number of players necessary to begin the game joins the match. After the Preround is complete, or if no Preround was needed, players proceed to the Warmup. While warming up, players can select their load-out and get ready to go into combat. Players are frozen in place until the match is ready to begin. After a brief countdown, the players unfreeze and are able to begin the battle. While playing, if the number of players drops below the minimum threshold, the match will return to the Preround to give other players a chance to join and repopulate the match. This ensures that every server is appropriately populated for combat.

COMBAT MISSION

When arming or disarming explosives at objectives, always have at least one teammate watch your back.

In Combat Mission, the coalition forces are attackers and the OPFORs are the defenders. Coalition forces must clear five consecutive objectives to win. OPFORs are tasked with stopping the coalition forces at any cost. As the coalition team clears objectives, new areas of the map are unlocked, which then reveals the next objective of the coalition forces. After each round, the sides switch, allowing both teams to have a chance to be on the offensive. The Team Health meter, in the bottom left corner of the screen, represents the remaining coalition reinforcements. If the Team Health meter is depleted before the current objective is cleared, the match ends and the coalition forces are stopped in their tracks. If the coalition forces complete all five objectives before their Team Health reaches zero, they claim victory.

M3 Cavalry Fighting Vehicle

The M3 light tank is the only vehicle available in multi-player mode and it appears exclusively during Combat Mission matches on the coalition's side—OPFORs can't even steal the vehicle. For the coalition attackers, the M3 offers some serious firepower, making it an asset that can turn the tide in tough fought battles. The driver controls the vehicle as well as its turret-mounted auto cannon. The auto cannon is capable of firing up to six high-explosive rounds in rapid succession. After six rounds are fired, there's a brief cool down period before more shots can be fired. However, the vehicle's ma-chine gun can be fired almost continuously.

Your peripheral vision is very limited while driving the M3, so make sure your machine gunner is constantly rotating to protect your flanks.

The machine gun is operated by a second player in the passenger position and is mounted on its own turret, allowing it to rotate independently of the auto cannon. But the machine gun is prone to overheating, leading to lengthy cool down periods. Fire the machine gun in short bursts, pausing a second or two in between each trigger pull. This keeps the weapon cool, allowing it to fire with minimal interruption. The machine gunner should rotate frequently, scouting the vehicle's flanks for enemy troops attempting to stage sneak attacks with rockets or explo-sives. Remember, the vehicle's armor is weakest on the sides and rear, so protect these vulnerable spots.

TIP

The M3 Cavalry Fighting Vehicle is best deployed as a stand-off weapon, suppressing enemy targets from long range. Avoid charging straight into swarms of enemy infantry, as this leaves the vehicle vulnerable to rocket and IED attacks.

SECTOR CONTROL

Capturing flags is a quick way to earn a lot of points, but don't forget to defend them as well.

Sector Control forces two sides to fight for possession of three sectors: Alpha, Bravo, and Charlie. These sectors are represented by flags. Holding an objective accumulates points over time. The more sectors you hold, the faster your points accrue. Stand close to flags to capture them. The more friendly units nearby, the faster the capturing process goes. Sectors can be lost and recaptured as the match goes on. The first team to earn 1,800 points wins. Study the team scores in the bottom left corner of the screen—the blue number represents your team's score and the orange shows the opposing team's score. If your team is trailing behind, capture and hold more flags. Each flag controlled generates approximately one point per second. If your team holds all three flags, that's 180 points per minute! Sectors can be lost and recaptured as the match goes on, so once you control a sector, take steps to defend it.

TEAM ASSAULT

Safety in numbers definitely applies to Team Assault. Move around with a small group of teammates and support each other.

Team Assault is a twelve-on-twelve no-holds-barred battle in a confined area where you fight for kills and points. The two teams struggle to reach 1,200 points to win the match. Each kill is counted, so take down your enemies to increase your team's points, represented by the blue number and scoring meter in the bottom left corner of the screen. The orange number is the opposing team's score. It's your choice whether to stick with your team or to go on a solo hunt. But be warned, the tempo is high and enemies can pop up from behind almost any corner. The

two teams struggle to reach a certain number of points to win the match. Each kill is counted, so take down your enemies to increase the team's points. Monitor the scoring meters to see how the fight is going, and make tactical adjustments as necessary. For example, if both teams are nearing 1,200 points, play it safe to avoid giving the enemy team the kills they need to win.

OBJECTIVE RAID

The two objectives are the focal point of this game mode, so attackers and defenders should expect heavy resistance at both locations.

In Objective Raid, OPFORs swarm across the map to sabotage two objectives (Alpha and Bravo) using explosives. Coalition forces must stop them and defend their installations. The OPFORs have five minutes to accomplish their objective. While players score points for attacking as usual, those points do not count toward the team's score. These points are displayed at the end of a round, but they are not used to calculate the winning team. If the OPFORs manage to clear both objectives before the time is up, they are the victors. If the coalition forces successfully defend at least one of the objectives and outlast the OPFORs for five minutes, then they are the winners.

TIP

You can aim and fire your weapon while setting or disarming a charge in Objective Raid and Combat Mission matches, so don't go down without a fight!

HARDCORE

Tired of the easy-to-use interface and minimap showing you exactly where to go? Then try Hardcore mode. This allows you to play Sector Control, Team Assault, and Objective Raid matches in hyper-realistic parameters. This mode removes most of the HUD elements, including weapon reticule. Therefore, you must aim using only your weapon's iron sight or scope. Even more notable, friendly fire is turned off, so you can injure and kill your teammates and vice versa, something that impacts poorly on your score. To up the realism even more, weapons inflict much more damage. Even if you get hit only once or twice, it's back to the spawn screen. This mode is intended solely for experts, so make sure you have plenty of experience before tackling Hardcore mode.

MULTIPLAYER TACTICS

Tactics is the combining of maneuvers and firepower to achieve an objective. Both movement and weapons have already been covered, so this section focuses on using the two together.

PLAN AHEAD

Before a round begins, take a few seconds to discuss tactics with your teammates. Any game plan is better than none.

There is an old saying that those who fail to plan, plan to fail. You need to come up with a plan before the bullets start flying. The best place to start is to look at your game mode's objectives, since those determine victory or defeat. While killing the enemy is always a goal, it is often a means to an end. Instead, focus on the objectives. Do you have to destroy a target, defend a position, or just get to a certain point on the map?

Once you know what you must do, look at the map and examine the terrain. Where are you located? Where is the objective? How will you get there? Are there any vehicles you can use? These are all questions you need to ask yourself. Once you have determined how to get to the target, you must then consider how to accomplish your orders. Will you need to get in close to plant an explosive charge on the target? If so, how will you secure the perimeter? Finally, you need to take into account your opposition. What does the enemy have and where are they located? Usually you will not know that type of information until you get in close to the target and can see the enemy with your own eyes. Therefore, planning continues on the fly as you learn new information about enemy positions and actions.

COVER

You can fire through some cover, such as this wrecked chopper in the Shahikot Mountains. If you suspect an enemy is hiding behind flimsy cover, open fire. If the bloom animation appears, you've scored a hit.

Combat is very dangerous. Bullets and other deadly projectiles fly through the air and can kill you outright if they make contact. The concept of cover is to place something solid between you and the enemy that will stop those projectiles and keep you safe. The multiplayer maps are filled with objects that you can use as cover—buildings, walls, trees, rocks, earthen mounds, and so on. Some types of cover will stop small arms fire such as rifle bullets, but not stop the heavier machine gun fire. Walls of buildings will stop machine gun fire, but not rockets or light tank rounds. Therefore, pick cover that will protect you from the current threat—objects constructed from wood or flimsy sheet metal won't stop a bullet.

Cover should become ingrained in your combat thinking. In addition to looking for enemies, you also need to be looking for cover. During a fire fight, always stay behind cover. The only reason you leave cover is to move to another position with cover. If the cover is low, you may need to crouch down behind it, standing only to fire over it. When moving from cover to cover, sprint to get there quicker.

While you want to stay behind cover, you also want to try to deny the benefit of cover to your enemies. Destroying their cover is a way to do that. Another way is to reduce the effect of their cover by moving to hit them from a direction for which they have no cover. This is called flanking. For example, if an enemy is taking cover behind a wall, move around to the side of the wall so that the wall is no longer between you and your target. In the single-player campaign, your squad is great at holding an enemy's attention, giving you the chance to flank, surprising threats from the side or rear. Try the same tactics in multiplayer, using teammates to provide support fire while you flank or vice versa.

LONG-RANGE COMBAT

When sniping, try to focus your fire down narrow choke points. Also, be sure to hold your breath to steady your aim—you can hold your breath for approximately seven seconds.

If possible, it is best to try to attack the enemy at long range before they're even aware of your presence. While sniper rifles work great for this type of combat, you can even use assault rifles, light machine guns, or rocket launchers to hit targets at long range. The key to winning at long range is to take your time. Crouch, stay still, and use iron sights or scopes to increase your magnification and accuracy. As always, make sure you have some good cover in case the enemy decides to shoot back. If you can see them, they can see you. Also remember to fire in short bursts to ensure that more of your bullets hit the target.

CLOSE-QUARTERS COMBAT

Quick reflexes trump accuracy in close-quarters gun battles like this. This is why shotguns are so effective.

This type of combat is the exact opposite of long-range combat. In close quarters, such as in a town or even within a building, you don't have a lot of time to aim before shooting. However, at such short ranges, accuracy is not really a factor. Instead, you need a weapon that puts out a lot of firepower with some spread so you are more likely to get a hit while moving. Shotguns and submachine guns are great for close-quarters combat. Your minimap is also an important tool, especially if a friendly UAV is in the air. Since you can see where enemies are located, use this info to set up shots while strafing around corners. Your weapon will already be aimed at the target as it appears on the minimap, which saves you just enough time to have the advantage and make the kill rather than be killed. Don't forget to use grenades, which can be

thrown around corners or over walls to hit enemies who think they are safe behind cover.

TIP

Have you just run out of ammo in the middle of a close-quarters duel? It's much faster to draw your pistol than to reload your main weapon. If your opponent is reloading too, rush in for a melee kill.

ENGAGING FIXED WEAPON POSITIONS

The rocket launcher at Mazar-i-Sharif Airfield is powerful, but offers little protection from snipers and offensive support actions. When playing as the coalition, take it out with an offensive support action before advancing through the hangar.

There are two types of fixed weapons positions—heavy machine guns and rocket launchers. Each must be manned by a soldier. These weapons can be extremely deadly during combat, so it is usually a top priority to silence these weapons either by destroying them outright or at least killing the soldiers manning them. Some machine guns have a shield to protect the gunner. However, if you take careful aim, you can shoot through the view slits in these shields to kill the gunner. Other options include using grenades or rockets to wipe out the weapon along with the gunner. Some of these weapons also have limited firing arcs and can't turn to fire at targets in all directions. If you can attack these guns from the flanks or sides, you can not only avoid being fired on by that weapon, but also possibly prevent the shield from protecting the gunner.

TIP

Offensive support actions can completely eliminate fixed weapons, so call in mortar strikes or other forms of artillery to take out these weapons and anyone standing nearby. The weapons eventually respawn, but only after several minutes have passed.

MULTIPLAYER: CLASSES

In *Medal of Honor,* you select one of three classes to play, each with its own unique flavor and appearance. Pick from rifleman, special ops, and sniper to find the class that best suits your style of play. In addition to this, as you gain rank, you can pick the weapon and customize it in terms of both function and appearance. Experiment to find the best combinations for different game modes and maps. Play to the strength of each class to win.

You can view the rank progress of each class in the Your Stats screen that appears at the end of each round.

Before spawning into a match, choose your class and customize your weapons. The various attachments can enhance or hinder the performance of your selected main weapon, so make your decisions carefully.

As your score increases, you will rank up your military career, gaining better and more advanced equipment. You can check the Unlock Tree screen to track your current progress. You have three separate careers, one for each soldier class in the game. Your rifleman might be better than your sniper if you play rifleman more, which dictates what weapons and gear you can choose from. You can try to get some play time in each class to keep them level or go for maximum ranking in your favorite class. In *Medal of Honor,* you shape your military career. With determination and skill you can even become a Tier 1 operator. Attaining the Tier 1 rank will not only change your appearance to other players, it will also set you on the path to unlock some really exciting and useful equipment.

There are many small arms to choose from in *Medal of Honor,* all with their advantages and disadvantages. As you progress through the ranks, you will unlock new weapons and accessories to put on your guns such as scopes, suppressors, and muzzle brakes. Each of these also has their own strengths and weaknesses, altering the performance of your selected weapon. Customize your weapon to fit your play style. Each weapon handles differently with different attachments, so it is wise to experiment to find combinations that suit the situation and game mode or map. Customizations are made on the Weapon Customization screen, available both in game and the multiplayer main menu. Extra ammunition in game can be found either by locating a weapon cache with the help of your minimap or by walking over dead enemies.

TIP

Want to try out a weapon you haven't unlocked yet? Pick up a weapon off a fallen opponent or teammate. Simply stand over the weapon and follow the on-screen instructions to pick it up. Walking past a dead player also restocks your ammo. Dropped weapons only appear for a few seconds, so grab it before it disappears.

MEDAL OF HONOR

RIFLEMAN

The rifleman is the basic fighter class. They tend to be front line combatants, leading the charge toward enemy positions and being the backbone of the armed forces. Riflemen generally use assault rifles and machine guns, with smoke grenades as an accessory.

COALITION RIFLEMAN

The coalition rifleman is ready for anything, equipped with an M16A4 assault rifle featuring an underslung M203 grenade launcher. Later on, the coalition rifleman can unlock the M249 light machine gun, for those occasions when suppressive fire is necessary. Whether attacking or defending, consider choosing the rifleman as your general-purpose combat workhorse.

Rifleman Rank 1-7

Rifleman Rank 8+

Standard-Issue Equipment

Weapon	Image
Combat Knife	
M9 Pistol	
M16A4 Assault Rifle	
M203 Grenade Launcher	
Smoke Grenade	

Coalition Rifleman Unlocks

Level	Rank	Points	Unlock	Image
1	Recruit	0	M16A4 Assault Rifle	
2	Regular	250	Extra Magazine	
3	Expert	350	Red Dot Sight	
4	Veteran	500	M249 Light Machine Gun	
5	Operator	800	Suppressor	
6	Commander	1,100	Open-Tip Ammunition	
7	Elite	1,500	Combat Scope	
8	Tier 1 Recruit	2,000	Muzzle Brake	
9	Tier 1 Regular	2,400	F2000 Assault Rifle	
10	Tier 1 Expert	2,800	Veteran M16A4 Assault Rifle	
11	Tier 1 Veteran	3,200	Veteran M249 Light Machine Gun	
12	Tier 1 Operator	3,600	AK-47 Assault Rifle	
13	Tier 1 Commander	4,000	Pistol Ammo	
14	Tier 1 Elite	4,400	PKM Light Machine Gun	
15	Tier 1 Warfighter	4,800	Extra Grenade	

OPFOR RIFLEMAN

Equipped with an AK-47 assault rifle and GP-25 grenade launcher, the OPFOR rifleman is a formidable combat unit even before unlocking any special gear. Keep playing as the rifleman to gain access to the PKM light machine gun and a host of other special weapons and attachments. Mix and match weapons and gear to counter the ever-changing conditions on the battlefield.

Rifleman Rank 1-7

Rifleman Rank 8+

Standard-Issue Equipment

Weapon	Image
Axe	
Tariq Pistol	
AK-47 Assault Rifle	
GP-25 Grenade Launcher	
Smoke Grenade	

OPFOR Rifleman Unlocks

Level	Rank	Points	Unlock	Image
1	Recruit	0	AK-47 Assault Rifle	
2	Regular	250	Extra Magazine	
3	Expert	350	Red Dot Sight	
4	Veteran	500	PKM Light Machine Gun	
5	Operator	800	Suppressor	
6	Commander	1,100	Open-Tip Ammunition	
7	Elite	1,500	Combat Scope	
8	Tier 1 Recruit	2,000	Muzzle Brake	
9	Tier 1 Regular	2,400	F2000 Assault Rifle	
10	Tier 1 Expert	2,800	Veteran AK-47 Assault Rifle	
11	Tier 1 Veteran	3,200	Veteran PKM Light Machine Gun	
12	Tier 1 Operator	3,600	M16A4 Assault Rifle	
13	Tier 1 Commander	4,000	Pistol Ammo	
14	Tier 1 Elite	4,400	M249 Light Machine Gun	
15	Tier 1 Warfighter	4,800	Extra Grenade	

NOTE

The veteran variants of each weapon only look different than the standard-issue versions. Operationally and statistically, these weapons are identical to the originals.

MEDAL OF HONOR

RIFLEMAN WEAPONS

M164A

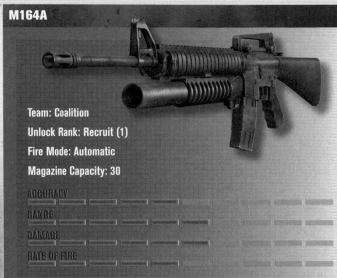

Team: Coalition
Unlock Rank: Recruit (1)
Fire Mode: Automatic
Magazine Capacity: 30

ACCURACY
RANGE
DAMAGE
RATE OF FIRE

Attachments

Name	Slot	Accuracy	Range	Damage	Rate of Fire
Red Dot Sight	Rail	+1	–	–	–
Suppressor	Barrel	–	-1	-1	–
Open-Tip Ammo	Base	-1	–	+1	–
Combat Scope	Rail	–	+1	–	–

FIELD NOTES

The M16A4 is the most recent variant in the legendary M16 family of assault rifles. The rifle is extremely versatile but is most effective when engaging targets at intermediate to long range. Attach a red dot sight or combat scope at the earliest opportunity to improve the rifle's accuracy while increasing the zoom magnification. With its impressive accuracy and stopping power, the M16A4 is a surprisingly effective long-range weapon.

AK-47

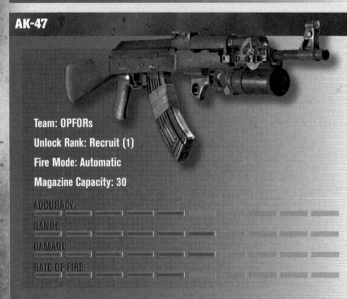

Team: OPFORs
Unlock Rank: Recruit (1)
Fire Mode: Automatic
Magazine Capacity: 30

ACCURACY
RANGE
DAMAGE
RATE OF FIRE

Attachments

Name	Slot	Accuracy	Range	Damage	Rate of Fire
Red Dot Sight	Rail	+1	–	–	–
Suppressor	Barrel	–	-1	-1	–
Open-Tip Ammo	Base	-1	–	+1	–
Combat Scope	Rail	–	+1	–	–

FIELD NOTES

Despite its age, the AK-47 remains one of the most popular and reliable assault rifles in the world. Statistically, the rifle performs similar to the coalition M16A4 and benefits from the same attachments. However, the AK-47 exhibits slightly heavier recoil, so go easy on the trigger. For best results, fire the rifle in short bursts to prevent the weapon from pulling off target. This is essential when engaging enemies at long range.

M249

Team: Coalition
Unlock Rank: Veteran (4)
Fire Mode: Automatic
Magazine Capacity: 100

ACCURACY
RANGE
DAMAGE
RATE OF FIRE

Attachments

Name	Slot	Accuracy	Range	Damage	Rate of Fire
Red Dot Sight	Rail	+1	–	–	–
Open-Tip Ammo	Base	-1	–	+1	–
Combat Scope	Rail	–	+1	–	–
Muzzle Brake	Barrel	+1	-1	-1	–

FIELD NOTES

The M249 Squad Automatic Weapon is the standard-issue light machine gun deployed by the U.S. Army. When it comes to suppressing targets with high volumes of fire, this is the right tool for the job. Install a muzzle brake on the weapon's barrel to dampen recoil and increase accuracy—the reduction in damage is a fair trade-off. But even with a muzzle brake, the weapon emits a large muzzle flash, potentially giving away your position.

PKM

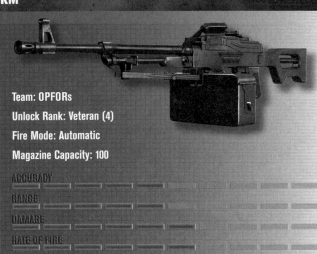

Team: OPFORs

Unlock Rank: Veteran (4)

Fire Mode: Automatic

Magazine Capacity: 100

ACCURACY

RANGE

DAMAGE

RATE OF FIRE

Attachments

Name	Slot	Accuracy	Range	Damage	Rate of Fire
Red Dot Sight	Rail	+1	—	—	—
Open-Tip Ammo	Base	-1	—	+1	—
Combat Scope	Rail	—	+1	—	—
Muzzle Brake	Barrel	+1	-1	-1	—

FIELD NOTES

The Russian designed and manufactured PKM light machine gun has been adopted worldwide by armies and rebel groups alike thanks to its rugged operation and reliability. However, the weapon exhibits heavy recoil and can greatly benefit from a muzzle brake attached to the barrel. Attaching optics can also increase the PKM's accuracy and magnification, making it rather effective for suppressing targets at intermediate and long range.

M60

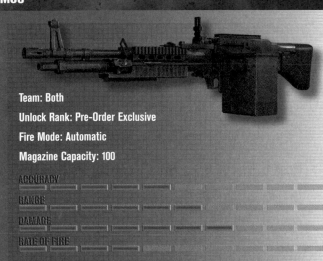

Team: Both

Unlock Rank: Pre-Order Exclusive

Fire Mode: Automatic

Magazine Capacity: 100

ACCURACY

RANGE

DAMAGE

RATE OF FIRE

Attachments

Name	Slot	Accuracy	Range	Damage	Rate of Fire
Red Dot Sight	Rail	+1	—	—	—
Open-Tip Ammo	Base	-1	—	+1	—
Combat Scope	Rail	—	+1	—	—
Muzzle Brake	Barrel	+1	-1	-1	—

FIELD NOTES

The M60 light machine gun is an exclusive pre-order unlock, available only from specific vendors. Once unlocked, it's immediately available to rifleman players on both coalition and OPFOR teams. This gives you access to a very formidable light machine gun before reaching the Veteran (4) rank. The M60 packs a bit more range and power than the standard M249 and PKM light machine guns too. But it also exhibits heavy recoil, despite its significantly lower rate of fire.

M240

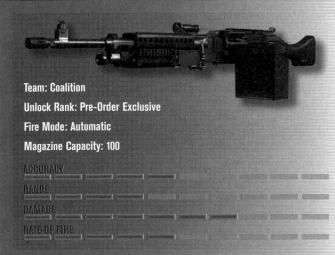

Team: Coalition

Unlock Rank: Pre-Order Exclusive

Fire Mode: Automatic

Magazine Capacity: 100

ACCURACY

RANGE

DAMAGE

RATE OF FIRE

Attachments

Name	Slot	Accuracy	Range	Damage	Rate of Fire
Red Dot Sight	Rail	+1	—	—	—
Open-Tip Ammo	Base	-1	—	+1	—
Combat Scope	Rail	—	+1	—	—
Muzzle Brake	Barrel	+1	-1	-1	—

FIELD NOTES

The M240 light machine gun is an exclusive unlock for players who pre-ordered *Medal of Honor* from the EA Store. This massive weapon packs some serious power but suffers from a lack of range and some fierce recoil. Attaching a combat scope and a muzzle brake can somewhat mitigate these deficiencies, but the weapon remains most effective at short-intermediate ranges.

RPK

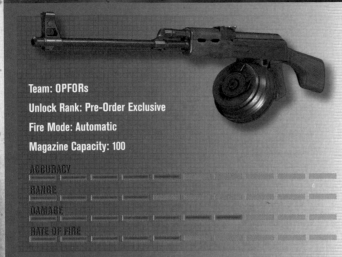

Team: OPFORs

Unlock Rank: Pre-Order Exclusive

Fire Mode: Automatic

Magazine Capacity: 100

ACCURACY

RANGE

DAMAGE

RATE OF FIRE

Attachments

Name	Slot	Accuracy	Range	Damage	Rate of Fire
Red Dot Sight	Rail	+1	–	–	–
Open-Tip Ammo	Base	-1	–	+1	–
Combat Scope	Rail	–	+1	–	–
Muzzle Brake	Barrel	+1	-1	-1	–

FIELD NOTES

Like the M240, the RPK is an exclusive unlock for EA Store customers, and is made available at the very start of your multiplayer career. Statistically, the RPK is identical to the M240. Both weapons are very powerful light machine guns that are most accurate when fired from a stable, fixed position. In other words, don't fire this weapon from the hip while on the run—you probably won't hit anything.

F2000

Team: Both

Unlock Rank: Tier 1 Regular (9)

Fire Mode: Automatic

Magazine Capacity: 30

ACCURACY

RANGE

DAMAGE

RATE OF FIRE

Attachments

Name	Slot	Accuracy	Range	Damage	Rate of Fire
Red Dot Sight	Rail	+1	–	–	–
Suppressor	Barrel	–	-1	-1	–
Open-Tip Ammo	Base	-1	–	+1	–
Combat Scope	Rail	–	+1	–	–

FIELD NOTES

This Belgian-designed fully automatic assault rifle utilizes a bullpup configuration offering great performance and mobility. The rifle has a slightly higher rate of fire than the M16A4 and AK-47, but also inflicts less damage. As a result, the weapon is best suited for engagements at close-to-intermediate ranges where its high rate of fire can chew through opponents. Equipping a suppressor reduces the rifle's effective range and damage but also dampens recoil, making the F2000 an absolute beast in close quarters.

SPECIAL EQUIPMENT

Grenade Launcher

The M16A4, AK-47, and F2000 are each equipped with an underslung grenade launcher. Grenades fired from this launcher explode on impact and can destroy light cover including wood fences, trees, and some stone walls. By raising the barrel you can launch these munitions impressive distances, especially if you're standing on a hill. Use the horizontal lines on the HUD to adjust your aim, raising the barrel to engage distant targets or lowering the barrel for a more direct firing arc. Grenades have a high splash damage and can kill or injure opponents within a modest blast radius. They're particularly effective at taking out fixed machine gun positions. However, they lack the penetrative power of the special ops rocket launcher and as such are less effective against armored vehicles like the M3 Cavalry Fighting Vehicle.

Smoke Grenade

Never underestimate the significance of a well-placed smoke screen. Instead of frag grenades, the rifleman is equipped with one smoke grenade useful for concealing yourself (and teammates) from incoming fire. On offense, smoke grenades are vital for concealing advances, particularly when there's little environmental cover. Use smoke grenades when crossing streets, streams, alleys, or other open areas known to be watched by enemy troops. But smoke screens are at their most opaque in the first five to seven seconds, so move out before the smoke dissipates.

NOTE

Smoke grenades don't function properly when thrown into water, no matter how shallow. Always toss your smoke grenades at dry land to ensure maximum concealment.

RIFLEMAN TACTICS

- Of all three classes, the rifleman is the most versatile, offering exceptional performance at any range. If you're not sure what the situation is on the ground, spawn in as a rifleman (equipped with an assault rifle) and lend your teammates a hand.

- The rifleman is the core unit of any attacking force, particularly when rushing an objective. Dash from one piece of cover to the next, using smoke as necessary to conceal your advance. Smoke can also be used to conceal the objective itself, especially if you need a few seconds to set a charge or capture a flag.

- Any of the assault rifles can double as a decent sniper rifle by attaching a combat scope. With 4x magnification, the combat scope's optics make it easy to score head shots at just about any range. Plus, the rifle's automatic capability makes it simple to fire a follow-up burst if you miss the first time. But don't hold the trigger down too long as recoil will cause the weapon to jump off target.

- The light machine guns greatly benefit from the addition of a muzzle brake. While the attachment reduces the weapon's range and damage, it greatly reduces recoil, making it much easier to keep the weapon on target, even during prolonged automatic bursts. However, muzzle brakes do very little to reduce the weapon's large muzzle flash and distinct sound, so be mindful of giving away your position—snipers have any easy time zeroing in on large muzzle flashes.

- Suppressors can only be fitted on the assault rifles in this class. The reduction in range and damage may seem like a hard sell, but suppressors have some great advantages. Obviously, a suppressor reduces the weapon's report, making it tough to hear. As a result, your position is not temporarily shown on the minimap when firing a suppressed weapon. The suppressor also eliminates muzzle flash, ideal when trying to hide from snipers and other long-range threats.

MEDAL OF HONOR

SPECIAL OPS

Special Ops are close-quarters combat experts. They use submachine guns or shotguns, and keep a rocket launcher ready for high explosive sabotage. Sneaking behind enemy lines and cutting off supply routes or waiting to ambush are two key strategies for Special Ops.

COALITION SPECIAL OPS

Packing an M4A1 carbine and a AT4 rocket launcher, the coalition special ops soldier is a front line specialist, perfect for staging sneaky flanking attacks. Unlocking the 870MCS combat shotgun gives the special ops soldier even more lethal close-quarters capability. Choose this class when you need to take the fight to the enemy in urban environments and other close-quarters situations.

Special Ops Rank 1–7

Special Ops Rank 8+

Standard-Issue Equipment

Weapon	Image
Combat Knife	
M9 Pistol	
M4A1 Carbine	
AT4 Rocket Launcher	
Frag Grenade	

Coalition Special Ops Unlocks

Level	Rank	Points	Unlock	Image
1	Recruit	0	M4A1 Carbine	
2	Regular	250	Extra Magazine	
3	Expert	350	Red Dot Sight	
4	Veteran	500	870MCS Combat Shotgun	
5	Operator	800	Suppressor	
6	Commander	1,100	Shotgun Slugs/Open-Tip Ammo	
7	Elite	1,500	Combat Scope	
8	Tier 1 Recruit	2,000	Laser Sight	
9	Tier 1 Regular	2,400	P90 PDW	
10	Tier 1 Expert	2,800	Veteran M4A1 Carbine	
11	Tier 1 Veteran	3,200	Veteran 870MCS Combat Shotgun	
12	Tier 1 Operator	3,600	AKS-74U Carbine	
13	Tier 1 Commander	4,000	Pistol Ammo	
14	Tier 1 Elite	4,400	TOZ-194 Combat Shotgun	
15	Tier 1 Warfighter	4,800	Extra Grenade	

OPFOR SPECIAL OPS

Whether armed with their standard AKS-74U carbine or their unlockable TOZ-194 combat shotgun, the OPFOR special ops soldier is crucial in both offensive and defensive operations. During Combat Mission matches, their RPG-7 is extremely useful for taking out the coalition's M3 Cavalry Fighting Vehicle. But they also excel in close-quarters attack roles, ideal or staging sneak attacks on enemy positions.

Special Ops Rank 1–7

Special Ops Rank 8+

Standard-Issue Equipment

Weapon	Image
Axe	
Tariq Pistol	
AKS-74U Carbine	
RPG-7 Rocket Launcher	
Frag Grenade	

OPFOR Special Ops Unlocks

Level	Rank	Points	Unlock	Image
1	Recruit	0	AKS-74U Carbine	
2	Regular	250	Extra Magazine	
3	Expert	350	Red Dot Sight	
4	Veteran	500	TOZ-194 Combat Shotgun	
5	Operator	800	Suppressor	
6	Commander	1,100	Shotgun Slugs/Open-Tip Ammo	
7	Elite	1,500	Combat Scope	
8	Tier 1 Recruit	2,000	Laser Sight	
9	Tier 1 Regular	2,400	P90 PDW	
10	Tier 1 Expert	2,800	Veteran AKS-74U Carbine	
11	Tier 1 Veteran	3,200	Veteran TOZ-194 Combat Shotgun	
12	Tier 1 Operator	3,600	M4A1 Carbine	
13	Tier 1 Commander	4,000	Pistol Ammo	
14	Tier 1 Elite	4,400	870MCS Combat Shotgun	
15	Tier 1 Warfighter	4,800	Extra Grenade	

SPECIAL OPS WEAPONS

M4A1

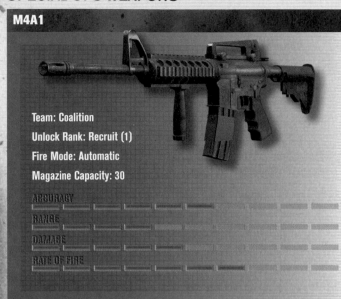

Team: Coalition

Unlock Rank: Recruit (1)

Fire Mode: Automatic

Magazine Capacity: 30

ACCURACY

RANGE

DAMAGE

RATE OF FIRE

Attachments

Name	Slot	Accuracy	Range	Damage	Rate of Fire
Red Dot Sight	Rail	+1	—	—	—
Suppressor	Barrel	—	-1	-1	—
Combat Scope	Rail	—	+1	—	—
Open-Tip Ammo	Base	-1	—	+1	—
Laser Sight	Barrel	+1	+1	-1	—

FIELD NOTES

The M4A1 is a carbine version of the M16, designed for close-quarters combat. The shorter barrel length makes it easy to maneuver in tight spaces, such as building interiors, making it ideal for urban combat. However, the weapon has limited range and is easily outclassed by the larger assault rifles when engaging targets beyond intermediate range. For best results, choose this weapon when operating in environments with limited sightlines and equip a red dot sight for improved accuracy.

AKS-74U

Team: OPFORs

Unlock Rank: Recruit (1)

Fire Mode: Automatic

Magazine Capacity: 30

ACCURACY

RANGE

DAMAGE

RATE OF FIRE

Attachments

Name	Slot	Accuracy	Range	Damage	Rate of Fire
Red Dot Sight	Rail	+1	—	—	—
Suppressor	Barrel	—	-1	-1	—
Combat Scope	Rail	—	+1	—	—
Open-Tip Ammo	Base	-1	—	+1	—
Laser Sight	Barrel	+1	+1	-1	—

FIELD NOTES

Designed primarily for use by Russian special forces, the AKS-74U is a fully automatic carbine with impressive performance and maneuverability. While it has less stopping power than its AK-47 counterpart, it more than makes up for it in its high rate of fire. Like the M4A1, the weapon has limited range and is best suited for close-quarters combat in urban settings.

MP7A1 PDW

Team: Both

Unlock Rank: Limited Edition Unlock

Fire Mode: Automatic

Magazine Capacity: 30

ACCURACY

RANGE

DAMAGE

RATE OF FIRE

Attachments

Name	Slot	Accuracy	Range	Damage	Rate of Fire
Red Dot Sight	Rail	+1	—	—	—
Suppressor	Barrel	—	-1	-1	—
Combat Scope	Rail	—	+1	—	—
Open-Tip Ammo	Base	-1	—	+1	—
Laser Sight	Barrel	+1	+1	-1	—

FIELD NOTES

The MP7A1 Personal Defense Weapon (PDW) is a special unlock available only to owners of the Limited Edition game. This compact automatic weapon is a little larger than a pistol but is capable of firing a laser beam-like string of lead thanks to its blistering rate of fire. This makes it extremely deadly at close range. But the weapon has very poor performance at greater distances, so avoid long-range duels with opponents packing an assault or sniper rifle.

MULTIPLAYER
CLASSES

870MCS

Team: Coalition
Unlock Rank: Veteran (4)
Fire Mode: Pump-Action
Magazine Capacity: 8 Shot/5 Slugs

ACCURACY
RANGE
DAMAGE
RATE OF FIRE

Attachments

Name	Slot	Accuracy	Range	Damage	Rate of Fire
Red Dot Sight	Rail	+1	—	—	—
Shotgun Slugs	Base	-1	+1	+1	—
Laser Sight	Barrel	+1	+1	-1	—

FIELD NOTES

The 870 Modular Combat Shotgun (MCS) is a pump-action military variant of the same weapon deployed by law enforcement agencies around the United States. Although it has devastating damage output at close range, you better make sure you hit your target with the first shot. In the time it takes to load a fresh shell (or slug) an opponent can easily perform a fatal counterattack. As with any shotgun, it's best deployed in close-quarters environments—it's perfect for clearing buildings.

TOZ-194

Team: OPFORs
Unlock Rank: Veteran (4)
Fire Mode: Pump-Action
Magazine Capacity: 8 Shot/5 Slugs

ACCURACY
RANGE
DAMAGE
RATE OF FIRE

Attachments

Name	Slot	Accuracy	Range	Damage	Rate of Fire
Red Dot Sight	Rail	+1	—	—	—
Shotgun Slugs	Base	-1	+1	+1	—
Laser Sight	Barrel	+1	+1	-1	—

FIELD NOTES

Designed for the Russian military, the TOZ-194 was never adopted for service, but has instead become a popular weapon among security forces around the world. Like the 870MCS, this is a pump-action shotgun capable of firing shot or slugs. When loaded with slugs, consider attaching the laser sight for improved accuracy. But make those shots count—when engaging an opponent face to face, chances are you won't get an opportunity to pull the trigger a second time.

P90 PDW

Team: Both
Unlock Rank: Tier 1 Regular (9)
Fire Mode: Automatic
Magazine Capacity: 50

ACCURACY
RANGE
DAMAGE
RATE OF FIRE

Attachments

Name	Slot	Accuracy	Range	Damage	Rate of Fire
Red Dot Sight	Rail	+1	—	—	—
Suppressor	Barrel	—	-1	-1	—
Combat Scope	Rail	—	+1	—	—
Open-Tip Ammo	Base	-1	—	+1	—
Laser Sight	Barrel	+1	+1	-1	—

FIELD NOTES

The P90 Personal Defense Weapon (PDW) packs some serious firepower into a very compact package. Like the MP7A1, the submachine gun has an extremely high rate of fire, made even more impressive by its large 50-round magazine. However, frequent reloads are still necessary due to the weapon's lack of power and inaccuracy when fired in long bursts. Initially the P90 is equipped with an integrated mini reflex sight but can be customized with a standard red dot sight or combat scope.

SPECIAL EQUIPMENT

Rocket Launcher

The coalition and OPFOR special ops soldier each comes equipped with a rocket launcher: coalition troops carry the AT4 while the OPFORs tote around an RPG-7. Each weapon system fires a high explosive rocket with armor-piercing capability. Rockets are most effective at damaging and destroying armored vehicles, such as the coalition team's M3 light tank on Combat Mission maps. When attacking the M3, always try to hit the sides or rear where its armor is weakest. Rockets are also great for taking out fixed machine gun positions. But rockets are only mildly effective against infantry, unless you manage to score a direct hit. When targeting opponents with the rocket launcher, aim for their feet—the splash damage alone should be enough to send them back to the spawn screen.

SPECIAL OPS TACTICS

- The special ops soldier excels in close-quarters combat, so consider choosing this class when operating in urban environments or when assaulting (or defending) an objective at point blank range. The unit's rocket launcher is also the most effective weapon against armored vehicles.

- When attacking the M3 Cavalry Fighting Vehicle with a rocket launcher, pay close attention to the vehicle's turret. The driver and machine gunner are often looking in the same direction, so avoid exposing yourself to their devastating weapons. Instead, look for opportunities to flank, attacking from just outside their narrow peripheral vision. For best results, hit the vehicle's side or rear armor to maximize damage. Even then, it may take several direct hits to destroy an M3, so ask for some help from your teammates or find an ammo crate to keep stocked on rockets during the attack.

- Both the MP7A1 and P90 submachine guns are awesome close-quarters weapons thanks to their high rates of fire. Attaching a suppressor not only silences these weapons but it also dampens recoil, helping you keep the weapon on target during lengthy automatic bursts. The reduction in range and damage is a small price to pay for the increased stability and stealth.

- The carbines bridge the gap between the assault rifles and submachine guns, and as such, are very versatile weapons. In tight quarters, a red dot sight is recommended for quick target acquisition, while at longer ranges the combat scope is a better option. Suppressors are best suited for close-quarters engagements, but the reduction in sound and muzzle flash is welcome in any situation.

- Shotguns are extremely deadly but require quick reflexes and precise targeting at close range to optimize their effectiveness. For best results, aim for your opponent's chest to score an instant kill with a single blast. This allows the shot to spread out across the target's upper torso and head to ensure the kill. Slugs are essentially large bullets, offering even less margin for error when targeting, but with the added benefit of increased range and damage. A single slug hit to the chest is enough to drop your target, regardless of range, as there is no spread to account for. But don't expect to snipe enemies at long range with your slug-loaded shotgun—it's still a close-quarters weapon.

SNIPER

Snipers are best when taking up positions behind the main line and taking out enemies from afar. While they can plant and detonate explosives, their primary function is long-range crowd control. Snipers need to take precautions to keep safe when in combat, since looking down a scope limits their field of view.

COALITION SNIPER

Starting with an M21 battle rifle, the coalition sniper only gets deadlier while progressing through their career. By unlocking weapon attachments and the powerful M24 sniper rifle, the sniper transforms into a feared long-range specialist. But the sniper can also surprise unsuspecting attackers by detonating C4 charges placed at strategic choke points or defensive positions.

Sniper Rank 1–7

Sniper Rank 8+

Standard-Issue Equipment

Weapon	Image
Combat Knife	
M9 Pistol	
M21 Battle Rifle	
C4 Explosives	
Frag Grenade	

Coalition Sniper Unlocks

Level	Rank	Points	Unlock	Image
1	Recruit	0	M21 Battle Rifle	
2	Regular	250	Extra Magazine	
3	Expert	350	Combat Scope	
4	Veteran	500	M24 Sniper Rifle	
5	Operator	800	Rangefinder	
6	Commander	1,100	Open-Tip Ammunition	
7	Elite	1,500	High Power Scope	
8	Tier 1 Recruit	2,000	Suppressor	
9	Tier 1 Regular	2,400	G3 Battle Rifle	
10	Tier 1 Expert	2,800	Veteran M21 Battle Rifle	
11	Tier 1 Veteran	3,200	Veteran M24 Sniper Rifle	
12	Tier 1 Operator	3,600	SVD Battle Rifle	
13	Tier 1 Commander	4,000	Pistol Ammo	
14	Tier 1 Elite	4,400	SV-98 Sniper Rifle	
15	Tier 1 Warfighter	4,800	Extra Grenade	

OPFOR SNIPER

The OPFOR sniper's standard-issue SVD battle rifle is a good training weapon before stepping up to the more powerful SV-98 sniper rifle. Both rifles are great in defensive situations, but can also prove invaluable when applying long-range pressure against fixed coalition positions. The sniper's cell phone-detonated IEDs are also great for staging ambushes on enemy infantry and vehicles.

Sniper Rank 1–7   Sniper Rank 8+

Standard-Issue Equipment

Weapon	Image
Axe	
Tariq Pistol	
SVD Battle Rifle	
IED	
Frag Grenade	

OPFOR Sniper Unlocks

Level	Rank	Points	Unlock	Image
1	Recruit	0	SVD Battle Rifle	
2	Regular	250	Extra Magazine	
3	Expert	350	Combat Scope	
4	Veteran	500	SV-98 Sniper Rifle	
5	Operator	800	Rangefinder	
6	Commander	1,100	Open-Tip Ammunition	
7	Elite	1,500	High Power Scope	
8	Tier 1 Recruit	2,000	Suppressor	
9	Tier 1 Regular	2,400	G3 Battle Rifle	
10	Tier 1 Expert	2,800	Veteran SVD Battle Rifle	
11	Tier 1 Veteran	3,200	Veteran SV-98 Sniper Rifle	
12	Tier 1 Operator	3,600	M21 Battle Rifle	
13	Tier 1 Commander	4,000	Pistol Ammo	
14	Tier 1 Elite	4,400	M24 Sniper Rifle	
15	Tier 1 Warfighter	4,800	Extra Grenade	

MULTIPLAYER
CLASSES

SNIPER WEAPONS

M21

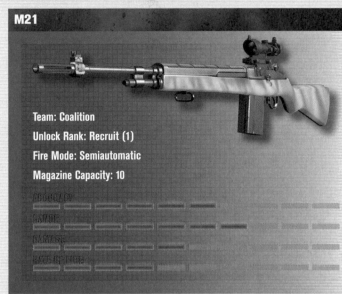

Team: Coalition
Unlock Rank: Recruit (1)
Fire Mode: Semiautomatic
Magazine Capacity: 10

ACCURACY
RANGE
DAMAGE
RATE OF FIRE

Attachments

Name	Slot	Accuracy	Range	Damage	Rate of Fire
Combat Scope	Rail	—	+1	—	—
Open-Tip Ammo	Base	-1	—	+1	—
Suppressor	Barrel	—	-1	-1	—

FIELD NOTES

The M21 is a semiautomatic sniper variant of the M14 with origins dating back to the Vietnam War. Initially the rifle is fitted with a red dot sight, offering minimal magnification. Add a combat scope as soon as possible to improve the rifle's range. Also, be ready to squeeze the trigger in rapid succession to down a target. Unless you score a head shot, it may take two or three hits to drop your target for good.

SVD

Team: OPFORs
Unlock Rank: Recruit (1)
Fire Mode: Semiautomatic
Magazine Capacity: 10

ACCURACY
RANGE
DAMAGE
RATE OF FIRE

Attachments

Name	Slot	Accuracy	Range	Damage	Rate of Fire
Combat Scope	Rail	—	+1	—	—
Open-Tip Ammo	Base	-1	—	+1	—
Suppressor	Barrel	—	-1	-1	—

FIELD NOTES

Also known as the Dragunov, the SVD is a Soviet-designed semiautomatic sniper rifle, first manufactured during the height of the Cold War. Like the M21, the rifle is equipped with a red dot sight by default, but can greatly benefit from the addition of a combat scope. While the rifle has decent power, you'll need to score a head shot to drop a target with only one bullet.

M24

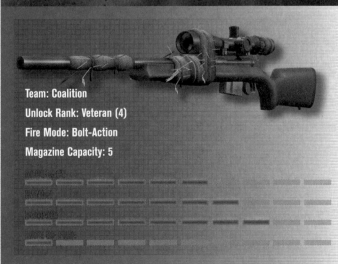

Team: Coalition
Unlock Rank: Veteran (4)
Fire Mode: Bolt-Action
Magazine Capacity: 5

ACCURACY
RANGE
DAMAGE
RATE OF FIRE

Attachments

Name	Slot	Accuracy	Range	Damage	Rate of Fire
Rangefinder	Barrel	—	+2	-1	—
Open-Tip Ammo	Base	-1	—	+1	—
High Power Scope	Rail	—	+2	—	—

FIELD NOTES

The bolt-action M24 is the standard-issue sniper weapon system of the U.S. Army. Initially the rifle is fitted with a powerful telescopic sniper scope, ideal for engaging targets at long range. But you must compensate for the rifle's vertical sway by holding your breath—this stabilizes the rifle for approximately seven seconds, giving you just enough time to center your sight on the target and squeeze the trigger. Even with the rifle's powerful scope, scoring head shots can be difficult. Aim for your target's torso to ensure an equally lethal hit.

PRIMA Official Game Guide

SV-98

Team: OPFORs
Unlock Rank: Veteran (4)
Fire Mode: Bolt-Action
Magazine Capacity: 5

ACCURACY
RANGE
DAMAGE
RATE OF FIRE

Attachments

Name	Slot	Accuracy	Range	Damage	Rate of Fire
Rangefinder	Barrel	—	+2	-1	—
Open-Tip Ammo	Base	-1	—	+1	—
High Power Scope	Rail	—	+2	—	—

FIELD NOTES

The Russian-designed SV-98 bolt-action sniper rifle is used primarily by law enforcement and counter-terrorist units. It performs identically to the M24, sporting the same telescopic sniper scope and a five-round magazine capacity. While sighting through the scope, hold your breath before firing to steady your aim. Since your peripheral vision is significantly narrowed while peering through the scope, make sure you choose a relatively safe location to snipe from to avoid being flanked or surprised by a knife-wielding opponent.

G3 Battle Rifle

Team: Both
Unlock Rank: Tier 1 Regular (9)
Fire Mode: Semiautomatic
Magazine Capacity: 20

ACCURACY
RANGE
DAMAGE
RATE OF FIRE

Attachments

Name	Slot	Accuracy	Range	Damage	Rate of Fire
Combat Scope	Rail	—	+1	—	—
Open-Tip Ammo	Base	-1	—	+1	—
Suppressor	Barrel	—	-1	-1	—

FIELD NOTES

The German-designed G3 is a legendary battle rifle popular with marksmen around the world. It performs much like the M21 and SVD battle rifles, but with less recoil and stopping power. Therefore, be prepared to fire two or three consecutive rounds into your target to produce lethal results—even when scoring head shots. The addition of a combat scope greatly enhances the rifle's effectiveness when engaging enemies at long range. Thanks to the rifle's limited muzzle climb it's possible to fire several shots without lifting the crosshairs off target.

SPECIAL EQUIPMENT

Explosives

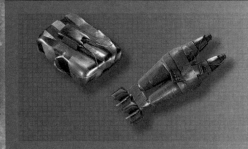

In addition to carrying a powerful rifle, snipers are also equipped with remote-detonated explosives. These explosives are devastating against infantry and armor alike, so look for opportunities to ambush your opponents. Drop them at known choke points on the map and wait for your opponents to walk into your trap before triggering your attack. These explosives are also the quickest way to slice through a M3's thick armor. For best results, slap a charge on the side or rear of the vehicle to optimize damage. If you have the time, toss two charges on a light tank and then escape to a safe distance before triggering the fireworks.

TIP

Explosive charges can be detonated by hand grenades or other explosives. If you're expecting an ambush, look for ways to eliminate the enemy's booby traps before advancing into the kill zone or simply kill the triggerman.

SNIPER TACTICS

- Of all the classes, the sniper is the most specialized, requiring practice and patience to master. Whether toting a battle rifle or sniper rifle, make a habit of staying back from the front lines and engage opponents at long range. Snipers are easily outclassed by rifleman and special ops soldiers at close and intermediate ranges, so do your best to keep your distance.

- Be mindful of your surroundings while peering through a scope. As the magnification of your sight increases, your peripheral vision decreases, allowing enemies to potentially flank your position. Try to find geographical features such as impassable rocks, cliffs, or the map boundary to protect your flanks. Also, don't stay glued to your scope view. Pull away from the scope frequently and pan left and right to watch for enemies approaching your position.

- Don't silhouette yourself. While it may seem logical to climb to the highest point on the map to get a better view, make sure there's always an object directly behind you. This is called your backdrop and prevents you from presenting enemy snipers with a crisp silhouette. Hills, rooftops, and towers make it tough to conceal your position, so consider sniping from lower positions, where your enemies are less likely to expect it.

- Sniper rifles can not be fired accurately from the hip at close range—no crosshairs appear on the HUD while toting around these weapons. When moving from one sniping spot to the next always equip your pistol. Although much less powerful, a pistol has a higher rate of fire, giving you a fighting chance should you come face to face with an opponent.

- Explosives aren't only great for blowing up armored vehicles, but they can also prove devastating against infantry. Identify areas on the map where enemies are likely to take cover and group up. Place an explosive charge at each of these popular cover locations, then retreat to a safe distance and wait for your opponents to approach. Explosive icons appear on the HUD and minimap showing you exactly where you planted the charges. If a friendly UAV is present you can see enemies on the minimap too, making it easy to determine when to set off your explosives. These charges have a very large blast radius, so it's possible to score multiple kills with a single detonation.

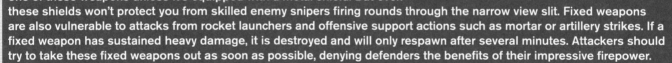

Fixed Weapons

Some maps feature stationary heavy machine guns and rocket launchers that can be manned by simply interacting with them. Such weapons are usually placed in a defensive position, covering predicable avenues of attack. While manning a fixed weapon, you can only aim and fire the weapon. This makes you rather vulnerable to sniper fire and explosive attacks, so think twice before taking control of one of these weapons unless it's equipped with a metal shield. But even these shields won't protect you from skilled enemy snipers firing rounds through the narrow view slit. Fixed weapons are also vulnerable to attacks from rocket launchers and offensive support actions such as mortar or artillery strikes. If a fixed weapon has sustained heavy damage, it is destroyed and will only respawn after several minutes. Attackers should try to take these fixed weapons out as soon as possible, denying defenders the benefits of their impressive firepower.

HELMAND VALLEY

MAP OVERVIEW

Combat Mission: Python 1 has been tasked to break through the southern province of Helmand in search of intelligence and weapon caches. Several antiaircraft emplacements in the area deny the coalition air superiority, which complicates the situation. The experienced operators of Python 1 prepare, knowing the area is infested with OPFOR fighters. As they start down along the stream, they detect rapid movement in the distant brush. The coalition forces must fight their way through the valley, clearing out several enemy strongholds and bunker systems to finally allow a wing of F-18 Hornets to deliver their deadly payload on target.

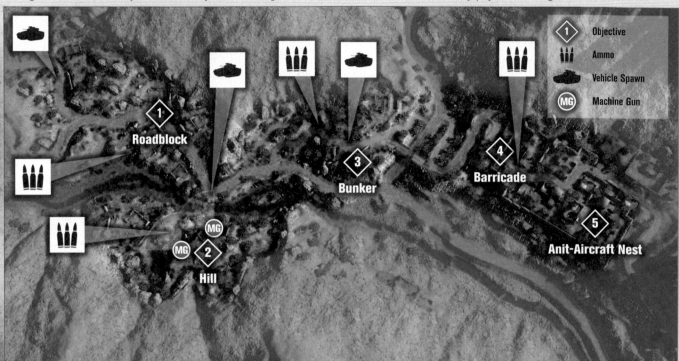

1 Roadblock

2 Hill

3 Bunker

4 Barricade

5 Anit-Aircraft Nest

1	Objective
Ammo	Ammo
Vehicle Spawn	Vehicle Spawn
MG	Machine Gun

1 ROADBLOCK

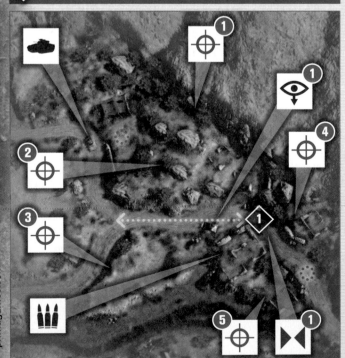

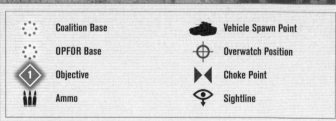

Coalition Base		Vehicle Spawn Point	
OPFOR Base		Overwatch Position	
1 Objective		Choke Point	
Ammo		Sightline	

MAP FEATURES
OVERWATCH POSITIONS

When playing as the coalition, move to this rocky hillside near the base for a great view of the objective. Providing covering fire from this elevated position can give your team the upper hand as they make the push toward the roadblock objective. You can even see the area behind the objective and hit OPFORs as they scramble from their spawn point. However, there's little cover here. Don't make a habit of camping here long, otherwise you're likely to gain the attention of OPFOR snipers. For a better view from this position, consider knocking down the trees in front of you with grenades.

The large rocks near the coalition base also provide an elevated position from which to cover the roadblock. Simply climb onto one of the two massive rocks and begin providing fire support. However, standing or crouching atop these rocks leaves you silhouetted against the sky, making you an easy target for your opponents. Pick off a few targets behind the roadblock and move to another postern before your victims can respawn and seek revenge.

This low ridge is a popular spot for coalition snipers seeking to cover the stream and roadblock area. The ridge itself provides decent cover while the nearby tree and plants offer some good concealment. Crouch and just barely peek over the ridge to limit your exposure. OPFORs attempting to flank your teammates at the roadblock are easy to pick off from this position. Just watch out for countersnipers positioned along the stream.

For the OPFOR team, this hillside near the objective is a perfect overwatch position. The nearby rocks provide excellent cover from incoming fire, allowing you to camp the objective from relative

safety. Opponents that try to arm the charge at the roadblock are easily picked off with the weapon of your choice. This is also a good position to guard the objective from flanking maneuvers. However, be aware of the coalition light tank—sustained fire from its auto cannon can make camping here hazardous.

Use explosives to blow away the bricks in these ruins to gain an unobstructed view of the stream. This is a great spot for picking off coalition attackers attempting to flank the objective from the stream. The ruins also offer excellent protection as long as you stay crouched.

CHOKE POINTS

The most significant choke point in this engagement is the roadblock itself. This is where the traffic is the heaviest, and as a result, this is where the most kills take place. Coalition troops are often pinned here, making it an absolute kill zone for OPFOR players looking to score some easy kills with explosives or offensive support actions. The coalition team is best served by saturating the area with smoke and flanking the objective from the stream. Once the coalition controls both sides of the roadblock they'll have a much easier time arming the explosives required to advance to the next area.

SIGHTLINES

Regardless of which team you're playing on, avoid traveling down the road whenever possible as it is one of the longest sightlines in this engagement. If you must cross the road, do so quickly while sprinting from one piece of cover to the next. Or better yet, drop smoke on the road to conceal your advance. Coalition troops that try to dash down the road toward the roadblock won't live very long.

COALITION TACTICS

The quicker the coalition team can push past this first objective, the better the chance they have at winning the battle. The light tank plays a pivotal role in this engagement and should provide covering fire from long range while infantry push toward the roadblock. Snipers positioned near the base can also lend a helping hand. But the bulk of the team should consist of riflemen and special ops troops attacking the roadblock at close range. Look for opportunities to flank the roadblock from the stream in an effort to secure both sides. Use smoke grenades as necessary, particularly when planting the charge.

OPFOR TACTICS

When playing as the OPFORs, do your best to hold out at the roadblock as long as possible. Keep a close eye on the roadblock, but don't forget about guarding the flanking path along the stream. The coalition light tank poses a serious threat here and is best countered by special ops troops firing RPGs. Use the ammo crate near the stream to stock up on rockets as needed. IEDs placed near the objective point are also good ways to stop close-quarter attacks by the light tank and infantry. But when not planting explosives, snipers should hold back in the ruins or cover the flanking approach along the streambed.

◈ HILL

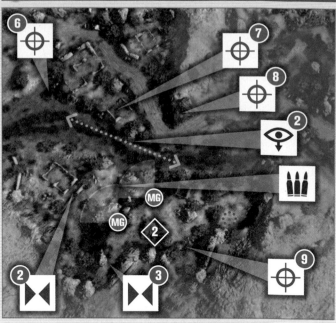

⬡ Coalition Base		⬡ Machine Gun	
⬡ OPFOR Base		⬱ Overwatch Position	
◈ Objective		▶◀ Choke Point	
▮▮▮ Ammo		◉ Sightline	

MAP FEATURES
OVERWATCH POSITIONS

Once the coalition team destroys the roadblock, this position near the stream is perfect for targeting the two OPFOR machine guns on the hill. The large rock nearby provides excellent cover, particularly when in a crouched position. This is also a good spot for engaging enemy traffic along the streambed.

CHOKE POINTS

Blow away the bricks in these ruins for another good view of the OPFOR machine gun positions on the hill. This is a great spot for engaging these two guns directly with a special ops rocket launcher—a direct hit from a rocket will knock out the gun as well as anyone manning it. But if you do come under fire, side step left or right to take cover behind the ruins.

The ruins just below the objective are a popular staging point for the coalition team. Coalition troops often gather here prior to storming the hill. While the low stone walls offer excellent protection, the two narrow doorways here are easily targeted by OPFORs on the hill. So when playing as the coalition, utilize smoke in this area before making a move on the hill.

Try hiding behind the rock at the bend in the road when playing as an OPFOR. Here you can intercept coalition foot traffic ascending the hill, hitting them from the back. The rock and map's boundary prevents you from getting flanked so you'll always have a fighting chance here, assuming the enemy ever sees you. For added stealth, consider equipping a suppressor to keep your opponents guessing.

This narrow passage near the objective is another popular gathering spot for coalition troops. OPFORs are well served by placing IEDs here or calling in offensive support actions. Since the coalition can't capture the objective from this spot, they're better served by spreading out. The structures containing the two machine guns offer decent protection and are both within the objective's capture radius.

SIGHTLINES

For the OPFORs, this hill overlooking the objective is a popular sniping spot. Not only does it offer a clear view of the objective, but it also has a line of sight on the coalition base across the stream. This little hillside plateau is also out of bounds for coalition soldiers, so there's no way they can sneak up behind you. However, do watch out for incoming hand grenades.

The stream is the lowest point in this engagement and the site of some heavy traffic as the coalition troops rush from their base toward the hill. It's in the interest of both teams to secure the stream. Snipers positioned at either end have long, unobstructed views. Therefore, never run down the stream. Instead cross while sprinting or under the concealment of a smoke screen.

META

MEDAL OF HONOR

COALITION TACTICS

Unlike the previous objective, this time the coalition must occupy a spot on the hill to secure the area. This requires a number of coalition troops to be within the capture radius of the objective, near the large rock behind the two machine gun positions. The machine guns pose a serious threat to a direct attack, so look for opportunities to flank, moving outside their firing arcs. But both machine guns can easily be destroyed with persistent rocket hits or fire from the light tanks. When capturing the objective, use the large rock for cover or hide in the structures where the machine guns are positioned. The status bar in the middle of the HUD shows you when you're within the capture radius, so stay put until you wrestle control from the OPFORs.

OPFOR TACTICS

The coalition team can attack from multiple directions here, so it's best to watch all avenues of attack. Pin the enemies at their base as long as possible with the machine guns and pick off targets as they cross the stream. When the objective icon flashes on the HUD it means that coalition units are within the capture radius. Hunt down all enemies as quickly as possible before their teammates can spawn on them. The two structures containing the machine guns are popular hiding spots, so fire rockets or toss grenades through the doorways if you suspect an enemy presence. Planting IEDs in these buildings early on in the fight is also a good defensive measure.

③ BUNKER

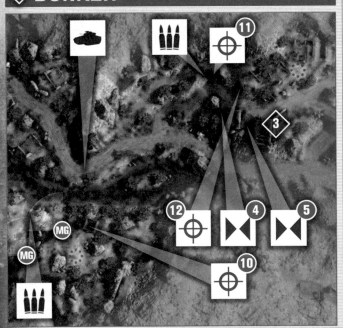

 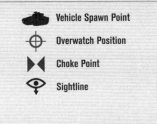

Coalition Base	Vehicle Spawn Point
OPFOR Base	Overwatch Position
Objective	Choke Point
Ammo	Sightline
Machine Gun	

MAP FEATURES
OVERWATCH POSITIONS

This small structure offers a decent view of the bunker complex across the stream, making it an ideal spot for coalition snipers. Side step left and right in front of the windows to alter your sight-lines. But don't get too close to the windows. It's best to hold back a few feet so the muzzle flash is contained within the building, otherwise you may draw immediate fire from your opponents.

When playing as the OPFORs, take cover behind this ammo crate and turn to cover the upper path leading to the bunker complex. Coalition troops seeking to take a less direct route to their objective often take this path, so it's important this area is covered at all times. The ammo crate not only provides decent protection, but it also keeps you stocked on bullets, grenades, and rockets. Special ops troops seeking to take out the incoming coalition light tank are well served by camping this spot.

Take cover near this tree across from the first bunker's entrance when you're defending this area from a coalition attack. The large rock near the tree prevents you from being flanked while the tree's shade makes you difficult to spot. But most importantly of all, from this spot you can cover the bunker's primary entrance, often by shooting opponents in the back as they sprint toward the doorway. You can also engage enemies as they scurry up the hill along the bunker's outer wall.

CHOKE POINTS

In most matches, the coalition team gets pinned at this spot as they climb the hill toward the bunker. While this is the most direct line of attack, it is also the deadliest. Even a rookie OPFOR team can have this area covered with small arms fire, not to mention offensive support actions. To avoid this funnel of death, consider spreading out the attack. At the very least, have the light tank run interference while storming up this hill, otherwise your team will be cut to pieces.

This narrow trench-like alley between the two bunkers is a hot point of contention in any match. As coalition troops advance along this path they need to know that the left side is completely exposed. Consider deploying smoke before advancing through this area toward the bunker where the objective is located. Saturating the neighboring bunker with rockets and grenades is also a good idea since the objective is probably heavily camped by your opponents. Enemies hiding inside the bunkers can also be killed with most offensive support actions.

COALITION TACTICS

Taking the bunker is one of the most difficult objectives in this battle. The enemy holds the high ground and can easily camp the objective both from inside and outside the bunker. But with some coordination and communication you can sweep through the bunker in no time. Charge the bunker complex with the light tank and use it to harass the defenders. Meanwhile, send riflemen and special ops troops toward the bunker. For best results, take the elevated path, go past the ammo crate, and infiltrate the ruins. Once you've established a presence on the hilltop, you have a much better chance of entering the bunker and planting a charge on the objective.

OPFOR TACTICS

With careful placement of resources, the OPFORs can hold out at this location until the coalition team runs out of reinforcements. Instead of camping the objective and bunker entrances, make an effort to keep the coalition troops off the hill. Special ops troops are needed to engage the coalition light tank. Try to take it out before it can get near the bunker complex. Once the light tank is down, cover all paths up the hill. If and when the coalition establishes a foothold on the hill, center your defenses around the objective in the bunker. Plant IEDs in and around the bunker and surprise your opponents as they rush forward. Be mindful of the coalition taking cover in the ruins across the road from the bunker as this puts them dangerously close to your team's spawn location.

◆ BARRICADE

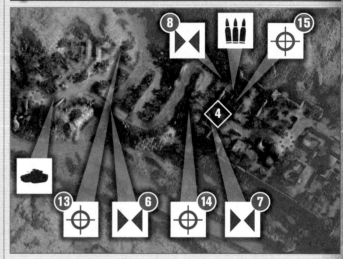

Coalition Base	Vehicle Spawn Point
OPFOR Base	Overwatch Position
Objective	Choke Point
Ammo	Sightline

MAP FEATURES
OVERWATCH POSITIONS

While fleeing the bunker site as an OPFOR, take cover along the side of the road here and engage the advancing coalition units as they proceed toward the next objective. This is a good spot to flank infantry from as well as advancing light tanks. Your life expectancy in this forward position isn't very long, so make the most of it.

In an effort to halt the coalition advance on the barricade, OPFOR defenders should take up positions just outside the village's perimeter wall. The crest of this hill offers some sweeping views of the valley below, ideal for sniping enemies near their base. But watch for coalition counter snipers located at the bunker complex.

This barricade objective is just one of two entrances into the village. Like the roadblock encountered earlier, launching a direct assault on this location is extremely dangerous. So when playing as the coalition, either deploy a lot of smoke before attempting to set the charge or look for another way around. Securing the other side of the barricade is a much safer way to approach this objective.

For the OPFOR defenders, this rooftop position near the barricade is ideal for picking off targets outside the village's perimeter wall. You can also cover both village entry points from this location. However, the high vantage point makes you easy to spot and hit. So make a habit of crouching beneath the low wall on the rooftop's perimeter. When you must stand up, do so quickly to fire a shot and then drop back down.

This low wall is the second entry point into the village and is the recommended route for flanking the barricade. While you can jump over the wall, it's easier to simply blow away the bricks with explosives such as a grenade or rocket launcher. But OPFORs on the nearby rooftop have a clear line of sight on this location, so make sure the path is clear before infiltrating the village. Once inside, coalition troops have a much easier time securing the area around the barricade.

CHOKE POINTS

This bridge is a classic choke point that the coalition is better off avoiding. While the bridge is the quickest path to the barricade objective, it offers no cover for infantry. OPFORs can also plant IEDs on the bridge and blow light tanks to bits. If driving a light tank, opt for the switchback path up the hill unless you're positive the bridge is free of enemy explosives. You can destroy enemy IEDs by shooting them with the vehicle's auto cannon.

COALITION TACTICS

Attacking the barricade is much like overrunning the roadblock at the start of the battle. Move your light tank into support range and hammer all visible OPFORs inside the village. At this point you may have two light tanks to use, so leverage this firepower to plow through the opposition. Meanwhile, send infantry over the low wall to the left of the objective. Once inside the village, establish a perimeter around the barricade, completely clearing the area of hostiles. Oncc both sides of the barricade are secure, plant the charge and get ready to make the final push to the last objective.

OPFOR TACTICS

The key to this engagement is keeping the coalition troops out of the village. Fortunately, there are only two entry points to cover. Keep heavy fire focused on the barricade to prevent a frontal assault. But don't forget about covering the low, destructible wall on the barricade's flank. As usual, the coalition light tank is a constant source of harassment, so don't let it distract you from the task at hand. A couple of dedicated special ops troops should be more than enough to stop any light tank attacks. But if your team spawns in with no antitank capability, this objective may be tough to hold.

5 ANTIAIRCRAFT NEST

Symbol		Symbol	
	Coalition Base		Overwatch Position
	OPFOR Base		Choke Point
1	Objective		Sightline
	Ammo		

MAP FEATURES
OVERWATCH POSITIONS

Located equidistant between the coalition and OPFOR bases, this rooftop is beneficial to both teams. For the OPFORs, this rooftop provides a clear view down the main road where the coalition team spawns. The coalition team can also benefit from this rooftop when attacking the objective on the neighboring rooftop. But the rooftop provides little cover for either team, so stay low and try to avoid drawing too much attention to your location.

This spot can work for both teams, but OPFORs are more likely to rack up points here as the coalition rushes toward the objective. This walled-off perimeter position near a well is rather isolated, but provides a great view of the objective building. Players from either team can engage the cross-traffic in and around the objective building. For best results, remain crouched among the vegetation and attach a suppressor to your weapon.

Here's an OPFOR rooftop position across from the target building that the coalition troops can't access—it's out of bounds for them. OPFOR troops can hold here and cover the objective directly without fear of getting knifed from behind. Still, the roof offers little protection from small arms fire, so don't expect to camp here long without being spotted.

CHOKE POINTS

This narrow alley between the objective building and the village's perimeter wall is a high-traffic area likely to see a lot of action. Coalition troops attempting to avoid the main road must rush down this alley to access the objective building's interior. Both teams should attempt to secure and control this corridor.

SIGHTLINES

The road running down the center of the village is an absolute kill zone and should be avoided whenever possible. The long sightline here allows players at either end to mow down opponents at will. Fortunately, the alleys flanking both sides of the road offer much more protection, especially for the advancing coalition troops.

COALITION TACTICS

The antiaircraft nest is the final objective in this battle, but it's not an easy one to take. Light tanks cannot enter the village, so the objective must be secured solely by infantry. Light tanks can still provide support fire from the village entrance. From the barricade, spread out among the village, flanking both sides of the road and steadily push the OPFORs back toward the objective building. Try to secure both entry points into the building before making a move on the rooftop objective. The objective is somewhat exposed on the building's rooftop so be sure to saturate the area with smoke before attempting to arm the explosives. Once the explosives are set, secure the building's interior and rooftop until the charge detonates, securing your team the victory.

OPFOR TACTICS

This is the OPFOR team's last stand, and it isn't an easy point to defend. The porous nature of the village allows the coalition team to attack the objective building from multiple directions. The OPFORs are most effective at pinning the coalition near their base, before they can spread out deeper into the village. Press forward and attack the village's entry points aggressively. But don't forget to leave some personnel back at the objective building. No matter how effective your counterattack is, some enemy troops are likely to slip through. For this reason it's important to keep nearly half of the team on defense, positioned in and around the objective building. If you can hold out long enough you'll walk away with a hard-fought win.

MAZAR-I-SHARIF AIRFIELD

MAP OVERVIEW

Combat Mission: Coalition forces are preparing to assault the northern airfield of Mazar-i-Sharif. OPFOR fighters have set up a strong defensive perimeter among wrecks of Russian tanks and airplanes. Intel indications that a high value target is hiding somewhere by the airstrip makes the need for surgical precision all the more crucial. Python 1 prepares to enter what looks like a graveyard. Coalition forces must first gain entry to the airfield by destroying a barricade and then fight their way through hangars and wrecks before they can reach the air tower at the end of the airstrip. Along the way, OPFOR marksmen have dug in deep to wait for the attackers.

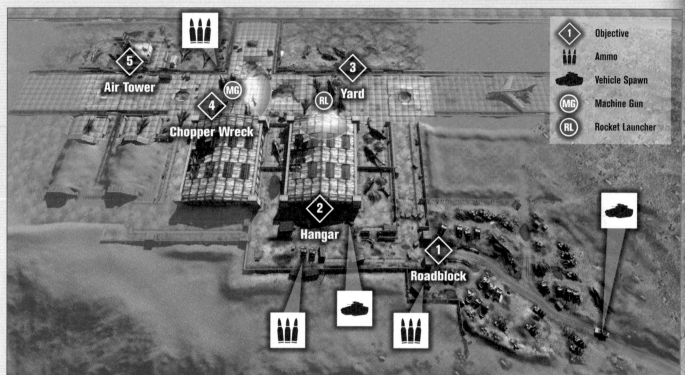

1	Objective
Ammo	Ammo
Vehicle Spawn	Vehicle Spawn
MG	Machine Gun
RL	Rocket Launcher

◇ ROADBLOCK

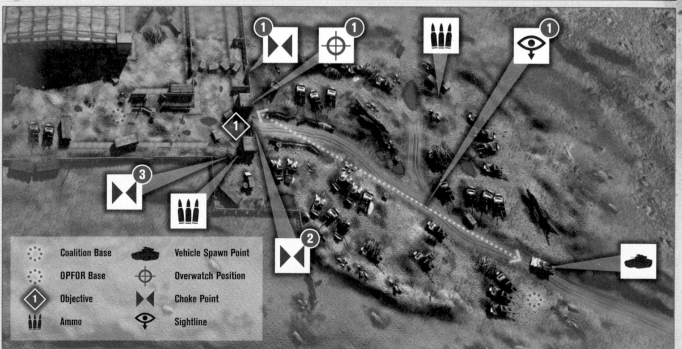

Coalition Base	Vehicle Spawn Point
OPFOR Base	Overwatch Position
Objective	Choke Point
Ammo	Sightline

MAP FEATURES
OVERWATCH POSITIONS

The two concrete guard towers flanking the roadblock are ideal overwatch positions for the OPFOR team. While they don't provide much elevation, these short towers do offer excellent protection from incoming fire. Stand on the step in front of each forward-facing window for a clear view of the junkyard. If you come under fire, simply crouch to take cover. Spotting enemy movement among the graveyard of tanks may be difficult, but any advances along the road are easily countered—be ready to blast the coalition light tank as it approaches. But keep an eye on the objective, too. From this elevated position you can easily pick off coalition troops attempting to plant a charge at the roadblock.

CHOKE POINTS

When attacking as the coalition, this breach in the wall to the right of the roadblock is a perfect infiltration point, allowing you to flank the OPFOR defenders gathered around the objective. However, be mindful of enemies camping around this area. Defenders can easily cover this narrow hole in the wall with automatic fire and explosives. Always conceal your advance with smoke grenades and then consider taking cover in the nearby guard tower.

The roadblock itself is another obvious choke point—one that coalition troops should avoid until the airfield is properly infiltrated. As long as the OPFORs hold the area around the roadblock, including the two guard towers, this area is an absolute kill zone. However, if the coalition light tank provides support fire at close range, it may be enough to distract the defenders, allowing coalition troops to sneak in and plant a charge on the roadblock. But it's much safer for the coalition team to sneak in through the holes in the perimeter wall before attempting to destroy the objective.

Here's another entry point in the airfield's perimeter wall. When playing as the coalition, stay to the left of the roadblock to sneak through this narrow passage. OPFORs should always keep any eye on this entry point as it gives the coalition team a dangerous flanking angle on defenders surrounding the objective. Coalition troops bunched up in this area near the ammo crate are very vulnerable to offensive support actions, so look for some opportunities to score some easy kills. Still, this is the preferred path of attack for coalition troops attempting to secure the objective from both sides.

SIGHTLINES

Given the plentiful cover provided by the scores of abandoned Russian tanks in the junkyard, there's no reason to charge down the middle of the road unless you're driving the coalition light tank. The road offers absolutely no cover and is a kill zone for snipers positioned at either end of the map. Do yourself a favor and stick to either side of the road where there's plenty of places to hide. The light tank, on the other hand, can score some easy kills by pounding enemies dumb enough to charge out into the middle of the road.

COALITION TACTICS

The coalition team starts in the junkyard outside the airfield. Fortunately, the old Russian tanks provide excellent cover during this advance. But instead of charging straight for the roadblock, perform flanking maneuvers, infiltrating the airfield through the holes in the walls on the objective's flanks. Meanwhile, keep the light tank back near its spawn point and use it to provide suppressive fire on the two short concrete guard towers on either side of the roadblock. Keeping the enemy out of these guard towers makes it easier on the infantry to get in close and flank the roadblock. Once the roadblock's rear has been secured, plant explosives at the objective and defend it until it explodes.

OPFOR TACTICS

Don't make the mistake of waiting for the coalition to come to you. Take the fight to them in the junkyard, ambushing them with shotguns and carbines at close range. While half the team goes on the offensive, keep some teammates back near the objective, particularly near the perimeter wall choke points. It's vital to keep the coalition troops pinned in the junkyard as long as possible. Once they attain a foothold inside the airfield's walls, it is increasingly difficult to halt the roadblock's destruction as they can spawn closer to the objective than you can. An aggressive and prolonged defense here can greatly increase the OPFOR team's chances of winning the battle.

② HANGAR

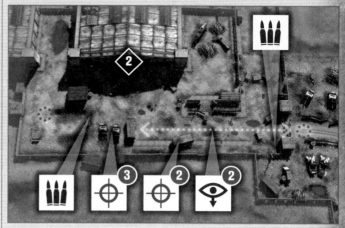

⋯ Coalition Base	⊕ Overwatch Position
⋯ OPFOR Base	▶◀ Choke Point
◇1 Objective	👁 Sightline
⫴ Ammo	

MAP FEATURES
OVERWATCH POSITIONS

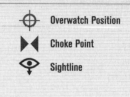

When playing as the coalition, the corner of this shipping container offers decent protection and some good sightlines. Aim along the perimeter wall to spot OPFORs near their base spawn point—this is a great way to score some kills as the OPFORs rush toward the objective. The hangar door is also visible from this position, allowing you to provide supporting fire to teammates attempting to set a charge.

For the OPFORs, defending the hangar doors is difficult as there aren't too many safe positions near the objective. However, if you duck down between these two tanks, you have a clear view of the doors, allowing you to pick off any coalition troops moving in to set a charge. However, your back is completely exposed. Turn around periodically to ensure you're not being flanked, otherwise you may get a knife in the back. The coalition team can also benefit from this position when it's time to defend the charge on the hangar door.

SIGHTLINES

The road leading from the roadblock area, where the coalition team spawns, to the hangar is fairly open and unobstructed, allowing for a very long sightline. Coalition troops advancing along this road are vulnerable to OPFOR sniper fire. Likewise, coalition snipers positioned near the coalition base can also engage distant OPFORs setting up defenses near the hangar.

COALITION TACTICS

In this engagement, the coalition must blow open the hangar doors to continue their advance through the airfield. The area around the hangar doors is relatively open, with little cover. Therefore, bring the light tank (spawned back in the junkyard) forward and use it as a mobile shield for your team's infantry to hide behind while advancing and setting the charge on the hangar door. Even if the light tank is destroyed, the wreck remains in place for a few minutes, giving your team a chance to set the charge. If the light tank is unavailable, the rifleman's smoke grenade is your best bet at approaching the hangar doors without getting cut to pieces by the OPFOR defenders camped near their base—you cannot enter the area where they spawn.

OPFOR TACTICS

As in the previous engagement, have half of your team defend the objective directly from fixed positions near the OPFOR base while the rest of the team aggressively attacks the advancing coalition troops. Although the area around the objective is devoid of cover, there are plenty of hiding spots between the hangar and the coalition base. Look for opportunities to ambush unsuspecting opponents as they race toward the hangar. Also, if the coalition tank is active, try to take it out with rockets or IEDs before it can provide fire support (and cover) near the hangar. Planting IEDs near the objective is also a good defensive measure when it comes to stopping coalition troops from setting the charge on the hangar doors.

◆ YARD

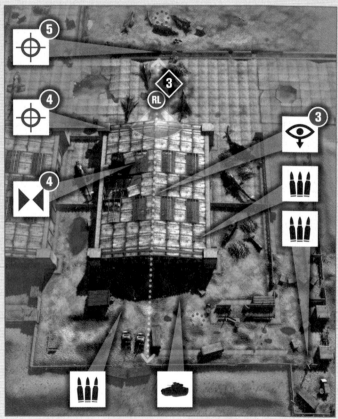

⋮	Coalition Base	RL	Rocket Launcher
⋮	OPFOR Base	⊕	Overwatch Position
◆1	Objective	▶◀	Choke Point
▮▮▮	Ammo	👁	Sightline

MAP FEATURES
OVERWATCH POSITIONS

The hangar's entrance and exit are major choke points ideal for ambushes. This spot outside the hangar's exit is a great place for OPFORs to intercept coalition traffic heading for the objective area. Simply crouch near this pile of rubble and mow down any opponents who race out of the hangar. Teammates positioned on the opposite side of the door can join the fun too, since you don't have to worry about friendly fire.

When playing as the OPFORs, take cover behind this grate and engage coalition troops gathered around the objective. The grate doesn't offer much in the form of cover, but it does make you harder to see, especially if you're crouched. For best results, attack with a suppressed weapon to avoid giving away your position. You can fire through the grate, but it reduces the damage dealt by your bullets. Likewise, your opponents can shoot through the grate too, so be ready to move to more suitable cover once your location has been revealed.

CHOKE POINTS

During this engagement, the coalition team must advance through the hangar to reach the next objective. There are no other routes available,

making the hangar a crucial choke point. The hangar is dark and filled with tons of cover in the form of old airplanes, barrels, crates, stacks of tires, and shipping containers. The OPFORs can seriously hamper the coalition advance by camping in the hangar and staging ambushes. Coalition troops should utilize smoke upon entry and work their way up the sides of the hangar where there is more cover.

SIGHTLINES

Players on both teams should avoid moving through the center of the hangar as it is a popular kill zone for snipers positioned on both sides of the map. Coalition snipers can hit OPFORs near the objective (or rocket launcher) while OPFOR snipers can engage coalition troops near their base. Expect these long-range sniper duels to persist throughout this engagement and make sure you're never standing motionless while in the crossfire.

COALITION TACTICS
This is the toughest objective the coalition team faces in this battle because they're forced to stage a frontal assault on the OPFOR position and maintain a fixed position in the objective's capture radius while withstanding counterattacks. As soon as the hangar doors are open, enter the hangar and quickly make a move for the objective, slipping along the sides of the structure. The light tank can offer some welcome support during the hangar advance, but be aware of the enemy's stationary rocket launcher at the objective point. Once at the objective, take cover among the wrecked MiG fighter jets within the capture radius. Get as many teammates in this area as quickly as possible to secure the objective, but watch out for OPFOR counterattacks originating from their nearby base.

OPFOR TACTICS
The yard is the OPFOR team's best chance at stopping the coalition team once and for all. As the coalition advances through the hangar, throw everything you have at them. Still, make sure at least one teammate holds near the objective and mans the rocket launcher, but only when the coalition light tank makes an appearance—otherwise the player manning the rocket launcher is an easy target for enemy snipers. The bulk of the team should take the fight into the hangar, hiding in shadowy corners and engaging the coalition attackers at close range. If the objective icon begins to flash on the HUD or minimap, coalition troops are in the capture radius. Instead of counterattacking directly from the base's spawn point, circle around the wrecked fighter jets and try to take your opponents by surprise. A powerful offensive support action can also be effective at completely clearing the objective area.

TIP

Rockets fired from the rocket launcher can be guided manually after launching. Simply place the weapon's sight where you want the rocket to impact. This makes it easier to hit moving targets.

◇4 CHOPPER WRECK

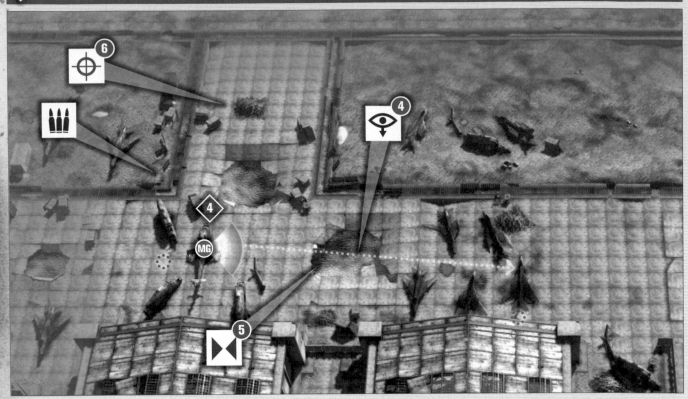

Legend

Coalition Base		MG Machine Gun	
OPFOR Base		⊕ Overwatch Position	
◇1 Objective		▶◀ Choke Point	
Ammo		👁 Sightline	

CHOKE POINTS

MAP FEATURES
OVERWATCH POSITIONS

Crouch near this pile of rubble while aiming at the nose of the wrecked chopper. This gives you the perfect vantage point of the objective, allowing you to pick off opponents that rush in to set (or disarm) a charge—you also have a clear view of the tunnel exit. The pile of rubble offers great protection and concealment as long as you stay crouched. But be mindful of enemies creeping over the pile to knife you. Consider equipping a suppressor to keep your position from appearing on your opponents' minimap.

There's an L-shaped tunnel running beneath the ground in this area, offering the coalition team a less direct route to the chopper wreck. Coalition troops often opt for this path as it's less exposed and allows them to flank the machine gun inside the chopper. However, it's also a narrow passage ideal for OPFOR booby traps. OPFORs should line the walls of this tunnel with IEDs and camp the exit near the objective. Direct attacks in the tunnel are equally effective, especially when armed with a shotgun or submachine gun. The blind corner at the tunnel intersection is a perfect place for defenders to camp.

SIGHTLINES

The area between the coalition base and the chopper wreck is relatively open with several long sightlines. Most notable is the OPFOR machine gun, capable of mowing down anyone dumb enough to attempt a direct attack. Coalition snipers can easily suppress the machine gun—simply fire through the view slit on the gun's front armor to kill the gunner. Rocket attacks can eliminate the gun entirely.

COALITION TACTICS

Now the coalition team must plant another charge at the wrecked chopper. Although this objective is relatively close to the coalition base, don't get lured into taking a direct approach. There's a fixed machine gun in the chopper's cargo compartment aimed directly at the coalition base. Take out the gun as early as possible (preferably with rocket attacks) to remove the threat. Offensive support actions are also very effective. Still, even with the machine gun out of the picture, avoid a direct assault. Instead, circle around the left and right flanks of the chopper. The subterranean tunnel is a quick way to reach the objective without exposing yourself to the chaos above. Once the charge is placed, form a defensive perimeter and prevent the OPFORs from disarming your explosives.

OPFOR TACTICS

This isn't an easy objective to defend as the coalition can attack from multiple directions. First of all, don't put too much faith in the machine gun positioned inside the chopper wreck as it can easily be destroyed by rockets or suppressed by coalition snipers. Instead, fan out and cover the flanking approaches. Pay particular attention to the short tunnel system by camping the interior and the exit. Meanwhile, use the nearby wreckage for cover while defending the objective located at the nose of the chopper. If the coalition team is pinned, look for opportunities to counterattack, engaging them closer to their base. The more casualties you can inflict here, the greater the chance of pulling off a win.

◇⑤ AIR TOWER

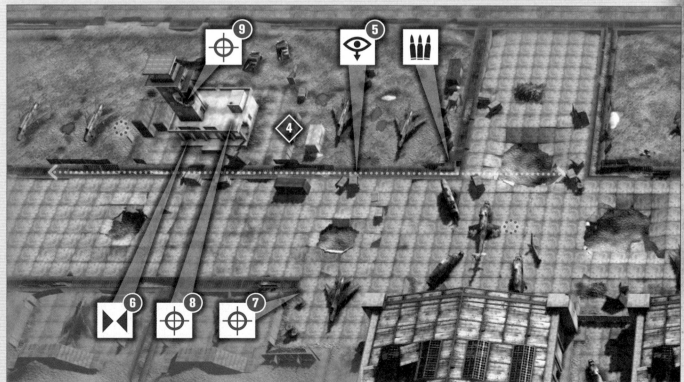

Coalition Base	⊕ Overwatch Position	
OPFOR Base	▶◀ Choke Point	
◇ Objective	⊙ Sightline	
▮▮▮ Ammo		

MAP FEATURES
OVERWATCH POSITIONS

Stand on the block near the concrete wall in this corner of the tarmac to gain great firing position on the tower. While standing, only your head is exposed. But if you take fire, simply crouch to duck behind the concrete wall. Since your whole right side is exposed, this position benefits the coalition team the most. Consider using this as a countersniping position when engaging OPFOR marksmen in and around the tower.

The sweeping view of the airfield offered by this low rooftop at the tower is great for OPFOR defenders looking to halt the coalition advance. However, there is very little cover on this rooftop and you're easily silhouetted against the sky for opponents on the ground. So don't linger in one spot for long or else you're likely to catch a sniper's bullet in your teeth.

A damaged staircase prevents you from climbing to the top of the tower. But this gaping hole in the stairwell's wall provides the map's highest vantage point, ideal for OPFOR snipers. The dark, shadowy stairwell offers great concealment but there's virtually no cover, so stay back way from the damaged wall in an effort to remain hidden within the tower. The high elevation makes it easy to spot coalition flanking maneuvers snaking through the wrecked planes and other obstacles. As the highest point on the map, this is a very predicable sniper position and is likely to draw lots of fire. Don't make a habit of camping here very long and never crowd the tower with more than two players at a time.

CHOKE POINTS

Some the battle's fiercest fighting occurs in the room containing the final objective. This is located on the ground floor of the tower, not far from the OPFOR base. There are two doorways here. The exterior doorway, at the back of the building, is often used by OPFORs while the interior doorway leads to a hallway that is often frequented by coalition troops. When guarding this room, it's a good idea to cover both entry points with a buddy as it's impossible to tell where an attack is coming from. Watch out for grenades coming in through the doors and windows and take evasive action as necessary.

SIGHTLINES

The partially covered drainage trench running between the tower and tarmac is a very long sightline exploited by snipers on both teams. While you can duck inside the trench to avoid incoming fire, as soon as you stand up and try to get out to the trench, you're completely exposed. For this reason it's best to avoid this area completely. Coalition snipers have the best cover from their end of the sightline, but OPFOR snipers positioned near the tower can also score some quick kills before seeking cover.

TIP

Crawling through the drainage trench is a great way to advance toward the tower unnoticed. The metal grate covering the trench makes it tough for enemies to see you, but it does very little to stop their bullets.

COALITION TACTICS

For the final objective, the coalition team must infiltrate the ground floor of the tower and download some data before calling in a JDAM strike on the structure. Expect stiff opposition from the OPFORs as they take up elevated positions in the tower. A few friendly snipers are essential for suppressing these threats, but the majority of the team should make an aggressive push toward the tower using the nearby wrecked planes for cover. Once you've gained a foothold on the tower's interior, spread out among the rooms to avoid getting wiped out by OPFOR booby traps near the objective. Continually spawn in the tower until you can download the data at the objective point then defend the area until you've achieved a victory.

OPFOR TACTICS

This is the OPFOR team's last stand, so it's important to take a diverse approach to defending the objective. While the tower's elevated positions make sniping tempting, your team is better off crowding around the objective on the tower's first floor—cover all the building's entry points. Once the tower is secure, look for opportunities to ambush the coalition team among the wrecked planes and drainage trench outside. The opposing team often moves in a straight line from their base toward the tower, so look for spots where you can flank their advance. By applying some offensive pressure you can often catch the attackers off-guard, potentially buying your team enough time to secure a tight win.

SHAHIKOT MOUNTAINS

MAP OVERVIEW

Combat Mission: A Chinook helicopter has crashed somewhere in the Shahikot mountains. These snow-covered mountain peaks, called The Place of the King in the local tongue, have been a rebel hiding place since ancient times. Python 1 is inserted to investigate and look for survivors in these eerie surroundings. As they embark from their helicopter they hear the first crackling sound of a sniper rifle roll between the steep mountain sides. A strong OPFOR presence in the area leaves the coalition forces stranded. They must fight their way up the mountains, past ammo caches and mortar stations, to clear any hostile antiaircraft emplacements to allow evacuation from the area.

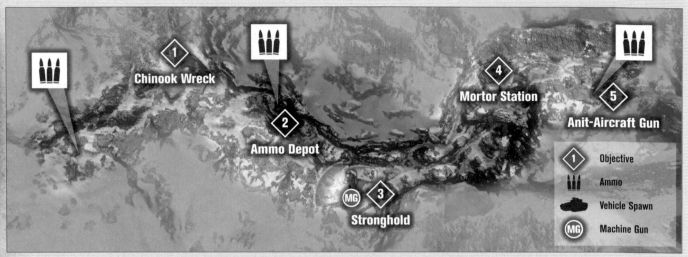

◇ CHINOOK WRECK

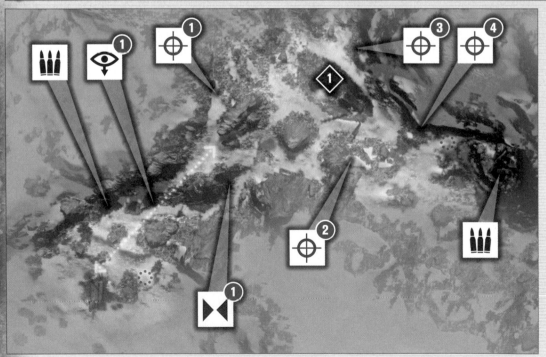

MAP FEATURES
OVERWATCH POSITIONS

When playing as the coalition, take the upper path from the base to reach this position overlooking the Chinook wreck. This is a great spot for providing support fire while your teammates gather around the objective. From here you have a clear, elevated view of the objective and the nearby rocks offer decent protection if you come under fire. Watch for OPFORs rushing toward the objective from their base and pick them off before they can harass your teammates below.

Duck through the small rock archway, beneath the camo net, to reach the elevated spot on this hill near the Chinook wreck. Both teams have a good chance of claiming this spot, so it's a good idea to check your surroundings frequently while camping here. The low rocks in front of this position offer little protection, so back up through the rock archway for better cover and concealment. Coalition players here should also be mindful of being flanked from the right, as the OPFOR base is only a few dozen meters away.

Looking for a safe place to hide while capturing the objective? Press your left shoulder up against this rock across from the chopper's cracked fuselage and inch forward until you enter the objective's capture radius. This low spot is tough for OPFORs to spot from a distance, but don't let your guard down. OPFORs patrolling the wreck are likely to spot you, so be ready for some close-quarters fighting. If you go unnoticed, this is an excellent place to hide while your teammates spawn on you, increasing the speed of the capture process.

For the OPFORs, this low spot near their base is ideal for engaging coalition troops gathered around the wreck. Crouch between this low rock archway and scan the crash site and distant hillside for enemy movement. A rifleman's light machine gun is very effective at this position, especially if enemy troops are hiding inside the chopper's fuselage—simply fire into the wreck. The chopper's thin outer skin is no match for even the weakest weapons, allowing you to score kills even if you can't see your targets.

CHOKE POINTS

There are two paths connecting the coalition base to the Chinook wreck: an upper path and a lower path. Both paths are narrow, but this lower path is particularly treacherous due to the OPFORs' ability to easily funnel fire down it. For this reason, always opt for the upper path. If you do find yourself pinned in the lower path, deploy smoke and retreat back toward the coalition base where you can take the safer fork in the road.

SIGHTLINES

OPFORs positioned on the upper path can peer over the crest of this hill and look directly into the coalition base, hitting anyone standing near the landed Chinook. While the coalition spawn area is out of sight, OPFOR snipers pose a serious threat to troops exiting the base. Coalition snipers positioned near the landed Chinook can also strike back at the OPFOR position, clearing a path for teammates. While sniper duels in this area are rare, they are possible. Just be sure you don't get caught in the crossfire.

COALITION TACTICS

At the start of the battle, the coalition team must secure the Chinook crash site by occupying the capture radius and holding it until the objective is complete. This is one of the toughest objectives and must be completed quickly if the coalition hopes to pull off a win. Filter into the crash site via the upper path out of the coalition base. When it comes to capturing the objective, take cover near the wrecked chopper's nose while teammates provide support fire from the nearby hill. The chopper's fuselage is a death trap, so fight the temptation to hide inside it—its light armor offers no protection at all. Get as many teammates in the objective's radius as quickly as possible to expedite the capture process. Taking control of this location early is essential in securing a victory.

OPFOR TACTICS

The objective at the Chinook wreck is the OPFOR team's best chance at completely halting the coalition advance, potentially leading to a quick victory. At the very least, a prolonged defense at this location can seriously eat into the coalition's team health, something they might not recover from. Fortunately, there are multiple cover positions surrounding the wreck, so find a good camping spot among the rocky hills and shoot anything that runs toward the objective. However, the OPFORs can't hold out by simply camping the perimeter. Once the objective icon flashes, it means coalition troops are in the capture radius. So be prepared to take the fight to close range and completely clean out the objective area. Offensive support actions targeting the wreck are also very effective at clearing out enemies.

2 AMMO DEPOT

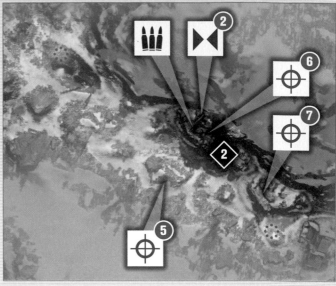

Coalition Base	Overwatch Position
OPFOR Base	Choke Point
Objective	Sightline
Ammo	

MAP FEATURES
OVERWATCH POSITIONS

Before storming the ammo depot, it's a good idea for coalition troops to occupy this hilltop position. From here players can cover one of the depot's entrances as well as approaches from the OPFOR base. Overall, this is a great staging point for the attack on the ammo depot. Hide among the rocks and engage enemies while allowing your teammates to spawn on your position. OPFOR troops can also benefit from this position, but can easily be flanked by advancing coalition troops.

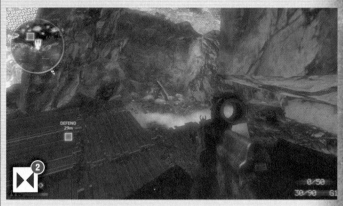

CHOKE POINTS

From the upper cave, just above the objective, slip through a narrow gap in the rocks along the trail to locate this hole in ground. This hole looks straight down onto the objective in the cave below. This spot can benefit both teams. Coalition troops looking for a sneaky way into the ammo depot can simply drop through this hole and plant their charge without having to fight through the depot's more traditional entry points. Likewise, OPFOR troops can camp this spot and blast any attackers who attempt to set a charge. By the time both teams are aware of this entry point, expect heavy fighting to occur on the nearby upper trail and cave. Whoever controls this spot controls the ammo depot.

OPFORs should expect heavy coalition traffic in this upper cave, above the ammo depot. Coalition troops must move through this cave to drop through the hole in the ammo depot's ceiling, so this is a good spot for OPFORs hold in order to prevent such sneak attacks. When camping this area, climb onto the crates across from the fire pit and mow down your opponents as they rush past your position. Even through you have little cover, hiding in this dark corner of the cave buys you more than enough time to get the jump on your enemies.

COALITION TACTICS

Occupying the high ground in this narrow valley is the key to securing the ammo depot. Stick to one of the two elevated paths on each side of the valley to avoid getting caught in the open. Once a base of fire is established on each side of the valley, make a push for the ammo depot. It's easiest to access this cave via the hole in its ceiling, but it may take a steady attack to secure the cave's interior before you've eliminated all defenders and their pesky booby traps. For best results, drop smoke into the cave before making a move for the objective. This will hamper the vision of defenders camped outside the cave, giving you just enough time to set the charge before the smoke screen dissipates. Once the charge is set, it's easiest to defend it through the hole in the cave's ceiling.

OPFORs seeking to cover the ammo depot from long range are well served by this distant position not far from their base. Hunker down among the rocks on this low hill and engage targets moving along the valley and nearby hills. From this angle you can also see directly into the cave's nearby entry point, offering a clear view of the ammo depot. When playing as a sniper, plant IEDs in the cave near the objective and detonate them as coalition troops attempt to set their charge. Snipers here can also engage targets approaching from the Chinook wreck.

OPFOR TACTICS

As with the coalition, controlling the high ground here is crucial to stopping the enemy's advance. Take up fixed positions on both sides of the valley, ensuring you've covered all entry points into the cave. While it's important to cover the objective, it's equally important to defend the paths leading to the cave. While some teammates hold back near the objective, the rest of the team should advance closer to the Chinook wreck, where the coalition team spawns, and harass the attackers before they can gain a foothold in the valley. It's most important to control the upper cave from which the coalition can attack the ammo depot from above. If this position is overrun, it's increasingly difficult to prevent the coalition from destroying the ammo depot.

◈ QALAT

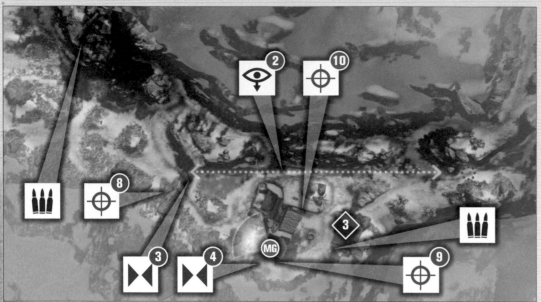

Legend:
- ⸭ Coalition Base
- ⸭ OPFOR Base
- ◇1 Objective
- 𝕀𝕀𝕀 Ammo
- (MG) Machine Gun
- ⊕ Overwatch Position
- ▶◀ Choke Point
- ◈ Sightline

MAP FEATURES
OVERWATCH POSITIONS

This damaged wall, near the gate, is a great spot for coalition troops to provide support fire from as their teammates assault. By standing, you can easily fire into the complex, hitting defenders on rooftops or in the buildings. And by simply crouching, you can avoid getting hit by incoming fire. Of course, you don't want to crowd this area with snipers as it only provides the OPFORs with a juicy target when it's time to call in an offensive support action.

The room just below the machine gun is a perfect sniper position for the OPFOR defenders. Peer through the damaged wall here to get a clear view of the gate choke point—an area likely to see heavy

traffic. To remain concealed, avoid stepping too close to the hole in the wall. Instead, crouch a few feet back from the hole in an attempt to conceal your weapon's barrel and muzzle flash. The longer you can hold here unnoticed, the more kills you're likely to score.

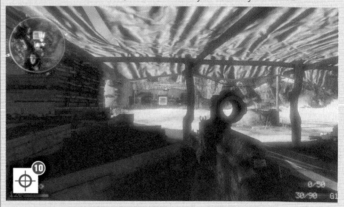

This is the sneakiest spot from which to cover the objective directly. Simply hide behind the crates beneath the awning across the courtyard from the objective. The awning makes this corner very dark, making you very difficult to see. For added concealment, attach a suppressor to your weapon for reduced muzzle flash. Both teams can benefit from this position, so don't forget to check this corner before rushing in to set or disarm a charge.

CHOKE POINTS

Located opposite of the OPFOR machine gun, this narrow gateway is an absolute kill zone and should be avoided whenever possible. The OPFOR defenders have a serious height advantage on this position as coalition attackers file through this opening. Furthermore, as coalition troops get pinned here they're vulnerable to offensive support actions such as mortar strikes. Coalition troops are better off circling around to the left when advancing on the objective.

This is another gateway choke point located on the machine gun's left flank. As a result, the machine gun cannot traverse to cover this area, but that doesn't mean it isn't watched by defenders. OPFORs hiding in the room below the machine gun can easily pick off coalition troops as they rush toward this gate. There are also several blind corners on the other side of the gate from which attackers can be cut down. So if you must move through this area, do so slowly and preferably with smoke.

SIGHTLINES

For the OPFORs, this is a very important sightline to exploit as it allows snipers to cover both paths toward the objective. By holding near the OPFOR base and hiding among the rocks it's possible to hit targets as far away as the distant gateway. But even more importantly, this vantage point offers a clear view of the coalition flanking path, too. However, coalition snipers can also utilize this sightline, so be on the watch for sniping operations at either end of this area.

COALITION TACTICS

Qalat is the Persian word for "fortress," and a fitting name for this objective. Expect the OPFOR team to be dug in around the objective's buildings and firing down on your team throughout this advance. For this reason, the rifleman's smoke grenade is essential for concealing your team's movement and denying the enemy long sightlines. Although the left flank offers less cover, it's the best route to take as it's outside the rooftop machine gun's firing arc. Just watch out for enemy snipers camped further back near the OPFOR base. Infiltrating the courtyard can also be dangerous, so be sure to enter with ample smoke and manpower to secure the area before planting a charge on the objective. Once the charge is set, establish a defensive perimeter around the courtyard until the objective is destroyed.

OPFOR TACTICS

Although this stronghold is a solid defensive position, don't get overconfident. The rooftop machine gun is sniper bait, so don't expect it to lend much to the defensive effort. Position a few snipers back by your base to cover the distant gate and the flanking path. The rest of the team should focus their efforts around the buildings and courtyard, ambushing the coalition troops as they rush toward the objective. There are many hiding spots within the courtyard, so spread out and cover both entry points on the southern and northern ends. If there's manpower to spare, send a few players out to challenge the coalition troops back by the cave, at the former ammo depot site. But the key to holding out here is locking down the courtyard and exploiting the choke points.

◈ MORTAR STATION

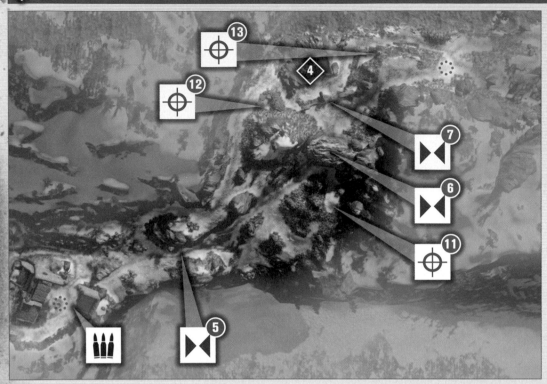

Legend	
⋰⋱	Coalition Base
⋰⋱	OPFOR Base
◇ 1	Objective
⁗	Ammo
⨁	Overwatch Position
▸◂	Choke Point
👁	Sightline

MAP FEATURES
OVERWATCH POSITIONS

⨁ 11

For the OPFORs, this is one of the best sniper positions on the entire map. Located on the high ridge near the rock tunnel, this area overlooks the narrow valley near the qalat, ideal for sniping coalition troops rushing toward the mortar station. With proper positioning you can even peer into the qalat's courtyard, hitting your opponents where they least expect it. Crouching gives you partial cover and concealment behind the low rocks. But if you take heavy fire, side step behind the larger rocks to the right. For better concealment, try to hide within the shadow of the large rock while sniping. Otherwise you're easy to spot, even from long range.

⨁ 12

This is an excellent staging area for the coalition team prior to their assault on the mortar station. While it doesn't offer a direct line of sight to the objective, the nearby rocks provide excellent cover from attacks originating near the OPFOR base. Plus, this is a good area from which to flank OPFOR defenders hiding among the ruins near the objective. When it's time to move out, hook left and infiltrate the mortar station from behind.

Located only a few steps from the OPFOR base, this hilltop position is ideal for defending the mortar station. It provides a clear, unobstructed view of the mortar, allowing you to pick off any troops attempting to set or disarm a charge. The rocks to the left offer some cover, but for the most part this area is fairly exposed. Remain in a crouched stance near the rocks to avoid silhouetting yourself. Due to its close proximity to the OPFOR base, this isn't a safe position for coalition troops. If you do defend from here as the coalition, make sure a buddy is always watching your back.

CHOKE POINTS

Like the other areas, there's an upper and lower path leading from the coalition base toward the mortar station. The lower path here is narrow, hemmed in by tall, impassable rocks on each side. As a result, this area is a popular kill zone for OPFOR snipers firing from the distant hilltop positions. Coalition troops should avoid this path whenever possible. The upper path, to the left, offers much more concealment and cover.

Coalition troops committed to the lower path must pass through this short, naturally formed tunnel in the rocks. For the OPFORs, this is a perfect ambush point. Stick IEDs to the walls and ceiling of this short tunnel and watch the exit point from a distance.

OPFOR riflemen with light machine guns can also unleash some serious carnage in this area, mowing down coalition troops as they emerge from the tunnel. Obviously, this is a good area for the coalition team to avoid. If your coalition forces stick to the upper path, you can completely bypass this kill zone.

Hoping to stage a frontal assault on the mortar station? Then you'll need to pass through this narrow opening in the wall just outside the objective location. The ruins surrounding the mortar offer the OPFORs plenty of hiding spots from which to defend the objective directly. Unless you have teammates in an overwatch position on the nearby hills, expect heavy resistance around the mortar. Saturate the area with smoke, then move in with a small team to secure the area before planting a charge.

COALITION TACTICS

Soon after destroying the objective at the qalat, mortar rounds begin falling from the sky. Eliminating this mortar is the coalition's next task. It's a long hike to the next objective, giving the OPFOR team plenty of time and space to set up ambushes along the way. Hug the left side of the narrow valley during the advance, taking the upper path toward the mortar station. This allows you to avoid the dangerous choke points in the lower elevations. Once near the objective, sneak up behind the building where the mortar is located and climb up the pile of rubble on the structure's collapsed corner to plant a charge. Pull back toward the upper path to defend the charge or simply hide among the ruins and blast any OPFORs that rush in to disarm your explosives.

OPFOR TACTICS

This is a very large area to defend, so take into account the size of your team before committing to a defensive strategy. If you have a small team, center your defenses around the mortar itself while covering the nearby upper and lower approaches. But if you have a large team, spread out into the valley and intercept the coalition troops as they advance from their base. Guard the upper path aggressively as it provides the coalition the safest route to the objective. But don't forget to cover the lower path as well—a good sniper can cover the lower path on their own, killing enemies as soon as they exit the qalat. If the coalition gains a foothold near the objective, fall back around the mortar until all enemies are eliminated, forcing them to spawn back at their base. A skilled and diverse OPFOR team stands a good chance of stopping the coalition here once and for all.

MEDAL OF HONOR

◇⑤ ANTIAIRCRAFT GUN

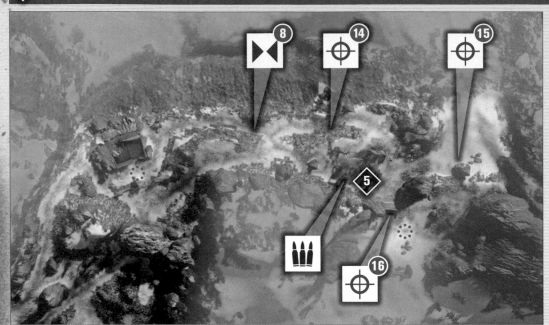

Icon	Label
Coalition Base
OPFOR Base
Objective
Ammo
Overwatch Position
Choke Point
Sightline

MAP FEATURES
OVERWATCH POSITIONS

The rocks near the objective from a short tunnel offer a clear view of the two approaches from the mortar station. This is an ideal defensive position for OPFORs. While it's possible to jump up on top of this large rock formation, doing so leaves you completely exposed and silhouetted against the sky. It's better to hunker down in the tunnel where the shadows can better conceal your location. Assault rifles and light machine guns are most effective at this range, but a well-concealed sniper can do some serious damage from this spot, too.

When playing as the OPFORs, you can access this area behind the antiaircraft gun. While this position doesn't provide the clearest view of the objective, it's still easy enough to spot any coalition troops approaching the area. The real benefit of this position is its isolation and nearly complete rock enclosure, ensuring nobody sneaks up behind you.

The area around the OPFOR base is also a great place to cover the objective from. This area is off-limits to the coalition team, so you don't need to worry about being flanked. The ruins surrounding the antiaircraft gun prevent you from getting a clear view of the objective, but it's still possible to spot traffic moving in and out of the location. If you can't get a clear shot at your opponents, consider launching grenades or rockets in their direction.

CHOKE POINTS

This narrow passage is located on the lower path between the mortar station and the antiaircraft gun. OPFOR defenders can take advantage of this cramped terrain by planting IEDs along the rock walls and ambushing coalition troops as they rush through. So when playing as the coalition, avoid this narrow passage by taking the upper path. You can also escape this kill zone by stepping out around the rocks to the left, on the ledge of the mountain—just watch your step!

COALITION TACTICS

Before the coalition troops can withdraw from the area, they must first destroy the mountainside antiaircraft gun. Only then can a Chinook land for extraction. The fighting here is frantic as the coalition team pushes toward the last objective. The OPFORs have nothing to lose, so expect stiff resistance at the objective as well as along the two paths leading there. From the mortar station there are two parallel routes to choose from. The upper path offers less cover, but it's also wider and less likely to be camped by OPFORs. But when it comes to reaching the objective, try to move through the short tunnel on the lower path. The tunnel is a great staging area for your attack on the antiaircraft gun—one player should hold here and serve as a forward spawn point. This allows your team to apply steady pressure against the objective until you can get close enough to set a charge on the antiaircraft gun. Afterward, set up a defensive perimeter around the objective and prepare for direct close-quarters attacks originating from the hillside where the OPFORs spawn. Defend the charge for the required 30 seconds to knock out the antiaircraft gun and secure the victory.

OPFOR TACTICS

There isn't much time to prepare for the coalition attack on this location once the mortar station has been overrun. So when spawning near the antiaircraft gun, stay put and take up strong overwatch positions covering the objective and the two incoming paths. Planting IEDs around the antiaircraft gun is also a good idea. Once the objective is well defended, send a few teammates forward to harass the advancing coalition troops back at the mortar station. Any pressure applied to the coalition base helps the defenders back at the antiaircraft gun. This is the OPFOR team's last stand, so attack aggressively but not stupidly. Look for blind corners and other hiding spots among the rocks that allow you to flank advancing coalition troops. Attaching a suppressor to your weapon can greatly increase your lifespan, allowing you to covertly mow down enemies without giving away your position. Also, look for opportunities to call in devastating offensive support action when your opponents are grouped up on the narrow paths leading to the objective. With plenty of skill, and a little luck, your team has a good chance of pulling off an upset.

DIWAGAL CAMP

The inhospitable terrain and complex cave networks of the Kunar province has made it a favored spot for OPFOR activity. A Taliban base has been found in the south parts of the Diwagal Valley close to a small settlement of mud huts. Coalition forces insert to clear the area and meet with heavy OPFOR resistance.

SECTOR CONTROL AND TEAM ASSAULT

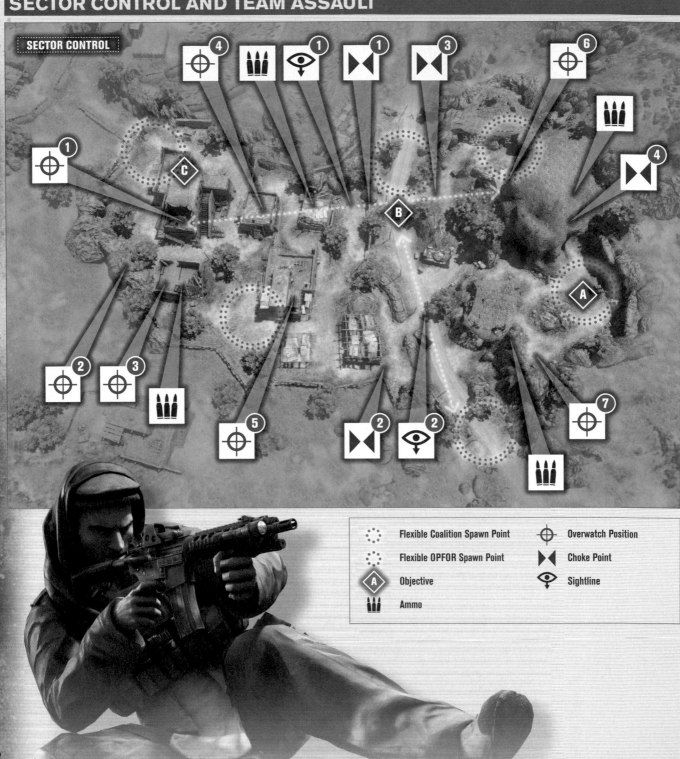

Flexible Coalition Spawn Point		Overwatch Position
Flexible OPFOR Spawn Point		Choke Point
Objective		Sightline
Ammo		

MULTIPLAYER
DIWAGAL CAMP

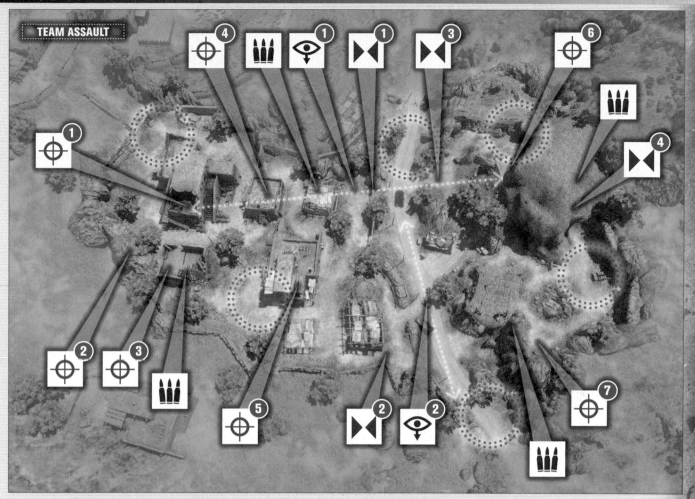

TEAM ASSAULT

Symbol	Description
⋮ Flexible Coalition Spawn Point	⊕ Overwatch Position
⋮ Flexible OPFOR Spawn Point	▶◀ Choke Point
🔫 Ammo	👁 Sightline

Team Assault: Although this is an excellent sniping location, don't linger here too long. Opponents looking to boost their melee kills are likely to frequent this position, looking for a sniper to knife. However, this can be a very strong location if defended by a group of two or three teammates.

MAP FEATURES
OVERWATCH POSITIONS

Sector Control: Located near Sector Charlie, the second floor of this building offers an excellent view of the map. Crouch and creep up to the hole in the corner of the building and engage opponents as far away as the cave near Sector Alpha. However, don't get too comfortable here as enemies can easily sneak up behind you. So if you plan on holding this position for any significant amount of time, ask a teammate to watch your back. Also, keep an eye on the minimap—if the objective icon at Sector Charlie flashes, there are enemies nearby.

Sector Control: Climb onto these rocks at the edge of the map for an elevated, but very exposed, view of the map. From here you can cover Sector Charlie as well as engage opponents near Sector Alpha. More importantly, you can flank the traffic moving between these two objectives. Although the view is spectacular, jump down to the ground as soon as you take incoming fire. There's simply nowhere to hide up here.

Team Assault: If you can stay low and minimize your muzzle flash, this rocky area can be a great sniping position. However, keep an eye on your minimap to ensure that teammates are nearby as you can easily be flanked while peering through your scope.

Sector Control: If you're looking for better concealment and protection, drop off the rock and take cover near the ammo crate in these ruins. This spot is best suited for intercepting traffic moving between Sectors Alpha and Charlie. When possible, stick behind the ammo crate for cover. This also keeps you stocked on ammo. In a pinch you can also turn to your left and engage opponents trying to capture Sector Charlie.

Team Assault: This is a decent solo camping spot for those who prefer to hold at one location. The low wall and ammo crate offer great protection and concealment.

Sector Control: The interior of this building is perfect for covering Sector Bravo on the road below. At this range, a carbine is just as effective as an assault or sniper rifle. Hold back in the shadows and blast any opponents that rush into view. For better concealment, attach a suppressor to your weapon. This makes you very difficult to detect. This small room only has one entrance, opposite of the makeshift window. Listen for enemy footsteps to avoid being surprised from behind. The loose bricks around the damaged wall can be destroyed for an even better view, but at the cost of protection.

Team Assault: While there's no objective to cover in this mode, this room is still a great spot for covering the road and the cave. In particular, this is a great spot for sniping enemies near overwatch position 6.

Sector Control: This is another elevated position with no direct view of any of the objectives. But given this structure's central location, this rooftop is a good area to monitor traffic from. The low wall surrounding the roof's perimeter also offers decent protection, at least while crouching. For extra concealment, hide within the shadows created by the small awning. This is a great area for covering the choke point between Sectors Alpha and Charlie.

Team Assault: Located near the center of the map, this rooftop is very dangerous in this game mode, so it's best to stick to the ground unless your team has a UAV in the air. When you can verify the security of the surroundings, this rooftop can be a great spot to engage enemies positioned near the cave. But be aware—they can probably see you too.

Sector Control: Looking for a premium sniping spot? This high perch near the cave is a popular location for long-range engagements. A sniper posted here can easily cover Sector Bravo as well as the area directly around the flag at Sector Charlie. However, this is a very predictable sniping spot, so don't linger here too long. As long as the opposing team is on the other side of the map you should be fine. But consider moving out once Sectors Alpha or Bravo are compromised.

Team Assault: As one of the highest accessible points on the map, this is the most utilized sniper perch. In this game mode it's perfect for hitting targets dashing around the village. But watch out for enemies sneaking up on you from the cave. If you don't see teammates nearby, vacate this position immediately.

Sector Control: Look for the mattress on the ground in the small alcove near Sector Alpha and take cover behind the nearby rocks. This out-of-the-way spot offers great protection and a nice view of the road below. This is the perfect spot for picking off enemies rushing from Sector Charlie to Sector Alpha. However, watch for attacks originating from the cave. If the Sector Alpha icon blinks on the minimap or HUD, turn around and get ready for a close-quarters fight.

Team Assault: This dead end area is another popular sniping position for covering the village. While it's possible to climb on the nearby rocks for an even greater view, doing so leaves you completely exposed. It's best to remain crouched behind the rocks, even if it does limit your view.

CHOKE POINTS

Sector Control: This narrow gateway near Sector Bravo is popular kill zone, ideal for blasting opponents at close range. This makes it a great place to ambush enemies moving between Sectors Charlie and Bravo. Hide nearby with a submachine gun or shotgun and surprise your opponents as they rush through this high-traffic choke point. This is also a good area to watch when defending Sector Bravo.

Team Assault: Traffic often flows in a circular fashion around the perimeter of the map, making this gateway a particularly brutal kill zone. So if you're not camping this spot, try to avoid it altogether, because one of your opponents is probably lying in wait with a shotgun or explosives.

Sector Control: The racetrack-like layout of the map makes this narrow spot another deadly choke point as players rush between Sectors Alpha and Charlie. This path between the perimeter wall and the small structure sees plenty of traffic, so look for opportunities to watch this area from a distance. When possible, avoid moving through this area, especially when approaching from the low road running down the middle of the map.

Team Assault: For players following the perimeter boundary of the map, this is another high-traffic area. Given the limited sightlines, fights often take place at close range, so consider equipping a pistol if your primary weapon is a sniper rifle.

Sector Control: This steep path near Sector Bravo is another high-traffic area, great for intercepting opponents moving out of or toward the cave. When staging an ambush here, hold the high ground and aim toward the flag at Sector Bravo—this is a great spot for guarding the flag. But there is no one great spot along this path, so keep moving, especially if Sector Alpha is secured by the opposing team.

Team Assault: When moving through this area, always try to advance down the slope instead of up it. There may be enemies hiding among the rocks in the upper elevations, making it extremely risky to climb this path from the road.

Sector Control: Exercise extreme caution when moving through the cave near Sector Alpha. Not only is it dark, but there's plenty of blind corners for enemies to hide in. There are three entrances to this small cave system. Pay close attention to which team holds the nearby sectors and adjust your travel accordingly. But no matter how careful you are, point-blank encounters with enemies are unavoidable here. Most weapons are effective at close range, but snipers should strongly consider equipping their pistol before moving through here.

Team Assault: The cave is the site of many close-quarters fights. Shotguns are extremely effective here, so consider finding a dark corner and scoring some cheap kills. Opponents are guaranteed to move through here at some point, so hold your ground and wait for your victims to come to you. A tight group of three or four teammates can completely lock down the cave.

SIGHTLINES

Sector Control: Sniper duels between overwatch positions 1 and 6 are very common on this map. But snipers at these two positions can also pick off enemies moving anywhere between these two points. Players moving between Sectors Bravo and Charlie are particularly vulnerable to sniper fire in this area. Pay close attention to your surroundings and utilize cover to prevent enemy snipers from scoring an easy kill.

Team Assault: This is one of the longest and most popular sightlines on the map, so exercise extreme caution when attempting long-range attacks from either side of this line. There's a good chance an opponent is looking back at you. Make a quick scan for targets, take a shot or two, then move out. The action is far too frantic to get comfortable in any one position.

Sector Control: The dirt road between the cave and village offers a very long sightline, ideal for watching Sector Bravo from a distance. But due to the locations of the other objectives, traffic often flows across this road instead of down it. Still, players camped at either end of this road can rack up some big points by simply intercepting the cross traffic here. So when crossing the road, always do so at a full sprint to minimize your exposure. Better yet, deploy a smoke grenade before moving out.

Team Assault: As in Sector Control, traffic often flows across the road. Look for opportunities to flank the cross-traffic by taking up a position at either end of the road, or camp both ends of this sightline with a teammate and catch your opponents in a brutal crossfire. Assault rifles and light machine guns are best suited for mowing down sprinting opponents here.

SECTOR CONTROL: TACTICS
In this battle, Sectors Alpha and Charlie are the two strong points on the opposing edges of the map while Bravo is located in the difficult-to-defend no man's land on the road in the center. Traffic usually flows in a circular fashion as each player races from one flag to the next. However, the quickest way to achieve a team victory is by taking and holding Sectors Alpha and Charlie, forcing the opposing team to spawn at the low point near Sector Bravo. Set up strong defensive positions in the cave and within the village and wait for your enemies to bring the fight to you. As long as your team holds two out of the three sectors and forces the enemy to attack uphill throughout the battle, you have a very good chance of securing a win.

TEAM ASSAULT: TACTICS
As with most Team Assault maps, the team that picks a location and defends it is more likely to win here. On this map the village is the best defensible spot, with plenty of hiding spots from which to ambush an unorganized opposing team. Split up into squads of three or four players and scatter throughout the village, always staying within support range of your teammates. Avoid rooftops and other elevated locations that may leave you silhouetted against the sky. Instead, stay in the low alleys and building interiors, picking off opponents that wildly run into view. By concentrating your team in the village, you can effectively lock down the location and make it a total kill zone.

OBJECTIVE RAID

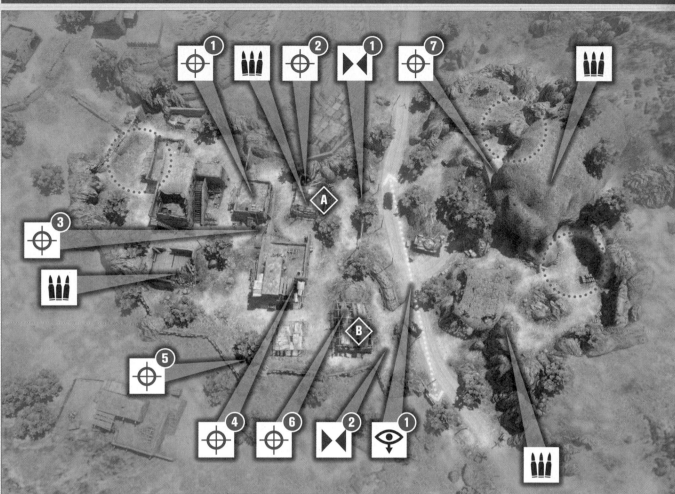

Coalition Spawn Point	Overwatch Position
OPFOR Spawn Point	Choke Point
A Objective	Sightline
Ammo	

MAP FEATURES
OVERWATCH POSITIONS

This dark room overlooking Objective Bravo is the perfect defensive position for the coalition team. Not only does this room have a perfect view of the objective, but snipers posted here can also pick off OPFORs near their spawn point by the cave. For best results, hold back from the opening in the wall to avoid giving away your position. Adding a suppressor to your weapon can also make a big difference.

If you're looking to defend Objective Bravo from close range, this corner is an excellent spot, especially for OPFORs. Hide back in this corner near the ammo crate and wait for opponents to approach the objective. However, your left side is completely exposed, making this a better position for the OPFORs than the coalition. After setting the charge on Bravo, hide in this corner and prevent the coalition from disarming your explosives.

This is another great defensive spot for the coalition team gathered around Objective Bravo. Crouch down in this alley and aim toward the road. The path ahead is often traveled by OPFORs rushing toward Bravo. The narrow gateway near the road is the perfect spot to focus your fire.

If you want to defend Objective Alpha at close range, hide in this corner within the structure, directly across from the objective. This is a well-concealed location for players on both teams. Simply blast anyone that barges through the doorway. However, you can be flanked from the rocks directly behind this position, so consider attaching a suppressor to your weapon to prevent giving away your hiding spot.

The rooftop in the center of the village is a versatile defensive position, allowing coalition players to defend both objectives. But you can't watch both Alpha and Bravo at the same time, so pick a side of the roof to defend. The low wall on the roof's perimeter offers some protection but OPFOR snipers positioned near the cave can still hit crouched players on this rooftop.

This high perch near the cave is a premium sniping position for the OPFOR attackers. This location is best suited for providing support fire for teammates attacking Objective Bravo. It's also a good counter-sniping spot for picking off coalition marksmen hiding in the village, but don't hold here too long. This is a well-known and obvious sniping location. Score a few kills and move out before your victims can respawn and seek revenge.

Here's a spot that both teams can utilize for defending Objective Alpha. Back up into this corner near the tree and aim toward Alpha. From this spot you can hit anyone moving through the structure's main entry point. This spot is also out of the way, obscured partially by the tree and nearby grass. This makes it a great and unpredictable spot for OPFORs to hide after arming the explosives at Alpha.

CHOKE POINTS

OPFORs rushing Objective Bravo often dash through this narrow gateway near the road. From this gate, they can easily access the objective's structure by climbing up the rubble pile in the collapsed corner. When playing as the coalition, consider defending this area to prevent quick rush attacks on Bravo.

Here's another path frequented by OPFOR attackers on the other side of the map. This narrow path near Objective Alpha is the quickest route for the attackers to move from their spawn point, near the cave, to the objective. As a result, this area should be monitored by coalition defenders.

SIGHTLINES

The road running down the center of the map is a key sightline benefitting the coalition defenders. Since the OPFORs always spawn near the cave, they must cross this road to reach either of the objectives. This gives coalition defenders camped at either end of the road the ability to intercept the cross-traffic. Therefore, OPFORs should never linger on the road. Always sprint across the road, preferably under the concealment of smoke.

COALITION TACTICS

At the start of this battle, Objective Alpha is the most vulnerable as it's the most distant from the coalition spawn point. So get half of your team to Alpha as soon as possible while the rest of the team heads to Bravo. Expect early rushes from the OPFORs on both locations, so get to each objective before they can set a charge. If your team withstands the initial rush, continue defending both objectives, but send a couple of teammates forward to harass the attackers near the choke points at the road. Applying pressure in these areas can yield some easy kills, catching the attackers by surprise. But it may also make them rethink their approach, so look out for different maneuvers.

OPFOR TACTICS

The coalition has the upper hand in this battle thanks to their strong defensive positions in the village. It takes a concerted team effort to pull off a win against an organized coalition team here. Start off by attacking Objective Bravo with the full force of your team. For the coalition, this is the most defensible position, so hit it while their team is divided between the two locations. Once Bravo is destroyed, make a move on Alpha. This location is furthest from the coalition spawn point so it's a bit harder for them to defend. For this task, use half of your team to attack the objective directly while the rest of the team infiltrates the village and intercepts the defenders as they rush from their spawn point toward Alpha.

GARMSIR TOWN

Through the village of Garmsir, situated in the southern part of Afghanistan, runs a canal that feeds the surrounding irrigations with water from the Helmand River. This central hub becomes a violent inferno as coalition Special Forces insert to clear the town of anti-coalition militia.

SECTOR CONTROL AND TEAM ASSAULT

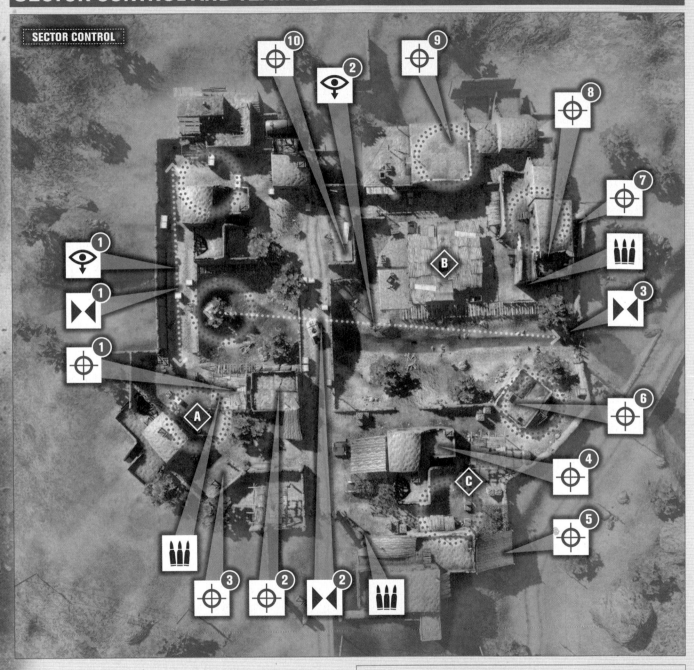

Flexible Coalition Spawn Point		Overwatch Position
Flexible OPFOR Spawn Point		Choke Point
A Objective		Sightline
Ammo		

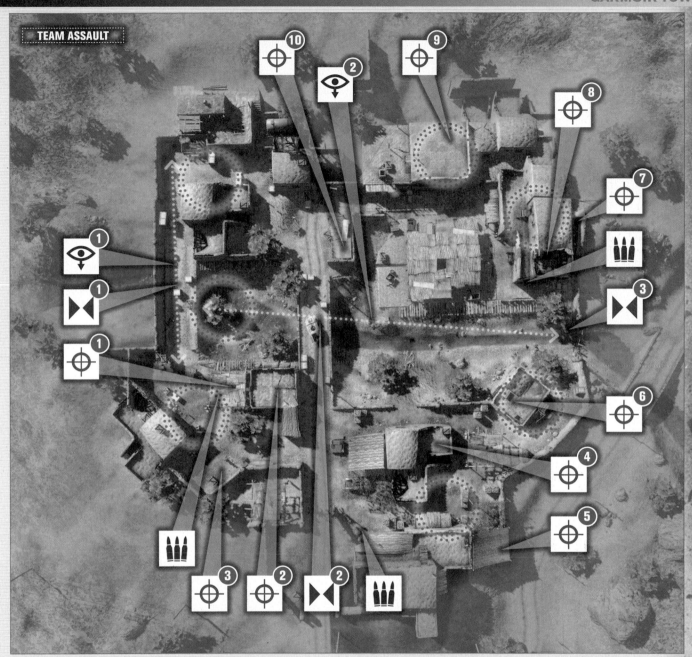

TEAM ASSAULT

Legend

⠂ Flexible Coalition Spawn Point		⊕ Overwatch Position	
⠂ Flexible OPFOR Spawn Point		◤◥ Choke Point	
⦙⦙⦙ Ammo		👁 Sightline	

MAP FEATURES
OVERWATCH POSITIONS

Sector Control: Crouch beneath this shady awning and partially conceal yourself behind the crates in the corner. This is a decent close-quarters defensive spot for covering Sector Alpha. From here you can ambush enemies rushing over the nearby bridge or approaching from Sector Charlie. While the shade makes you hard to see, there isn't a ton of cover here. If you plan to camp here for a prolonged amount of time, strongly consider attaching a suppressor to your weapon to avoid detection.

Team Assault: Although there's nothing to defend in this game mode, this is still a sneaky hiding spot, ideal for ambushing traffic rushing through this courtyard. Do your best to conceal your right side with crates and other objects to avoid being hit from the canal or opposite side of the map. Otherwise, there's no flanking you from this position.

Sector Control: While it's impossible to cover any of the flags from this makeshift window near Sector Alpha, this dark room is perfect for monitoring the two bridges crossing the canal. Shift to the right side of the room to cover the bridge running along the map's perimeter to the left, or shift to the left side of the room to cover the central bridge.

Team Assault: As in Sector Control, this dark little room is great for covering the two bridges as well as traffic moving along the opposite side of the canal. As usual, hold back from the window to prevent exposing your muzzle and its flash. Or better yet, attach a suppressor to your weapon to reduce your muzzle flash and weapon's report. If you make too much noise here, you're likely to get knifed in the back.

Sector Control: This is perhaps the best position for covering Sector Alpha. This little alcove is tucked away from the main thoroughfare, plus three walls completely cover your flanks, ensuring nobody sneaks up on you. Peek around the corner of this wooden fence to get a clear view of the flag and any opponents within the capture radius. Instead of staring at the flag constantly, hide in the corner and only peek out when the Sector Alpha icon flashes, indicating an enemy is trying to capture it. At that point, peek out and eliminate the threat.

Team Assault: This is another sneaky place to hide out and flank the cross-traffic moving along the map's heavily traveled circular path. This area also serves as a spawn point for both teams, but as long as you're here, no enemies will spawn on top of you. Consider holding this spot with a teammate for increased coverage and firepower. At this range, shotguns and carbines are very effective.

Sector Control: This rooftop is a unique location in this game mode as it allows you to cover both Sectors Charlie and Bravo. It's also possible to see the area around Sector Alpha. But this versatility comes at a price. While standing on this rooftop you're completely exposed and silhouetted against the sky. Therefore, always assume a crouched stance and use the low wall surrounding the rooftop's perimeter for cover. But even then, you're not completely safe from snipers positioned on the opposite side of the canal.

Team Assault: As a central, elevated position, this rooftop certainly has its appeal. But the traffic in the surrounding alleys is heavy, so you don't want to hold here very long. While moving out, stop here to scan your surroundings and then move on. Don't bother camping here unless you have a tight group of three or four teammates to lock down this position.

Sector Control: When defending Sector Charlie, hide in this area beneath the green tarp and further conceal yourself behind the crates and other objects in this isolated alcove. This is easily one of the best spots from which to babysit Sector Charlie. It's off the beaten path, plus the three walls completely secure your flanks, protecting you from getting blindsided with melee attacks.

Team Assault: In this game mode most players stay on the move, racing around the map's perimeter like a race track. If you want to avoid the chaotic race, step off to the side in this alcove and ambush any opponents that run by. Since most of your targets will be running past your location, choose a weapon with a high rate of fire, ensuring you score the kill before they move out of your line of sight. Carbines, submachine guns, and light machine guns are all very effective in this location.

Sector Control: If your team already controls Sector Bravo, this building on the opposite side of the canal is a perfect defensive position for holding it. While the rooftop of this building is accessible, it's much safer to hide inside the structure. The window here overlooks the marketplace where Sector Bravo is located, allowing you to easily pick off any intruders. Although it's on the other side of the canal, the range isn't that great, so a carbine or assault rifle should suffice.

Team Assault: The marketplace across the canal is a high-traffic area, making this an ideal spot for engaging opponents racing through. But in this game mode it's vital that you avoid the rooftop of this building. The interior offers much more cover and concealment, surely extending your lifespan in this chaotic game mode. Attaching a suppressor to your weapon can also increase your lifespan here by making you more difficult to detect.

Sector Control: While this location offers no benefit to capturing or defending Sectors, it is a very effective spot for monitoring traffic in the canal below. Climb up the narrow staircase of this building and turn around, aiming toward the canal. You can improve the sightline here by knocking over the nearby tree with explosives. The shadows make you very difficult to see, especially if firing a suppressed weapon.

Team Assault: The crossing at the canal is another high-traffic area worth covering in this game mode. Back up into this corner and blast enemies as they race through the shallow water. However, watch out for enemies moving though the building's interior. If you're not careful, they can flank you through the door on your right.

Sector Control: This upstairs room offers a great view of the marketplace, including Sector Bravo. But it's also possible to hit opponents crossing either of the two bridges. While assault rifles or carbines are well suited for covering Sector Bravo, you may want something with a bit more range when engaging the more distant targets from this location—a battle rifle or sniper rifle should do the trick. But if performing long-range shots, make sure you have a buddy nearby to watch the room's entrances.

Team Assault: Fight the urge to snipe from this room unless you have a dedicated group of teammates posted around the building's perimeter. This is one of the map's more predictable sniping locations, so don't expect to hold here long unnoticed. Still, the view is great, so scan for targets through the hole in the wall before moving out. You can often find enemy snipers here, so look for opportunities to score some easy melee kills.

Sector Control: This isolated room near the marketplace is prime real estate for defending Sector Bravo. Move to the very back of the room and turn around, aiming toward the flag. For added cover and concealment, move in behind the crates and other objects at the back of the room. Enemies approaching the flag will have a very difficult time spotting you here thanks to the shadows.

Team Assault: The stall-like rooms near the marketplace are equally effective in this game mode, allowing you to mow down opponents dashing through this high-traffic area. The neighboring room (to the left) is narrower and darker, ideal for ambushing enemies moving in and out of the building at overwatch position 8. Anyone attempting to take you out must attack directly as the walls protect you from flanking attacks.

Sector Control: This abandoned market stall near the central bridge is a good spot to cover the traffic in and out of the marketplace, allowing you to better secure Sector Bravo. Take up a position in this corner near the wooden fruit stand and ambush opponents moving through this otherwise neutral corner of the map. Given its distance from the flags, players usually let their guard down and sprint though this area, making them particularly vulnerable to surprise attacks.

Team Assault: As in Sector Control, this is an excellent spot from which to engage enemy traffic moving through this corner of the map. But don't get too greedy. After scoring a few kills from this spot, move on before your victims can respawn and hunt you down.

CHOKE POINTS

Sector Control: This bridge on the perimeter of the map is a popular thoroughfare as players move between Sectors Alpha and Bravo. With the exception of a few crates, there isn't much cover here, so move through this area quickly. If smoke grenades are available, use them to conceal your advance.

Team Assault: The long sightline down this bridge and the lack of cover make this a route best avoided in Team Assault matches. But if you must move across this bridge, do so while sprinting from one crate to the next. Also, do your best to minimize your exposure to snipers that may be camped at either end of the bridge or down in the canal.

Sector Control: The central bridge is a safer crossing point for players moving from one side of the canal to the other. The wrecked Humvee at the bridge's center not only provides some welcome cover, but it also prevents long-range duels from breaking out at either end.

Team Assault: This bridge is the safer of the two to cross during Team Assault matches. However, it's still exposed to enemies camped in the surrounding buildings. Therefore, always cross this bridge at top speed and never stop to return fire. If necessary, hunker down near the wrecked Humvee. But it's much safer to sprint all the way across the bridge.

TIP

Explosives planted beneath the central bridge are a great way to ambush enemies moving along the canal.

Sector Control: This canal crossing is a high-traffic area frequented by players moving between Sectors Bravo and Charlie. As a result, it is usually watched by enemies, so exercise extreme caution when moving through this area. There's virtually no cover, so speed and smoke grenades are your best defenses here.

Team Assault: The circular flow of traffic around the perimeter of this map makes this one of the more heavily traveled areas. Players hiding below the central bridge can easily pick off opponents moving through this area. The nearby stairs at overwatch position 7 are also a popular camping spot for players looking to score some easy kills at this choke point.

SIGHTLINES

Sector Control: By aiming between the crates at the center of the bridge, it's possible to score some long-range kills. In this game mode, the sightline is ideal for both attacking and defending Sector Alpha. On defense, hold near the flag and sidestep left and right to adjust your view down the bridge. When attacking from the opposite end, perform the same lateral maneuvers to scan for defenders hiding near the flag.

Team Assault: Long-range duels are very common on this bridge, so if you don't want to get pinned down here, avoid the bridge altogether. But by holding at either end of the bridge you can also score some quick kills. Traffic along this bridge is rather heavy, so there's never a shortage of targets. But don't get so focused on covering this bridge that you forget to watch your flanks.

Sector Control: The canal is the lowest spot on the map, but also offers the longest sightline. Crouch down at either end of the canal to engage cross-traffic moving from one side of the map to the other. Since flags are located on each side of the map, there's always a steady flow of traffic. You can even hit enemies rushing across the central bridge.

Team Assault: Movement along the canal is rather uncommon during Team Assault matches, as traffic tends to flow around the perimeter. Still, this sightline is still useful for picking off enemies moving across the central bridge or the low spot at choke point 3. An assault rifle or battle rifle with a good scope is more than sufficient at this range.

SECTOR CONTROL: TACTICS

While it's possible to take and hold all three flags, it's much easier to lock down two locations. When taking this approach, choose Sectors Alpha and Charlie as your defensive positions. Since they're located on the same side of the canal, your defensive efforts at each location somewhat overlap, making it much tougher for your opponents to gain a foothold on this side of the map. Once Alpha and Charlie are locked down, send a few teammates forward to harass enemies attempting to cross the canal. The bridges are ideal choke points, perfect for staging ambushes. Even if the enemy team holds Bravo throughout the battle, maintaining control of Alpha and Charlie guarantees your team the win.

TEAM ASSAULT: TACTICS

With some organization and communication it's possible to turn this otherwise chaotic match into a complete rout for your opponents. First of all, find a good defensive position and communicate its location with the rest of your team. The buildings and stalls around the marketplace are good places to set up camp. But really, any corner of the map is just as effective as long as you have the manpower dedicated to make a stand at a static location. Monitor your teammates' positions on the minimap and make sure all approaches are covered. Your team's most skilled players are best utilized as skirmishers, pushing out of your team's position and engaging the enemy in unpredictable locations. This helps create the illusion that your team is on the move.

OBJECTIVE RAID

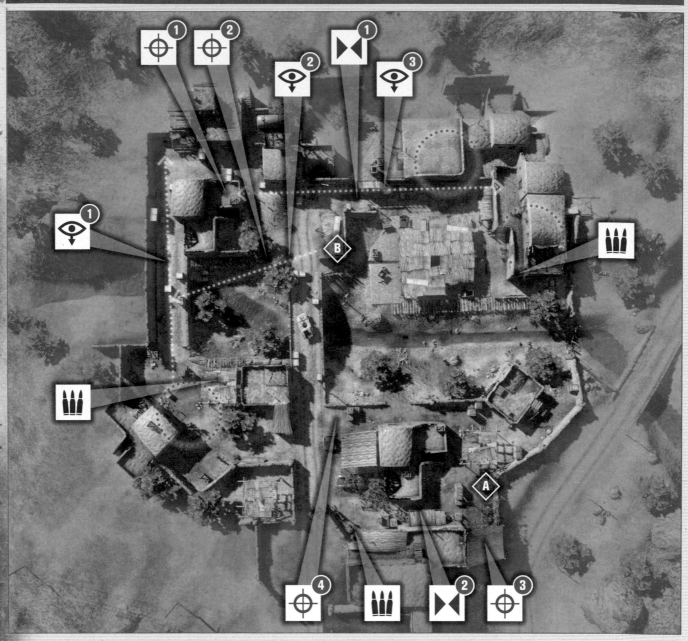

	Coalition Spawn Point	⊕	Overwatch Position
	OPFOR Spawn Point	◤◢	Choke Point
Ⓐ	Objective	◉	Sightline
▮▮▮	Ammo		

MAP FEATURES
OVERWATCH POSITIONS

This is one of the most versatile overwatch positions on the map, with sightlines to three key locations. For one, you can cover

Objective Bravo directly, ideal for either team. From this same rooftop, coalition troops can turn toward the OPFOR spawn point and pick off enemies as they rush across the bridge. On the other hand, OPFORs on this rooftop can turn toward the coalition spawn area and mow down opponents in the marketplace. So pay close attention to what team you're on and where the action is when positioned on this rooftop. The low wall around the perimeter offers solid protection as long as you remain crouched.

After setting the charge at Objective Bravo as the OPFORs, take cover along this brick wall near the canal. While the alarm is sounded at Bravo, you don't need to worry too much about the area to your right and the coalition can't access the area behind you. Stay focused on the objective and blast any coalition troops that dash in to disarm your team's explosives. Pay particular attention to the narrow alley at choke point 1.

Either team can make use of this awesome defensive position near Objective Alpha. Simply hide in this alcove and shoot anyone who tampers with the objective. The three walls surrounding this location make it impossible for anyone to sneak up on you. However, rockets and grenades fired into this cramped space can prove lethal, so do your best to avoid giving away your position. A suppressed weapon can help conceal your location, making you invisible on your opponents' minimaps.

Once Objective Alpha has been destroyed, OPFORs should take up flanking positions on this side of the canal. From this angle, you can hit coalition troops as they rush from their spawn area toward Objective Bravo. The marketplace is filled with destructible cover, so there aren't too many places for the coalition troops to hide. If you can pin them inside the buildings where they spawn, you can clear the way for the rest of your teammates to plant the charge at Bravo.

CHOKE POINTS

This narrow alley linking the marketplace to Objective Bravo is a popular kill zone leveraged by OPFOR forces. Freshly spawned coalition troops usually rush through this alley while moving to secure Bravo, making it a perfect ambush point of OPFORs. Plant IEDs here or simply lob grenades or launch rockets into this narrow choke point to score some easy kills. If multiple coalition troops are pinned at this bottleneck, an offensive support action can really do some damage.

Located near Objective Alpha, this narrow alley is the site of some brutal close-quarters fights. Coalition defenders should camp this spot and blast OPFORs rushing from their spawn point on the opposite side of town. Both shotguns and carbines are well suited for the point-blank battles in this alley. The majority of incoming OPFOR traffic passes through here, so take the opportunity to stop them before they can even lay eyes on Objective Alpha.

SIGHTLINES

The bridge near the OPFOR spawn point offers one of the map's longest and most controversial sightlines. Coalition troops positioned at the opposite end of this bridge can engage OPFOR forces soon after they've spawned. While spawn camping is often frowned upon, it's something all players should be prepared for. For this reason, OPFORs should secure the far side of the bridge to ensure this sightline is not exploited by the coalition team.

If you knock down the tree by the central bridge with explosives, you can create a long sightline between the perimeter bridge (by the OPFOR spawn point) and Objective Bravo. This allows OPFOR snipers posted on the bridge to get a clean angle on Bravo. This is ideal for covering the objective once the charge has been placed. But the sightline goes both ways, giving coalition troops near Bravo a clear sight of the bridge, potentially opening the door for some long-range spawn camping.

The area between the coalition spawn point and overwatch position 1 is a high-traffic area, especially when Objective Bravo is in contention. Players positioned at either end of this sightline can almost fire completely across the map. Sniper rifles or battle rifles are best suited for these long-range shots, but an assault rifle with a decent scope can also prove sufficient.

COALITION TACTICS

For the coalition team, Objective Alpha is the easiest spot to defend, but it's also the most distant from their spawn area. At the start of the match, it's important to get at least half of the team moving to Alpha as quickly as possible. Chances are that OPFOR attackers will reach the site first, so it may be necessary to wrestle control from the enemy before a defensive perimeter can be established. Meanwhile, Objective Bravo poses different problems. It's easiest to defend this site from overwatch position 1 where you can also apply pressure to the OPFOR spawn area. But if the OPFORs manage to take overwatch position 1, this objective can be very difficult to defend without leaving yourself open to flanking attacks. Therefore it's best to center the bulk of your defenses around Objective Alpha. A solid defensive effort here can earn you the win even if Bravo falls.

OPFOR TACTICS

An OPFOR victory on this map is usually decided in the first minute, all hinging on the ability to destroy Alpha before the coalition can dig in. Take advantage of the coalition team's distance from Objective Alpha by rushing it with the entire team in the opening moments of the match. OPFOR players can always reach and secure Alpha before the coalition team arrives, but make sure you have the firepower in place to maintain control until your team's charge goes off. With Alpha down, shift your focus to Bravo. First, secure overwatch positions 1 and 4 and then suppress the coalition troops at Objective Bravo and the marketplace, near their spawn points. With the coalition troops pinned at the marketplace, setting and defending the charge at Bravo is rather painless. Just keep applying the pressure until the final charge explodes, securing your team a victory.

KABUL CITY RUINS

Pillars of smoke rise high from the ruins in the ancient city of Kabul. On the outskirts, coalition soldiers try to rid the area of OPFOR activity. Warriors on both sides dart between piles of rubble and burning car wrecks as rooftop snipers take pot shots at anyone daring to move in the open.

SECTOR CONTROL AND TEAM ASSAULT

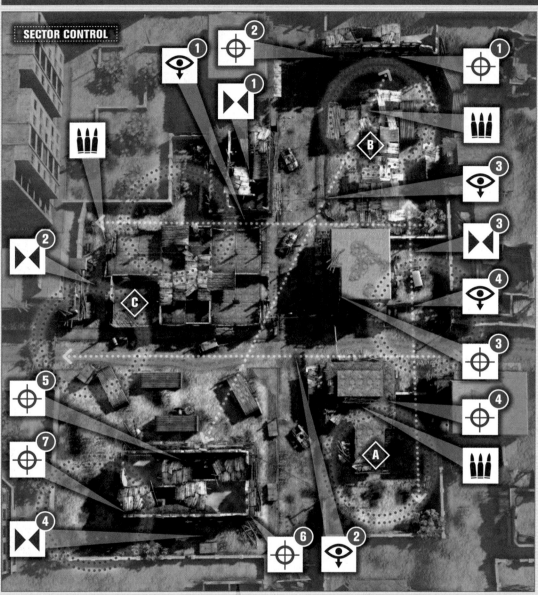

Flexible Coalition Spawn Point	
Flexible OPFOR Spawn Point	
A	Objective
	Ammo
	Overwatch Position
	Choke Point
	Sightline

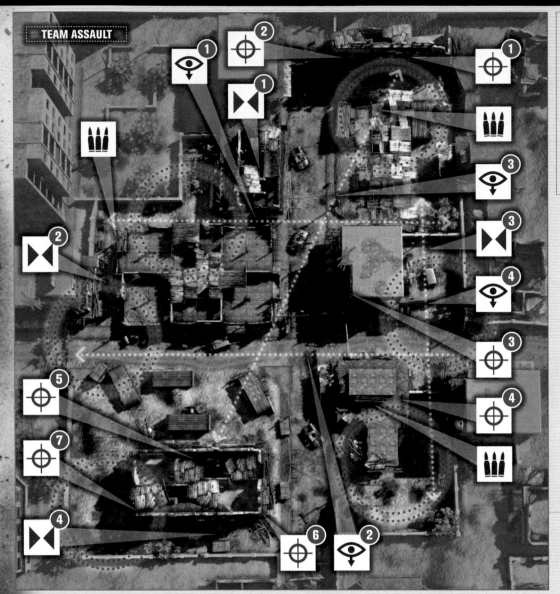

TEAM ASSAULT

Legend:
- Flexible Coalition Spawn Point
- Flexible OPFOR Spawn Point
- Ammo
- Overwatch Position
- Choke Point
- Sightline

MAP FEATURES
OVERWATCH POSITIONS

Sector Control: This second-story window near Sector Bravo is a popular but somewhat obvious sniper spot. From here you can cover the flag and narrow alley at choke point 3. Step back from the window for better concealment and be ready to side step behind a wall (or back down the stairwell) if you take heavy fire. When assuming a position here, make sure teammates are nearby to watch your back, otherwise knife-wielding enemies can easily

sneak up the stairs and surprise you from behind. Counter-snipers in the building at overwatch position 5 also pose a serious threat.

Team Assault: During these chaotic matches, never hold this position alone. At the very least, check your minimap to ensure teammates are nearby. If you don't see any friendly units, pick up camp and move out. It really takes two players to secure this position—one to snipe from the window and one to cover the stairwell.

Sector Control: Step out of the window at overwatch position 1 and onto this corner ledge for a great view of the street. This street is an obvious kill zone and as such does not see much foot traffic. However, enemies may wander down the street bounding from one wrecked vehicle to the next. This spot puts you in a great location to pick off any hostiles brave (or dumb) enough to charge down this street. However, crouching on this ledge gives you no concealment or cover. If you're spotted, quickly drop to the ground and find a place to hide before attempting to return fire.

Team Assault: This is a particularly dangerous position due to its complete lack of cover. However, if your team has the area around the marketplace locked down, this can be a very advantageous sniper position with an unobstructed view stretching to the opposite side of the map.

TIP

In Sector Control matches, Sector Bravo can be captured by standing atop the metal awning over the marketplace. However, it's safer to stay on the ground, where there's much more cover.

Sector Control: Climb the staircase in the marketplace between Sector Bravo and choke point 3 to reach this upper-level walkway. The shaded balcony and pillars offer excellent concealment when firing down on enemies rushing through the intersection as well as the rooftop where Sector Alpha is situated. This is also a good spot to pick off enemy units occupying the second floor of the unfinished building across the street. For best results, equip a suppressor to eliminate muzzle flash and reduce the report of your weapon. There aren't too many long sightlines available from this walkway, so be prepared to engage enemies at close to intermediate ranges.

Team Assault: This is a popular spot for engaging traffic at the intersection as well as in front of the building near overwatch position 5. Use the shadows for concealment and the crates and

concrete pillars for cover. But don't hide behind the rug hanging over the balcony—it won't block bullets. However, keep an eye on the minimap to monitor the positions of your teammates. If you have no teammates in the marketplace, there's a good chance an opponent can climb the same staircase you used to get up here and knife you from behind.

Sector Control: This rooftop perch near the ammo crate at Sector Alpha is ideal for covering the alley at choke point 3. This spot also offers a clear view into the second floor window at overwatch position 1. Unfortunately the rooftop here is completely exposed, so don't make a habit of camping here long. Instead, step into position, scan for targets, then move away. If you're not playing as a sniper, this is also a good spot from which to launch grenades and rockets at incoming troops advancing through the narrow alley below.

Team Assault: When engaging targets at choke point 3 or overwatch position 1, crouch behind the ammo crate and slowly step out to the right to peek around the corner. This prevents you from exposing your entire body, making you a tougher target to see and hit. However, don't get tunnel vision peering down this alley. The situation is always fluid in this game mode with enemies potentially swarming all around you. So if you don't see any teammates nearby, it's time to move on.

Sector Control: This upper-story window is much like the one at overwatch position 1, but on the opposite side of the map. So always watch for enemy snipers in the opposing building before getting too comfortable up here. This is the perfect spot for defending Sector Charlie, located on the second floor in the unfinished building across the street. Defending this flag can be as simple as sniping opponents that move into view, or you can get creative by planting explosives around the flag and triggering them once your enemies attempt to capture it.

Team Assault: Just like overwatch position 1, it's best to hold this spot with a buddy. If you become too fixated on sniping through this window, it's only a matter of time before an opponent sneaks up the stairwell and knifes you in the back. If you want this to be your sniper post, enlist a friend to provide rear security or take turns sniping and defending this location.

Sector Control: The damaged awning on the back side of the building serves as a ramp that you can climb to reach this narrow concrete ledge, ringing the entire structure. This is a great spot for defending Sector Alpha from a distance. There's minimal cover around Alpha, allowing you to hit anyone positioned near the flag. But there's not much cover on this little ledge either. You're particularly vulnerable to enemies moving through the alley below at choke point 4. Make sure a few teammates are nearby before getting too comfortable here.

Team Assault: In addition to covering the rooftop across the street, you can also peek around the building's corner to engage opponents in the intersection or as far away as the opposite side of the map at overwatch position 2. Still, this is a risky place to remain for very long, so make sure your teammates have your back.

Sector Control: This ledge is easiest to access via the ramp at overwatch position 6. Follow the ledge to this corner and aim toward Sector Charlie. Not only is this a great cover point for Charlie, but you can also engage enemy traffic moving through the alley at choke point 2. But just like overwatch position 6, you're vulnerable to enemies passing through the alley behind this building.

Team Assault: During these frantic matches, traffic is always heavy in the alley at choke point 2, making this one of the best spots to counter enemy movement through this bottleneck. Assault, battle, or sniper rifles are all very effective at picking off targets at this range. Of course, you're quite exposed up here, so don't expect to hold this spot indefinitely. Score a few easy kills and move on.

CHOKE POINTS

Sector Control: Always be ready to fire when moving through this narrow hall near Sector Bravo. This is a high traffic area often frequented by players moving between Sectors Charlie and Bravo. Avoid sprinting, otherwise you won't have enough time to bring your weapon up to fire should you encounter an enemy at close range. This can also be a very effective ambush point, so watch for enemies hiding on the stairs here.

Team Assault: As in Sector Control, this is also a very high-traffic area during Team Assault matches. Shotguns and submachine guns rule in these tight quarters, so if you're carrying something else, consider finding another route. But even if you survive moving through this hall, there may be more opponents camped near the exits. Watch your corners when exiting.

Sector Control: This alley near Sector Charlie is another notorious kill zone. The stairs in this alley are the quickest way to access the flag at Charlie, but this area is often watched by opponents at overwatch positions 5 and 7. Always deploy smoke when moving through this area, and especially when attempting to make a move on Sector Charlie via the exterior stairs. The building's interior staircase is a much safer path to the building's second floor.

Team Assault: Players moving through this alley are at a constant risk of both long- and short-range attacks. The alley itself offers some decent hiding spots, particularly behind the dumpsters. Watch out for enemies camped here, or take up these sneaky positions yourself. But the biggest threat in this alley comes from opponents at overwatch position 7. When entering this alley, always peek toward this position to make sure the path is clear before exposing your entire body.

SIGHTLINES

Sector Control: This alley between Sectors Alpha and Bravo is an absolute kill zone made even more dangerous by the narrow gate-like passage leading to and from the marketplace. If you must move through here, do so slowly and while crouched. The van in the alley offers decent protection, so stay behind it to avoid giving snipers at either end of the alley an easy kill. Dropping a smoke grenade can greatly increase your chances of getting out of here alive.

Team Assault: While moving through the narrow passage by the van is always dangerous, it can also benefit a bloodthirsty camper. There are plenty of hiding spots in this alley, ideal for staging ambushes. Hide behind the van or one of the dumpsters and blast the cross-traffic with a shotgun or submachine gun. Explosives are also very effective in this confined space—just be careful not to blow yourself up.

Sector Control: This sightline spans the width of the entire map, perfect for engaging opponents moving between Sectors Bravo and Charlie. Players positioned near the marketplace, by Bravo, can aim down through the nearby stairs and hit opponents as far away as choke point 2. Meanwhile, players positioned in the alley near Sector Charlie can kill enemies passing through the narrow passage at choke point 3. Such long-range shots are easiest with a battle rifle or sniper rifle.

Team Assault: Since there are no defined defensive locations in this game mode, it's never wise to camp at either end of this sightline. However, when passing through, take a moment to scan down this path and search for targets of opportunity. There's always plenty of traffic in this area, so you're likely to find something to shoot.

Sector Control: The alley behind this building is another high-traffic area, especially for players attempting a more indirect approach between Sectors Alpha and Charlie. While it is one of the wider alleys on this map, enemies positioned on the ledges at overwatch positions 6 and 7 always pose a threat, not to mention enemy cross-traffic. For this reason, never sprint here. Keep your weapon raised and ready to fire.

Team Assault: As one of the perimeter pathways, this alley sees a lot of traffic during this game mode. Although cover is minimal, it is available, especially near the corner spawn point. If you're looking to intercept traffic moving through here, you're better off doing it from the ground where you have more cover and concealment. The nearby building's elevated concrete ledge offers neither.

Sector Control: This is another long sightline, perfect for engaging the cross-traffic between Sector Alpha and the two other flags. At some point, every player must cross this street. So why not camp at either end of the sightline? Traffic rarely flows down this street, so you'll need to hit your targets as they dash across. This doesn't give you much time to aim and fire before your target moves out of view. That's why sniper rifles are so effective here. All it takes is one hit to bring down any sprinting target. But if your prefer a weapon with a higher rate of fire, then go with an assault rifle.

Team Assault: This is one of the most effective and under-utilized sightlines in this game mode. Granted, it does take a certain level of skill to score a kill from these positions. But once you have the proper optics and firepower, this can be a very lucrative camping spot. It's best to hold near the map boundary by choke point 3, taking cover behind the dumpster and steel obstacles. The opposite end of the sightline offers much less cover for campers, so don't make a habit of loitering there.

Sector Control: The areas between overwatch positions 1 and 5 are almost constantly watched by snipers. For this reason, it's best to avoid the streets as snipers at either end of this elevated sightline can easily pick off targets here. Furthermore, snipers at these locations can also cover Sectors Bravo and Charlie. Always be mindful of these two second-story windows on opposite sides of the map. If a team can occupy both of these spots, they can control a large portion of the map while effectively locking down Bravo and Charlie.

Team Assault: If you're not occupying one of the windows at overwatch positions 1 or 5, at least be aware of what areas snipers in these windows can see. As a rule, it's safest to stay in the alleys and buildings where the sightlines are short. If you must move out into the open, do so while sprinting. Snipers in either window can also be suppressed (or outright killed) by firing rockets or grenades into these small elevated rooms.

Sector Control: The alley at choke point 3 offers another long sightline useful for engaging traffic moving between Sectors Alpha and Bravo. Players positioned at either end of this sightline can score some long-range kills. But this line most benefits players positioned near Sector Alpha. Crouch near one of the crates and aim past the van and through the narrow passage at choke point 3 to hit targets near the marketplace by Sector Bravo.

Team Assault: Traffic in this area is equally heavy during Team Assault matches as players from both teams rush along this perimeter pathway. Still, regardless of which side of this line you're holding, your flanks are completely exposed. Don't get distracted by constantly peering through your scope and only take up these positions if you have teammates around to serve as a defensive buffer. If you're all alone, sighting down this line can leave you open to embarrassing melee kills.

SECTOR CONTROL: TACTICS

This is a very large map, so it's difficult to lock down all the flags. Therefore, it's best to capture and hold two, so set your sights on Sectors Alpha and Charlie. These two flags are closest to each other, allowing your team's defensive efforts to overlap. When defending these positions, the building at overwatch position 5 is vital. From this building and its ledges your team can cover both flags from long range. Supplement your long-range defenses by positioning skirmishers near the flags to intercept attackers at close range. If one of the flags is captured, quickly recapture it to maintain overall supremacy. If your team manages to hold Alpha and Charlie for most of the match, you have a very good chance of pulling off a win.

TEAM ASSAULT: TACTICS

On a map this large, it's difficult to keep your team together as one cohesive unit unless you identify a suitable rally point. Consider setting up a location for your team to defend. The buildings at overwatch positions 1 and 5 are ideal locations for such a rally point. Concentrating your team at either of these locations makes them virtually untouchable. Study the position of your teammates on the minimap and make sure all approaching angles are covered. If the opposing team isn't expecting you to be holding a fixed position, the balance of power can quickly swing in your team's favor. At the very least, a strong defensive action early in a match can give your team the score boost they need to secure a victory.

OBJECTIVE RAID

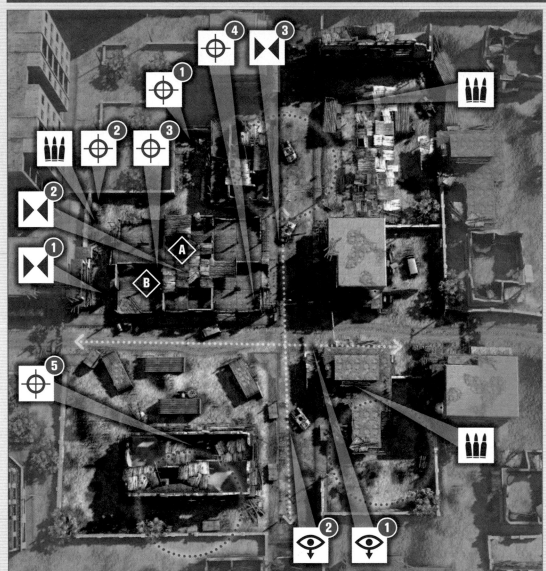

Coalition Spawn Point	
OPFOR Spawn Point	
Objective	
Ammo	
Overwatch Position	
Choke Point	
Sightline	

MAP FEATURES
OVERWATCH POSITIONS

This is the perfect coalition camping spot for defending Objective Alpha on the first floor. This section of the alley is completely off limits to OPFOR players, so you don't have to worry about being flanked. Instead, aim straight ahead and blast anyone tampering with Alpha. An assault rifle or carbine works well from this range, but a shotgun with slugs is equally effective if your aim is true.

For the OPFORs, this corner in the alley is a great flanking position for hitting coalition troops rushing toward the objectives. Intercepting the coalition defenders in this alley can alleviate some much needed pressure on the objectives, giving your teammates time to set charges and form defensive perimeters around each. Consider equipping a light machine gun when holding here as you'll need to expend a great deal of ammo to keep this alley filled with flying lead.

There are very few direct positions for defending Objective Bravo on the second floor. So consider hunkering down in this corner, right next to the objective. From here you can easily spot anyone entering this exposed room, including those moving up the nearby exterior staircase—a popular attack route for the OPFORs. At this range, shotguns are most effective. Just stay low and out of sight to avoid giving OPFOR snipers at overwatch position 5 a clear shot.

This second floor position is an ideal defensive location for coalition defenders attempting to halt the infiltration of the objective building. From here you have a clear view of the street below. Also, the room below is a popular entry point for OPFOR attackers. Surprise them from above with a blast to the face before they can sneak into the building. Stopping the attackers in the street below is much easier (and safer) than facing them inside the building.

Only the OPFOR team can enter this building across the street from the objectives. While it's difficult to attain a solid line of sight on any of the objectives from this location, it's still possible to hit coalition troops moving in and around the target building. Providing support from this location can help your teammates gain a foothold on the building's interior.

CHOKE POINTS

This exterior staircase is a popular attack route for OPFORs looking to rush Objective Bravo on the second floor. As one of three access points to the second floor, coalition troops should take action to defend these steps. Planting explosives on or near the steps is effective, but so is camping overwatch position 3. In any case, don't let the attackers rush up these steps unchallenged.

The interior staircase at the middle of the building is a high-traffic area likely to see some heavy action. Coalition troops should camp this staircase from the second floor. The height advantage and blind corners upstairs make this a relatively easy spot to defend. OPFOR attackers are better off utilizing one of the two exterior staircases.

The second exterior staircase sees the least amount of traffic, but should still be guarded by coalition troops. If left unguarded, defenders at overwatch position 4 are compromised, along the with entire second floor. Whenever possible, OPFOR attackers should use this staircase as it's relatively isolated and often forgotten by the coalition team.

SIGHTLINES

Most OPFOR attackers must cross this street to reach the objective building, so it only makes sense for the coalition defenders to take advantage of this long sightline. Applying pressure on the attackers before they can even reach the building is very effective, and may even slow their advance, buying your teammates more time to fortify the objectives. But sightlines go both ways, so OPFORs should quickly counter any attempts to camp this street.

Both teams should post at least one sniper at each end of this long sightline. Players posted at the other end can pick off enemies shortly after they spawn. OPFORs have an almost perfect view of the coalition spawn area. From their side of the line, coalition snipers can intercept enemy traffic in and around the street intersection. The team that exploits this sightline to its fullest has a good chance of tilting the odds in their favor.

COALITION TACTICS

Coalition defenders often make the mistake of centering their defenses too tightly around the objectives. While covering the objectives is critical, it's equally important to halt the OPFOR attack before OPFORs can even enter the building. While half of the team camps Alpha and Bravo, the rest of the team should aggressively attack the invaders, taking the fight to the streets outside the target building. Suppressing the OPFOR advance in the streets prolongs the battle, increasing your team's chances of pulling off a win. Remember, you only need to hold out for five minutes, so do everything possible to keep the OPFORs out of the building. If manpower isn't available to properly defend both objectives, make your stand at Objective Alpha, downstairs. It's closer to your team's spawn point and is much easier to defend than Bravo.

OPFOR TACTICS

Speed is the key to securing a quick victory here, so waste no time and make an aggressive push toward the building where both objectives are located. Instead of heading upstairs, stay on the ground floor and swarm Objective Alpha while the coalition team's defenders are split. It's important to take Alpha first, otherwise the coalition team will have an easy time defending it by concentrating their whole team at this cramped location. Save Bravo, on the second floor, for last. Bravo is the furthest from the coalition spawn point, plus they have to defend all three staircases to effectively lock it down. Furthermore, your team's snipers can provide fire support at Bravo from overwatch position 5, across the street.

MEDAL OF HONOR

KANDAHAR MARKETPLACE

Kandahar in the south is one of the oldest human settlements known. Once a bustling trade center, it is now torn by centuries of war. A marketplace in one of the northern parts of the city becomes the scene of a heated battle between coalition soldiers and OPFORs in a fight to the death between narrow alleys and market stands.

SECTOR CONTROL AND TEAM ASSAULT

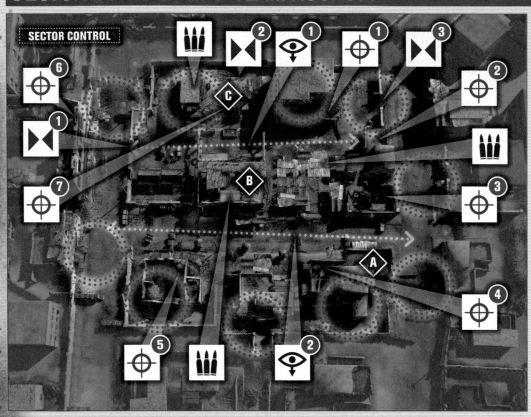

SECTOR CONTROL

Flexible Coalition Spawn Point	
Flexible OPFOR Spawn Point	
A Objective	
Ammo	
Overwatch Position	
Choke Point	
Sightline	

TEAM ASSAULT

Flexible Coalition Spawn Point	
Flexible OPFOR Spawn Point	
Ammo	
Overwatch Position	
Choke Point	
Sightline	

MAP FEATURES
OVERWATCH POSITIONS

Sector Control: This perimeter balcony offers a great view of the street below as well as the flag at Sector Bravo. While it's not possible to cover the entire room where Bravo's flag is positioned, a rocket or grenade launched through the hole in the wall can, at the very least, injure enemies' attempt to convert this Sector. If you continue along the balcony, you can also cover Sector Charlie. There isn't much cover here, so stay in the shadows and utilize the crates and other objects up here for cover.

Team Assault: While there are no objectives to attack or defend in this game mode, this spot is equally effective for scoring kills by engaging traffic in the street or marketplace. The marketplace is a particularly lethal kill zone as most of the wooden fruit stands and crates are destructible. Even if your victims manage to find a hiding spot, their cover won't last long.

Sector Control: This rooftop position utilizes sightline 1, perfect for engaging traffic moving along or across this street. This is a great spot for hitting cross-traffic between Sectors Bravo and Charlie. Players often race over the narrow arches between the two upper floor locations, leaving them completely open to fire from this position. However, watch for enemies camped at the opposite end of the street, especially in the window at overwatch position 6.

Team Assault: The view here is hard to pass up, but this rooftop is very exposed and vulnerable to flanking maneuvers. If your teammates are nearby to watch your back, climb to this rooftop to pick off targets moving along this street. It's even possible to hit enemies moving through the narrow green doors at choke point 1, assuming your weapon has the range and optics to pull off such a long-distance shot.

Sector Control: Climb to this rooftop for a great view of Sector Alpha. Unless you want to defend the flag at point blank range, this spot is a good alternative. Enemies gathered near the flag probably won't notice you here, especially if you remain in the shaded portion of the rooftop. But act fast to score the kill before they can convert the flag or take cover behind the low wall or in the second floor room nearby.

Team Assault: Utilizing sightline 2, it's possible to hit anyone moving down this street, making this rooftop a great sniping position. But like any rooftop, you're very exposed, so consider heading downstairs and knocking out the wooden door with your melee weapon. Removing the downstairs door opens a similar sightline down the street, but the cover afforded by the structure's walls is well worth any obstructions that may impede your vision.

Sector Control: The second floor room near Sector Alpha offers a great view of the street and marketplace below. If you look just beyond the marketplace, you can see Sector Charlie on the opposite side of the map. While the view isn't perfect, you can still hit enemies attempting to convert the flag at Charlie. Of course, at this range a sniper rifle is your best shot at scoring quick kills.

Team Assault: As one of the few upper-level positions on the map with suitable cover, this is a great sniping spot with sight-lines stretching across the map. Look for enemies on the balcony at overwatch position 1 or in the window at overwatch position 6, or simply pick off targets in the street or marketplace below. However, don't hold here long unless you have a dedicated group of teammates nearby to watch your back.

Sector Control: Located far away from any of the flags, this bombed-out building is the perfect spot to ambush unsuspecting opponents moving along the nearby road. Players usually sprint past this position without even glancing in the direction of this spot. For best results, hide in the shadows and attach a suppressor to your assault rifle or carbine. If you remain concealed, you can score multiple kills from this position, often without facing any sort of retaliation.

Team Assault: In this game mode, players aren't focused on flags or objectives, making this a slightly less safe place to camp. Players often move through this building to avoid getting cut down in the street, so there may be some heavy traffic here as well as the neighboring structures on this side of the street. But if moving through here, take a moment to scan for enemies, including snipers positioned in the window at overwatch position 6.

Sector Control: This building, directly below Sector Charlie, is a nice hiding spot. Although it offers no direct view of any of the flags, it's a great spot for monitoring and engaging enemy traffic around Sectors Bravo and Charlie. To enhance your concealment in this dark room, attach a suppressor to your weapon to eliminate muzzle flash. However, watch out for enemies sneaking up behind you via the alley at choke point 2.

Team Assault: Given the fluid action of this game mode, avoid stopping in this room for very long, at least while you're by yourself. It's a great spot to catch enemies by surprise, moving through the street and the alley at choke point 2. However, the action in the street often forces the traffic in and around this building, so it's never clear where the enemies are going to appear. But if you can hold this interior with a group of teammates, each covering an entry point, you can make a formidable stand and rack up some impressive kills in the process.

Sector Control: This window is the premiere sniping spot on this map. However, in this game mode it offers no clear views of any of the flags. But much like overwatch position 2, on the opposite side of the map, it's a great spot for engaging the cross-traffic between Sectors Bravo and Charlie. While sniper rifles are ideal at this range, a battle or assault rifle equipped with a combat scope is sufficiently effective here.

Team Assault: While this window offers a great view, it's also the single-most predictable sniper location on the map. So if you're camped up here, be prepared to take incoming fire from spots all around the map. Incoming rockets and grenades are particularly dangerous. Also, watch out for enemies sneaking up the stairs to knife you. In other words, don't make a habit of holding here. Peer through the window, take a few shots, and vacate the position before you draw too much attention.

NOTE

Check this wall outside overwatch position 7 to spot some familiar imagery from previous DICE games.

Sector Control: Positioned near Sector Bravo, peer through this doorway to get a great view of Sector Charlie. From here you can essentially cover two flags. If an enemy tries to convert Bravo, you can take them out at close range. Or if an attack is underway at Charlie, simply peek through this doorway and counter them. While you can't see both flags at once, rely on the Sector icons on the minimap. If they flash, an enemy is attempting to capture it. Take this as your cue to move into action.

Team Assault: Located in the center of the map, this two-story building sees a lot of action, so don't go here by yourself. However, if you can occupy this location with your team, you can unleash all sorts of carnage. The second floor has several windows and doorways, giving your teammates plenty of angles on the rest of the map. But make sure someone guards the two staircases leading up here at all times, otherwise your team could be wiped out by a single enemy.

CHOKE POINTS

Sector Control: Avoid rushing through these doors when spawning on this side of the map. Enemies positioned as far away as overwatch position 2 have a clear view of this bottleneck and can pick off anyone that dashes into view. You're better off passing through one of the wider or more concealed entry points nearby.

Team Assault: Look for opportunities to ambush enemies rushing through this gate. You can either watch it from a distance or simply hide on the opposite side and blind side them as they run past you. It may not be the most sporting way to boost your kill count, but it can help your team gain the upper hand in a tightly contested match.

Sector Control: The alley running along the perimeter near Sector Charlie is often a high-traffic area due to players avoiding the chaos in the street. There's also a staircase here leading up to Charlie, giving players yet another reason to frequent this alley. If your team already holds Charlie, consider defending this alley, as this can be a sneaky way for attackers to convert the Sector without much fanfare.

Team Assault: Players seeking to avoid the nearby street often race through this alley, with the assumption that it's safer. You can shatter those delusions by ambushing opponents from within the nearby building at overwatch position 7. There isn't much cover in the alley itself, so avoid stalling in the open.

Sector Control: Just like the gate at choke point 1 on the opposite side of the map, exercise caution while moving through here. There are no extremely long sightlines trained on this location, but enemies at Sector Bravo have a good view of this area. Enemies camped on the opposite side of the wall also have an easy time blasting players moving through this point.

Team Assault: As at choke point 1, look for opportunities to score some easy kills at this location. It's easiest to simply hide on the opposite side of this gate and mow down freshly spawned enemies as they rush through. There's no guarantee enemies will spawn in the adjacent street, so you might have to wait a while before you score your first kill.

SIGHTLINES

Sector Control: The area between Sectors Bravo and Charlie is always busy, making this street the perfect sightline for picking off the enemy traffic in this congested area. Set up at either end of the street and watch for enemies dashing between the two Sectors. Pay particular attention to the two archways, as players often dash across these narrow structures to quickly move between Bravo and Charlie.

Team Assault: The street here is a kill zone in Team Assault matches, so it's best to avoid running down the middle. If you must cross, do so at fast speed and a perpendicular angle, so as to make yourself a difficult target for opponents camped at either end of this long sightline.

Sector Control: This sightline is even longer than the one on the parallel street, allowing for some extreme long-range kills. Use this view to monitor traffic moving between Sectors Alpha and Bravo. The crates at either end of this street offer decent cover and concealment, but don't get so focused peering through your scope that you ignore your surroundings—enemies can still circle around and surprise you from behind.

Team Assault: This street is another popular kill zone and is best avoided during these frantic and unpredictable matches. Traffic usually flows along the perimeter alleyway, but at some point all players must cross this street. As usual, cross at a full sprint, moving to some piece of cover on the opposite side of the street. Tossing a smoke grenade in the street prior to your advance can obscure the sightline, making it relatively safe to cross regardless of how much fire is channeled down this road.

SECTOR CONTROL: TACTICS

All of the flags on this map are located on upper levels. Therefore, it's beneficial for your team to hold the high ground as much as possible in order to capture and defend these flags. The strongest defensive position on this map is around Sectors Bravo and Charlie. Both Bravo and Charlie are very close to each other and allow for overlapping defenses. By comparison, Sector Alpha is completely isolated, requiring its own defensive effort to hold. Make sure your team utilizes overwatch positions 1, 2, 6, 7, and 8 to secure this area and prevent the enemy from taking Bravo and Charlie. If your team can lock down this area throughout the match, you all but guarantee yourself a win.

TEAM ASSAULT: TACTICS

Due to the long sightlines and high vantage points, there's never a shortage of snipers on this map. To avoid being picked off, avoid the streets completely. Instead, move through the buildings and perimeter alleyways with a group of teammates. Perform orbits around the map's perimeter, visiting each of the overwatch positions and choke points along the way. But unless you have overwhelming manpower, don't linger at any one spot for long. Halt at each point of interest, scan for targets, then move on to the next spot. A small group of skilled teammates sweeping the map in this fashion can rack up an impressive amount of kills, giving their team's score a boost.

OBJECTIVE RAID

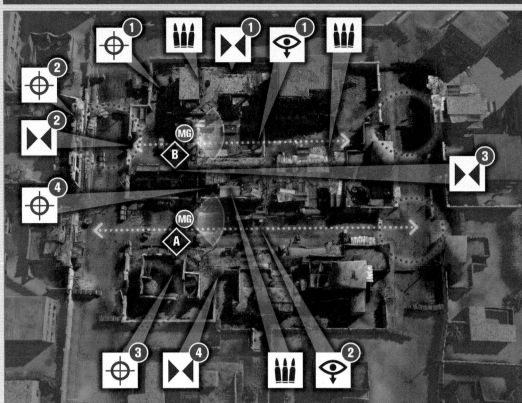

⋯	Flexible Coalition Spawn Point
⋯	Flexible OPFOR Spawn Point
Ⓐ	Objective
MG	Machine Gun
▮▮▮	Ammo
⊕	Overwatch Position
◤◥	Choke Point
👁	Sightline

MAP FEATURES
OVERWATCH POSITIONS

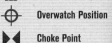

This is a great spot for watching Objective Bravo. However, it benefits the OPFOR team more as they're less likely to be flanked via the alley at choke point 1. Coalition troops are better off positioned in the gateway on the other side of this dumpster. From either position you have a clear view of Bravo, allowing you to pick off anyone attempting to set or disarm a charge. OPFORs attacking from this direction also have the chance to sneak up behind the defenders and evade the machine gun covering the street.

The window here is only accessible by coalition troops—the entire building is off-limits to the OPFOR team. This allows coalition snipers posted here to provide covering fire for Objective Bravo without having to worry about opponents sneaking up the stairs and knifing them. Pay close attention to OPFOR snipers posted on the rooftops at the opposite end of the street and deal with them before they can pick off your teammates positioned near the objective. Unfortunately, the view of Objective Alpha is rather limited from this position.

This is an excellent flanking and cover position for Objective Alpha. When playing as the OPFORs, sneak along the perimeter alley to reach this bombed-out building. This allows you to bypass the machine gun near the objective and potentially catch the coalition defenders by surprise. Once the charge is set at Alpha, return to this position and pick off the defenders that attempt to disarm your explosives. When playing as the coalition, occupy or patrol this building to prevent such flanking attacks.

The building between the two objectives is a critical overwatch position benefitting both teams. From here, both objectives can be covered from the second floor windows. But the tactical significance of this building probably won't go unnoticed by your opponents, so avoid lingering in front of one window for very long. Move around, patrolling the interior while scanning for enemies outside.

CHOKE POINTS

This alley is a popular flanking path for OPFORs looking to flank Objective Bravo. As such, coalition troops should keep an eye on this choke point. A rifleman with a light machine gun can do some serious damage by firing down this dusty alley. Unfortunately there isn't much cover, but the occasional gust of wind kicks up enough dust to conceal your position. For OPFORs, the alley can

be bypassed by moving along the nearby rooftop, but doing so leaves you open to sniper fire from overwatch position 2.

Both teams should make note of this gate near Objective Bravo. One of the coalition spawn points is located in the street right next to this gate. As a result, coalition players often rush through this narrow choke point, so OPFORs should keep an eye on this area to score some easy kills. OPFOR snipers posted at the opposite end of the map can score several kills just by zooming in on this one spot. Therefore, coalition troops spawning nearby should avoid this gate and choose one of the other entry points when moving toward the objectives.

The two objectives are separated by a wall, with only two narrow passages. Opponents camped at overwatch positions 1 or 3 can cover these two choke points, intercepting any traffic that moves through them. While movement here is relatively light for most of the match, traffic increases as the coalition shifts their attention from one objective to the other, such as when a charge is placed. OPFORs should prepare for movement through this area and take steps to exploit this bottleneck.

OPFORs often sneak through the perimeter alley when advancing on Objective Alpha. But they must exit the alley at this point before approaching the objective or continuing on to overwatch position 3. When defending as the coalition, watch this area from the upstairs windows at overwatch position 4 and pick off the sneaky attackers before they can place a charge on Alpha.

SIGHTLINES

As in Sector Control and Team Assault, this street is still a kill zone made even more perilous for the OPFORs due to the coalition machine gun posted near Objective Bravo. Even OPFOR snipers should think twice about taking up positions within view of the machine gun while it's pumping out rounds. But if the machine gun isn't manned, the street is a target-rich environment for snipers posted at both ends of the street.

The street leading to Objective Alpha is another avenue best avoided by OPFOR troops. A second machine gun posted near Alpha can cover both sides of the road, accurately hitting targets on the far side of the map. Even if the machine gun isn't manned, coalition snipers can still cover the street from long range, so the OPFORs should stick to the perimeter alley to avoid getting cut down in the street.

CAUTION

The machine guns near the objectives are very effective at suppressing OPFOR movement along the streets. However, if you man one of these guns, you're completely exposed to enemy sniper fire. Furthermore, the machine guns can be completely destroyed with explosive attacks, so watch out for incoming rockets and offensive support actions.

COALITION TACTICS

The coalition team definitely has the advantage in this battle, but it doesn't take much for the OPFORs to generate momentum. At the start of the battle, get both machine guns at Alpha and Bravo firing to effectively shutdown traffic along the streets. This usually pushes the OPFORs into the perimeter alleys, so make sure you have personnel in place to halt these flanking advances. Meanwhile, position troops around the objectives, making use of all the overwatch positions to create overlapping fields of fire. If manpower allows, send a few skirmishers toward the OPFOR spawn zones to harass them in areas where they least expect it. Every attempt to suppress, delay, and pin the OPFORs buys you time, helping ensure your team lasts the requisite five minutes to secure the victory.

OPFOR TACTICS

This map is nearly symmetrical so it doesn't matter which objective your team attacks first. However, it's a good idea to push against the same objective simultaneously, so communicate with your teammates and call out your first target before the match even begins. Once an objective is picked, focus on taking out the nearby machine gun first. A simple mortar strike is more than sufficient to wipe out the gun and anyone standing nearby. With the machine gun eliminated, snipers positioned on rooftops near your spawn zone can provide support fire while your team advances toward the objective. With your whole team attacking one objective simultaneously, you should have enough firepower to roll over the coalition defenders. Once one of the objectives is destroyed, repeat the same steps to take the second one, starting off by eliminating the machine gun to pave the way for sniper support.

KUNAR BASE

The sector designated N2KL along the Afghanistan-Pakistan border is teeming with violent activity. A coalition forward operating base comes under attack as OPFORs mount an aggressive assault. The remote hilltop is slowly covered in smoke from constant artillery strikes as soldiers huddle in the maze-like trenches.

SECTOR CONTROL AND TEAM ASSAULT

⋮⋮	**Flexible Coalition Spawn Point**	⊕ **Overwatch Position**
⋮⋮	**Flexible OPFOR Spawn Point**	◄► **Choke Point**
Ⓐ	**Objective**	👁 **Sightline**
☰	**Ammo**	

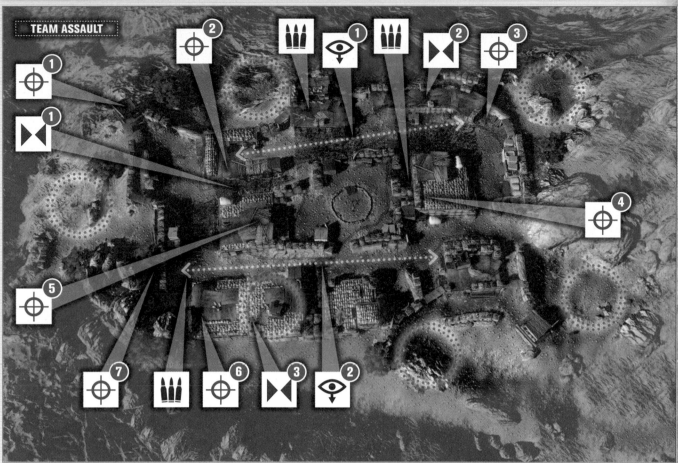

TEAM ASSAULT

⠿	Flexible Coalition Spawn Point
⠿	Flexible OPFOR Spawn Point
⫶⫶⫶	Ammo

⊕	Overwatch Position
◀▶	Choke Point
👁	Sightline

MAP FEATURES
OVERWATCH POSITIONS

Sector Control: This guard tower is the perfect defensive position for covering Sector Alpha. From here you have a perfect angle on the flag, allowing you to hit anyone that enters its capture radius. Furthermore, the position offers excellent protection, with high, thick walls completely encircling your flanks. Nobody is going to sneak up behind you here.

Team Assault: There's nothing to guard at this location in Team Assault, but this position is still awesome for intercepting traffic in the area below. Of all the guard towers, this one offers the best

view of a high-traffic area. Plus, knowing you can back up into a corner without worrying about getting knifed can give you some much needed peace of mind on this cramped and chaotic map.

Sector Control: There's plenty of great hiding spots in this small command center near Sector Alpha. While it's not a great spot for watching any of the flags, this is an excellent ambush spot for hitting enemies moving between Sectors Alpha and Bravo. Blind side opponents moving in through the doorway on the right, or take out more distant enemies moving along sightline 1.

Team Assault: There's plenty of cover and concealment opportunities in this room, ideal for the habitual camper. Hide near this table, or take cover between the crates on the right. Since most traffic flows along the perimeter pathways on this map, you're guaranteed to encounter enemies in this room. It's up to you to aim and pull your trigger before they uncover your hiding spot.

Sector Control: Due to the crates and other objects surrounding the flag at Sector Charlie, it's difficult to get a clean angle on this position from a distance. But by hiding among the crates in this corner, you can make out the base of the flag pole, making it easy to pick off anyone nearby. It may be difficult to prevent an enemy capture from this position, but at least you can hit anyone moving away or toward the flag.

Team Assault: This position is just a little too exposed for this game mode, but if you can remain concealed in this corner, you can definitely score some surprise kills. Don't bother camping here unless you have a suppressor attached to your weapon however, otherwise your weapon's bright muzzle flash and loud report may give away your position, making you easy to spot and kill.

Sector Control: Located just opposite of overwatch position 4, the rooftop of this bunker is littered with weight lifting equipment. When you're not pumping iron, scan the perimeter to gain great views of Sectors Alpha and Bravo. This area is easiest to access via the ladder near sightline 2, so make sure this alley is clear before climbing up top. The room below offers more protection, but greatly hinders your view of the nearby objectives.

Team Assault: Only move up to this elevated position if your team has the surrounding trenches covered. Otherwise, enemies moving along the trench behind this bunker can easily surprise you. Still, this is a great spot for engaging the cross-traffic moving through the center of the map. Just watch out for enemies camped at overwatch position 4 and the surrounding rooftop positions.

Sector Control: The roof of this bunker is great for covering both Sectors Bravo and Charlie. However, the higher elevations often leave you exposed on this map, so stay low and avoid poking your head too high above the ballistic barriers. For better protection and concealment, consider heading downstairs and hiding in the projection room. However, this limits your view drastically, only allowing you to see Sector Bravo.

Team Assault: Use elevated positions like these sparingly, as they can easily be flanked. However, if your flanks are covered by teammates, this bunker offers a great view of the map, including the kill zone in the middle. An assault rifle or battle rifle is more than sufficient for hitting distant targets on this compact map. Plus, the higher rate of fire (over a sniper rifle) can be a life saver.

Sector Control: Hide in the corner of this bunker to gain a distant view of Sector Alpha. This is a sneaky spot from which to defend this flag, often catching attackers by surprise. However, enemies moving through the bunker may flank you from the right. To avoid this, consider setting up outside, behind the stairs to the left. The view is a bit more limited from behind the steps, but you're completely safe from flanking attacks.

Team Assault: This is a great place to monitor traffic moving through this corner of the map. Blind side your opponents with a shotgun blast as they rush past your position. But just as in Sector Control, enemies moving through the bunker can still flank you here, so consider setting up outside behind the nearby staircase. The view still allows you to hit traffic moving toward and away from this corner.

CAUTION

You cannot walk across the camo netting hanging over the trenches. If you try, you'll fall through.

Sector Control: This is one of the few true sniper spots on this map. Stay on the outside of these perimeter barriers and aim down sightline 2 toward Sector Charlie. Anyone moving along this long trench is within your line of sight, as well as any opponents attempting to capture Sector Charlie. Of course, this position can be flanked from the left, so make sure you're not caught off guard by constantly peering through your scope. Having a buddy watching your back is the best way to avoid getting surprised here.

Team Assault: This is the best position from which to take advantage of the trench at sightline 2. Even if you don't have a sniper rifle, you can score multiple kills by pumping rounds down this trench—a light machine gun is very effective for suppressing traffic here. But this is a well-known spot, and likely to draw plenty of retaliatory fire and flanking attacks, so don't make a habit of camping here. If you're in the area, move here, score a few kills, and move on before your victims can respawn and hunt you down.

CHOKE POINTS

Sector Control: This narrow passage is frequented by players moving between Sectors Alpha and Bravo. The twisting path offers limited lines of sight, practically guaranteeing point-blank encounters. So if you don't want to move through the nearby command center at overwatch position 2, walk through this passage with your weapon at the ready. Don't sprint through here as you won't have time to stop, raise your weapon, and fire.

Team Assault: Unless you like close-quarters fights, this passage is best avoided by either moving through the command center at overwatch position 2 or the bunker at overwatch position 5. Though if you're looking to exploit this choke point, consider watching it from a distance near overwatch position 1 and blast anyone that exits.

Sector Control: This hall-like passage offers great protection, and is a wonderful way to avoid sightline 1. However, it is very narrow, offering little room to maneuver laterally. Therefore if you encounter an enemy here, there's no way to strafe to the right or left. As a result, the winner of fights in this passage often comes down to the player with the quickest trigger finger.

Team Assault: Traffic through this narrow passage can be heavy, especially if there's lots of bullets flying down sightline 1. To exploit this choke point, consider camping the exterior path outside the base and picking off enemies moving past the perimeter doorway. Explosives planted in this narrow passage are also very effective.

Sector Control: The rooms near overwatch position 6 are a popular refuge for players seeking to avoid sightline 2. As such, expect heavy traffic through here. As with most choke points, move slowly with your weapon raised and ready to fire. Pay particular attention to the narrow doorways—enemies may be covering them from a blind corner.

Team Assault: This is another high-traffic area and the site of some brutal close-quarters combat. Shotguns rule here, capable of scoring one-shot kills whether using standard shot or slugs. If you want to avoid this kill zone, consider cutting through the center of the map, moving through the bunker at overwatch position 5.

MEDAL OF HONOR

SIGHTLINES

Sector Control: The sightline down this trench is best covered by players near overwatch positions 2 and 3. Set up at either end of this sightline and pick off enemies moving between Sectors Alpha and Bravo. Players moving down this trench should always be prepared for enemies looking to exploit this sightline. Cut through the center of the map or move through the perimeter bunkers to avoid stepping into this kill zone.

Team Assault: Due to the transient nature of this game mode, players are rarely camped at either end of this sightline. But opponents simply moving through this area are reason enough to pay close attention. As a high-traffic area, avoid sprinting and keep your weapon raised. You can sometimes get the jump on your opponents by aiming down your weapon's sight while advancing through this trench.

Sector Control: The trench running between Sector Charlie and overwatch position 7 is the longest sightline on the map. This is also one of the most frequently traveled paths, making it a deadly kill zone for anyone caught in the middle. For this reason, avoid rushing down this trench whenever possible. Instead, cut through the center of the map, at Sector Bravo, or duck inside the perimeter bunkers, by choke point 3, for better concealment.

Team Assault: Just like sightline 1, snipers positioned at either end of this trench aren't the only threat. Enemies advancing down this trench have a clear view as well, so make sure you're ready to counter their attacks. As usual, avoid sprinting and aim your weapon straight ahead while advancing in preparation for the inevitable appearance of an enemy. If you need to take cover, move laterally into the center of the map or duck into one of the perimeter bunkers.

SECTOR CONTROL: TACTICS

This is a very small map, especially when played with 24 players. Organization is important to prevent this match from turning into a quasi-Team Assault free-for-all. First, split your team into three squads—Alpha, Bravo, and Charlie. Each squad is responsible for taking and defending one of the corresponding Sectors throughout the match. This allows each squad to become an expert at each location. While the opposing team frantically runs around from one flag to the next, hold your squads at their designated Sectors. Even if you temporarily lose a Sector, by following this gameplan you'll soon regain it and maintain a point advantage over the opposing team. If your team is short on players, focus your attention on Sectors Bravo and Charlie where your defensive efforts can overlap.

TEAM ASSAULT: TACTICS

As one of the smallest maps, Team Assault is fast paced and completely chaotic. However, don't lose your head in the frantic action. Make a consistent effort to stay with at least one other teammate at all times. Moving around the map as a small squad greatly increases your lifespan as you and your teammates gang up on lone wolf players racing around the map. Also, fight the temptation to climb to the upper levels. Doing so only leaves you exposed, making you an easy target for enemies. It's much safer to stay in the lower levels where there's more cover and concealment. Achieving a victory here often comes down to the individual skills of you and your teammates. But by moving and fighting together, you stand a greater chance of pulling off a win, even against a highly skilled team of individuals.

OBJECTIVE RAID

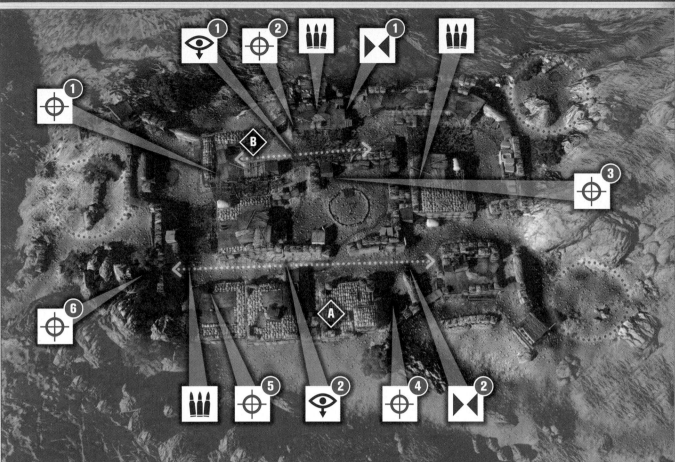

⊙ Coalition Spawn Point	⊕ Overwatch Position
⊙ OPFOR Spawn Point	◄► Choke Point
◈ A Objective	◉ Sightline
▥ Ammo	

MAP FEATURES
OVERWATCH POSITIONS

Whether playing as the coalition or OPFORs, this corner is an excellent spot for defending Objective Bravo. But this spot is particularly sneaky for OPFORs after a charge is set. Coalition troops often funnel into this room via the doorway on the right, allowing you to shoot them in the back as they attempt to disarm your team's charge. But this room also features a couple of other great hiding spots for covering the objective at close range, useful for both teams.

This spot is most beneficial to the OPFOR team when covering Objective Bravo. This is a good spot for covering the objective while teammates rush in to set the charge—hold here and defend the objective until the charge detonates. Due to the location of the coalition's spawn point, you're less likely to be flanked from behind here. However, keep an eye on the outer path to the right—opponents tired of getting mowed down by the objective may utilize this path in an attempted flanking maneuver on Bravo. The rooftop above this position offers an even better view, but provides little cover.

Locate suitable cover near the center of the map and aim toward Objective Alpha. If you align your position just right, you can see right through the bunker doorway where the objective is located. This is a great defensive spot for either team. As players attempt to arm or disarm the charge, they rarely turn in this direction. Go ahead and shoot them in the back as they tamper with the objective. However, watch out for cross-traffic moving between the two objectives and make sure you're not completely exposed.

The bunker in which Objective Alpha is located is small and cramped, offering very few great hiding spots. Consider covering the objective from this side doorway. This is most effective for the OPFOR team, as they're less likely to be flanked from behind due to the proximity of their spawn point. Coalition troops rushing from their spawn point or Objective Bravo often use the opposite doorway to enter the bunker, allowing you to flank them as they move toward Alpha.

The area between the coalition spawn point and Objective Bravo is off limits to the OPFOR team. However, OPFOR troops can still occupy this corner position, ideal for ambushing coalition troops rushing out of their spawn point. This flanking position is particularly effective when attacking Objective Bravo. If you can pin down the coalition reinforcements here, your teammates will have a

much easier time setting the charge and establishing a defensive perimeter around Bravo. Continue applying pressure from this position as the coalition team rushes to disarm the charge.

This spot is off limits to OPFOR players, making it the ideal sniping spot for coalition snipers. Utilizing sightline 2, aim down this trench and pick off OPFOR attackers swarming around Objective Alpha. Since you don't have to worry about enemies sneaking up behind you, choose a sniper rifle for dedicated long-range coverage from this spot. If you come under fire from the opposite end of the sightline, simply drop down behind the cover of the ballistic barriers and wait a few seconds before peeking out again.

CHOKE POINTS

This bunker is a popular route for OPFORs advancing toward Objective Bravo. Therefore, coalition troops should take steps to lock down this path, either by camping the bunker's interior, defending from the doorway, or hiding outside one of the bunker's windows and ambushing OPFORs once they're inside. Whatever your preference, prepare for heavy traffic here.

Sightline 2 cuts down this narrow spot in the trench, making it particularly dangerous for OPFORs rushing toward Objective Alpha. To avoid getting hit by coalition snipers positioned near overwatch position 6, deploy smoke ahead of your advance. If you don't have any smoke grenades, approach Alpha from a different angle, such as from the center of the map, by overwatch position 3. Racing across the trench makes you harder to hit.

While this sightline doesn't have a direct angle on Objective Alpha, players positioned at either end can engage the heavy traffic along this trench. OPFOR snipers near the radar dish often duel with coalition snipers at overwatch position 6. As the lead flies down this sightline, just be sure you're not caught in the middle. Never travel down this trench unless you've deployed smoke to conceal your advance, otherwise you're likely to catch a sniper's bullet in the teeth.

SIGHTLINES

This section of the trench sees some frantic fighting as both teams fight for control of Objective Bravo. Coalition troops should occupy the area near the objective early in the match and maintain constant watch down this trench to pick off approaching OPFOR attackers. Since the area around Alpha is usually heavily defended, OPFORs should attempt to clear out the bunker by utilizing an offensive support action, such as a devastating missile strike. The team that manages to dominate this sightline has the best chance at controlling Bravo.

COALITION TACTICS

At the start of the match, expect the OPFOR team to rush Objective Alpha. Alpha is the farthest from your team's spawn point, so get some teammates there are quickly as possible. Meanwhile, move a sniper or two to overwatch position 6 to cover the trench adjacent to Alpha, but don't forget about Bravo. Although it's close to your team's spawn point, Objective Bravo still needs to be defended against possible rush attacks. Concentrate teammates around the objective and post skirmishers in and round the bunker at choke point 1. If both objectives survive the early frantic moments of the match, maintain an even defensive split between the two locations. But if manpower doesn't allow for comprehensive coverage, center your defenses around Objective Bravo. This area is much easier to defend due to its close proximity to you team's spawn point. Hold out here for five minutes to secure the win.

OPFOR TACTICS

Instead of splitting your team between the two objectives, make an early, aggressive push toward Objective Bravo at the start of the match while the coalition team scrambles to defend both locations. Attack and destroy Bravo as quickly as possible with the full force of your entire team. If Alpha is destroyed first, the coalition team will have an easier time defending Bravo, concentrating all their defenses at this point within a few meters of their spawn point. With Bravo destroyed, focus on Objective Alpha. Coalition reinforcements have much further to travel to defend this location, giving your team the upper hand. Still, don't get overconfident. Attack Alpha from multiple directions and secure both entry points into the bunker before attempting to set the charge. While waiting for the charge to detonate, defend Alpha from overwatch position 3, picking off coalition troops as they frantically attempt to disarm the explosives. Even with a solid game plan, this is a tough fight for the OPFOR attackers, so stay focused and work together to achieve a victory.

APPENDIX

Tier 1 Mode Medals

Image	Medal Name	Mission	Par Time
	Afghan Star	First In	00:25:00
	Cross of the Coalition	Breaking Bagram	00:30:00
	Frontier Star	Running with Wolves...	00:20:00
	Sentry Cross	Dorothy's a Bitch	00:17:30
	Order of the Vanguard	Belly of the Beast	00:25:00
	Sniper's Cross	Friends from Afar	00:15:00
	Warrior's Badge	Compromised	00:12:30
	Shield of Valor	Neptune's Net	00:15:00
	Legion of Brotherhood	Rescue the Rescuers	00:28:30
	Conspicuous Gallantry Medal	Earn All Nine Tier 1 Mode Medals	–

Coalition Rifleman Unlocks

Level	Rank	Points	Unlock	Image
1	Recruit	0	M16A4 Assault Rifle	
2	Regular	250	Extra Magazine	
3	Expert	350	Red Dot Sight	
4	Veteran	500	M249 Light Machine Gun	
5	Operator	800	Suppressor	
6	Commander	1,100	Open-Tip Ammunition	
7	Elite	1,500	Combat Scope	
8	Tier 1 Recruit	2,000	Muzzle Brake	
9	Tier 1 Regular	2,400	F2000 Assault Rifle	
10	Tier 1 Expert	2,800	Veteran M16A4 Assault Rifle	
11	Tier 1 Veteran	3,200	Veteran M249 Light Machine Gun	
12	Tier 1 Operator	3,600	AK-47 Assault Rifle	
13	Tier 1 Commander	4,000	Pistol Ammo	
14	Tier 1 Elite	4,400	PKM Light Machine Gun	
15	Tier 1 Warfighter	4,800	Extra Grenade	

OPFOR Rifleman Unlocks

Level	Rank	Points	Unlock	Image
1	Recruit	0	AK-47 Assault Rifle	
2	Regular	250	Extra Magazine	
3	Expert	350	Red Dot Sight	
4	Veteran	500	PKM Light Machine Gun	
5	Operator	800	Suppressor	
6	Commander	1,100	Open-Tip Ammunition	
7	Elite	1,500	Combat Scope	
8	Tier 1 Recruit	2,000	Muzzle Brake	
9	Tier 1 Regular	2,400	F2000 Assault Rifle	
10	Tier 1 Expert	2,800	Veteran AK-47 Assault Rifle	
11	Tier 1 Veteran	3,200	Veteran PKM Light Machine Gun	
12	Tier 1 Operator	3,600	M16A4 Assault Rifle	
13	Tier 1 Commander	4,000	Pistol Ammo	
14	Tier 1 Elite	4,400	M249 Light Machine Gun	
15	Tier 1 Warfighter	4,800	Extra Grenade	

Coalition Special Ops Unlocks

Level	Rank	Points	Unlock	Image
1	Recruit	0	M4A1 Carbine	
2	Regular	250	Extra Magazine	
3	Expert	350	Red Dot Sight	
4	Veteran	500	870MCS Combat Shotgun	
5	Operator	800	Suppressor	
6	Commander	1,100	Shotgun Slugs/Open-Tip Ammo	
7	Elite	1,500	Combat Scope	
8	Tier 1 Recruit	2,000	Laser Sight	
9	Tier 1 Regular	2,400	P90 PDW	
10	Tier 1 Expert	2,800	Veteran M4A1 Carbine	
11	Tier 1 Veteran	3,200	Veteran 870MCS Combat Shotgun	
12	Tier 1 Operator	3,600	AKS-74U Carbine	
13	Tier 1 Commander	4,000	Pistol Ammo	
14	Tier 1 Elite	4,400	TOZ-194 Combat Shotgun	
15	Tier 1 Warfighter	4,800	Extra Grenade	

Coalition Sniper Unlocks

Level	Rank	Points	Unlock	Image
1	Recruit	0	M21 Battle Rifle	
2	Regular	250	Extra Magazine	
3	Expert	350	Combat Scope	
4	Veteran	500	M24 Sniper Rifle	
5	Operator	800	Rangefinder	
6	Commander	1,100	Open-Tip Ammunition	
7	Elite	1,500	High Power Scope	
8	Tier 1 Recruit	2,000	Suppressor	
9	Tier 1 Regular	2,400	G3 Battle Rifle	
10	Tier 1 Expert	2,800	Veteran M21 Battle Rifle	
11	Tier 1 Veteran	3,200	Veteran M24 Sniper Rifle	
12	Tier 1 Operator	3,600	SVD Battle Rifle	
13	Tier 1 Commander	4,000	Pistol Ammo	
14	Tier 1 Elite	4,400	SV-98 Sniper Rifle	
15	Tier 1 Warfighter	4,800	Extra Grenade	

OPFOR Special Ops Unlocks

Level	Rank	Points	Unlock	Image
1	Recruit	0	AKS-74U Carbine	
2	Regular	250	Extra Magazine	
3	Expert	350	Red Dot Sight	
4	Veteran	500	TOZ-194 Combat Shotgun	
5	Operator	800	Suppressor	
6	Commander	1,100	Shotgun Slugs/Open-Tip Ammo	
7	Elite	1,500	Combat Scope	
8	Tier 1 Recruit	2,000	Laser Sight	
9	Tier 1 Regular	2,400	P90 PDW	
10	Tier 1 Expert	2,800	Veteran AKS-74U Carbine	
11	Tier 1 Veteran	3,200	Veteran TOZ-194 Combat Shotgun	
12	Tier 1 Operator	3,600	M4A1 Carbine	
13	Tier 1 Commander	4,000	Pistol Ammo	
14	Tier 1 Elite	4,400	870MCS Combat Shotgun	
15	Tier 1 Warfighter	4,800	Extra Grenade	

OPFOR Sniper Unlocks

Level	Rank	Points	Unlock	Image
1	Recruit	0	SVD Battle Rifle	
2	Regular	250	Extra Magazine	
3	Expert	350	Combat Scope	
4	Veteran	500	SV-98 Sniper Rifle	
5	Operator	800	Rangefinder	
6	Commander	1,100	Open-Tip Ammunition	
7	Elite	1,500	High Power Scope	
8	Tier 1 Recruit	2,000	Suppressor	
9	Tier 1 Regular	2,400	G3 Battle Rifle	
10	Tier 1 Expert	2,800	Veteran SVD Battle Rifle	
11	Tier 1 Veteran	3,200	Veteran SV-98 Sniper Rifle	
12	Tier 1 Operator	3,600	M21 Battle Rifle	
13	Tier 1 Commander	4,000	Pistol Ammo	
14	Tier 1 Elite	4,400	M24 Sniper Rifle	
15	Tier 1 Warfighter	4,800	Extra Grenade	

Multiplayer Weapons

Name	Image	Team	Class	Unlock	Accuracy	Range	Damage	Rate of Fire
M16A4 Assault Rifle		Coalition	Rifleman	Recruit (1)	5	6	6	5
AK-47 Assault Rifle		OPFOR	Rifleman	Recruit (1)	5	6	6	5
M249 Light Machine Gun		Coalition	Rifleman	Veteran (4)	5	5	6	6
PKM Light Machine Gun		OPFOR	Rifleman	Veteran (4)	5	5	6	6
F2000 Assault Rifle		Both	Rifleman	Tier 1 Regular (9)	6	5	5	6
M60 Light Machine Gun		Both	Rifleman	Retailer Exclusive	5	6	7	4
M240 Light Machine Gun		Coalition	Rifleman	EA Store Exclusive	6	4	7	5
RPK Light Machine Gun		OPFOR	Rifleman	EA Store Exclusive	6	4	7	5
M4A1 Carbine		Coalition	Special Ops	Recruit (1)	6	4	5	7
AKS-74U Carbine		OPFOR	Special Ops	Recruit (1)	6	4	5	7
870MCS Combat Shotgun		Coalition	Special Ops	Veteran (4)	6	3	9	4
TOZ-194 Combat Shotgun		OPFOR	Special Ops	Veteran (4)	6	3	9	4
P90 PDW Submachine Gun		Both	Special Ops	Tier 1 Regular (9)	6	3	5	8
MP7A1 PDW Submachine Gun		Both	Special Ops	Limited Edition Exclusive	5	3	5	9
M21 Battle Rifle		Coalition	Sniper	Recruit (1)	6	7	5	4
SVD Battle Rifle		OPFOR	Sniper	Recruit (1)	6	7	5	4
M24 Sniper Rifle		Coalition	Sniper	Veteran (4)	6	7	8	1
SV-98 Sniper Rifle		OPFOR	Sniper	Veteran (4)	6	7	8	1
G3 Battle Rifle		Both	Sniper	Tier 1 Regular (9)	6	7	4	5

Multiplayer Weapon Attachments

Name	Image	Slot	Accuracy	Range	Damage	Rate of Fire
Extra Magazine		Base	–	–	–	–
Red Dot Sight		Rail	+1	–	–	–
Combat Scope		Rail	–	+1	–	–
Laser Sight		Barrel	+1	+1	-1	–
High Power Scope		Rail	–	+2	–	–
Suppressor		Barrel	–	-1	-1	–
Muzzle Brake		Barrel	+1	-1	-1	–
Open-Tip Ammo		Base	-1	–	+1	–
Shotgun Slugs		Base	-1	+1	+1	–
Rangefinder		Barrel	–	+2	-1	–